1993

# SONGS OF
# GLORY

# LINDA SEIDEL

# SONGS OF GLORY

## THE ROMANESQUE FAÇADES OF AQUITAINE

THE UNIVERSITY OF CHICAGO PRESS · CHICAGO & LONDON

THE UNIVERSITY OF CHICAGO PRESS, CHICAGO 60637
THE UNIVERSITY OF CHICAGO PRESS, LTD., LONDON
© 1981 by The University of Chicago
All rights reserved. Published 1981
Paperback edition 1987
Printed in the United States of America
96 95 94 93 92 91 90 89 88 87
6  5  4  3  2

LIBRARY OF CONGRESS CATALOGING IN PUBLICATION DATA

Seidel, Linda
    Songs of glory.

    Bibliography: p.
    1.  Façades—France—Aquitaine—Themes, motives.
2.  Sculpture, Romanesque—France—Aquitaine—Themes,
motives.     3.  Sculpture, French—France—Aquitaine—
Themes, motives.     4.  Churches—France—Aquitaine.
I.  Title.
NB1288.S4              730'.944'7              81-3342
ISBN   0-226-74513-9 (cloth)          AACR2
ISBN   0-226-74514-7 (paper)

L.S. to M.F.

# Contents

# Preface

THIS BOOK EVOLVED, OVER THE COURSE OF A DECADE, FROM AN initial interest in the equestrian figure as it appeared in the sculpture of the late eleventh and twelfth centuries to questions of a broader yet more fundamental nature concerning Romanesque sculpture in general. At the start, I sought only to account for the popularity of the antique motif of the rider in the art of western France. My goal was modest; it had been stimulated by the discovery of an unpublished carving of a crowned rider among Kingsley Porter's photos at Harvard. That image led me to the abundant scholarship on the Aquitainian horsemen who are celebrated in the literature under the name Constantine. As I studied this material, I was struck by how little attention it gave to practical matters. Why, for example, did the image appear primarily in coastal France whereas it was less popular either in regions closer to the reputed source in Rome or farther away in other regions to which pilgrims returning from the holy city also traveled? Nowhere did I find an explanation for the patronage of the numerous churches on which the rider was depicted; if the buildings were not monasteries, then what or who necessitated the construction of so many ecclesiastical structures? And finally, as my admiration for the richness and coherence of Aquitainian façade design grew, I became frustrated by the seemingly inappropriate inferior position to which these monuments had been relegated by scholars because of their purely *decorative* qualities—that is, the absence of an identifiable iconographic program and the rejection of the tympanum as the logical and meaningful surface for such expression.

The time had come, it seemed to me, to reconsider prevailing assumptions about Romanesque as these had been formulated by Mâle, Porter, Deschamps, and Focillon. By transferring my focus from the interesting and important iconographic motif of the rider, which could claim a distinguished lineage from imperial art, to the provincial, monotonous sculptural programs of which these riders form a part, I moved into the acknowledged backwaters of twelfth-century art. It was a necessary, inevitable, and, I believe, ultimately fruitful decision but one which, at the same time, was an intellectually lonely one.

The sole direction I had in my pursuit of what seemed to me to be very pragmatic issues was, of course, the best guide of all, indeed the only possible guide: the remarkable papers on the sculpture of southwestern Europe in the Romanesque period that had been published more than thirty years before by Meyer Schapiro. Although the articles, in particular the studies on Silos and Souillac, scarcely offer a prescription to be followed, except perhaps in their brilliant passages of descriptive analysis, they do make clear, in an uncompromising way, what it is necessary to ask about this art and, ultimately, to know. Without these exemplars I doubt that I would have been moved to pose unpopular questions and I probably would have lacked courage to persist in seeking their answers. Toward the end of my work, when the manuscript was written, Schapiro's papers appeared as a convenient collection. Only then did I fully realize how many of the points I labored so long and hard to demonstrate had been articulated or at least alluded to in those richly annotated pages: the sensitivity to Islam, the secularity, the bonds between art and poetry, the dependence upon Carolingian sources, the purposefulness of artistic decision, and much more. The extent of my indebtedness to Schapiro and his work, direct and indirect, cannot be adequately footnoted; it is the collective force of his arguments and the totality of his vision, rather than individual observations alone, that continually enriched and transformed my thinking during the course of this study.

At an early stage, this book profited in specific ways from the help of two friends, Qais Al-Awqati and Daniel Esterman. The knowledgeable advice and criticism of Ernst Kitzinger and the provocative lectures and papers of Oleg Grabar contributed significantly to the development of my ideas about Aquitainian art during the years in which I worked on this project in Cambridge. My colleagues at the University of Chicago, Peter Dembowski, Robert S. Nelson, and Karl J. Weintraub, all made valuable suggestions at various stages of the completed manuscript; I profited from their good judgment and deeply appreciate each of their special efforts in my behalf.

Above all else, I should like to thank my family, whose enthusiasm for my research and willingness to help shoulder its deflected stresses made work on this book both possible and pleasant. My gratitude to each one of them, Michael, Ezra, Ben, and John, for their good humor, understanding and, most of all, their unwavering support, knows no bounds.

# Foreground and Background

CROSSING THE LOIRE BELOW TOURS, THE TRAVELER THROUGH western and southwestern France cannot fail to be impressed by the large number of small churches that dot the rolling landscape. Hundreds of ecclesiastical structures appear by the roadside, on the crest of low hills, or overlooking the sea. Frequently they lie at the center of a modest-sized town; occasionally they rise at the edge of a wooded plain; at times there is little in their environs save the remains of a long-destroyed castle. These churches, which provide primary and sometimes even solitary animation of the terrain, were built in the late eleventh century and throughout the twelfth century in the region known at the time as Aquitaine. Occasionally they replaced smaller, earlier structures, but often the buildings were on entirely new foundations. In either instance, the churches survive with a substantial portion of their original, for the most part modestly proportioned, construction intact. By virtue of their number, location, and size, they testify to a remarkable popular diffusion of religious architecture in a period most frequently perceived as a time of relatively centralized monastic organization.[1]

*Figs. 1–12*

The churches of Parthenay, a town 50 kilometers west of the regional capital of Poitiers, provide an instructive example. Seven churches are known to have been newly built or under construction there in the early twelfth century. Five of these still survive—their location determined by the situation of the powerful local lord's castle, which, in turn, determined the organization of the developing medieval town. A walk through contemporary Parthenay directs the visitor along routes traced nearly a millennium ago. From the remodeled Saint-Laurent, which looms over a prominent intersection in *centre-ville,* the road rises toward the vast ruins of a château, home of the medieval lords Larchevêque, who controlled the area. It is not far to the church of Sainte-Croix, which borders this route as one approaches the citadel; Notre-Dame-de-la-Couldre, now only a fragmentary and freestanding façade, is just beyond, immediately adjacent to the fortified complex. Both monuments crowd the street and attest to the importance and austere grandeur of the feudal passage. On the ramparts below the castle there

*Fig. 10*

once stood another church dedicated to Saint-Jean. Enclosing this nucleus of four substantial religious structures were the churches of the newly established surrounding settlements. A modest chapel built in the faubourg of Saint-Paul now serves as a garage. The church of Saint-Sépulchre, established by the local lord after his visit to the Holy Land in the 1090s, survives only in memory, having given its name to another suburb and a street. Most handsome of all the extant structures
*Fig. 8*    in the region of the town is Saint-Pierre, the large, sparely adorned edifice planned to house the lords' tombs; it crowns a hillock in Parthenay-le-Vieux, an adjacent settlement to the southwest. Later in the twelfth century, additional churches were erected on the banks of the Thouet, across the bridge from Parthenay, to minister to the specific needs of pilgrims. Here, at Saint-Jacques and at the priory of la Madeleine, were received both the healthy travelers and the sick who passed by the town on their way to Santiago to venerate the relics of Saint James at his church in northwest Spain.[2]

The many churches of Parthenay appear to have served essentially local needs. There was neither cathedral nor monastery in the town and no church possessed a relic of singular power or fame that might have attracted worshipers from far off. Thus none of the early twelfth-century structures would have been reserved for the exclusive use of a particular religious community or devoted to a special religious ceremony. It is all the more difficult, therefore, to imagine, in very practical terms, why so many churches were built at about the same time within a reasonably small area. Although the town and the region were enjoying rapid growth in those years, thanks to the security provided by powerful lords, the accommodation of townspeople at regular liturgical ceremonies does not seem, in itself, to provide a sufficient explanation for the construction of so many buildings. Yet these multiple shrines, both in Parthenay and throughout the region, appear to have served for the most part as parish churches. It is a startling and seemingly excessive abundance.

Even more striking than their number is the fact that the churches throughout the Aquitaine countryside are remarkably homogeneous in appearance. These monuments, whether seen from a distance or at close range, confront the viewer with a highly uniform ensemble of architectural and sculptural forms. Exteriors of buildings are marked by the repetitive application of sculptured shafts and round arches to
*Fig. 13*    mural surfaces. Aisle walls and apses as well as soaring entry walls are emphatically adorned with columnar arcaded forms that appear to lighten the massive masonry of the building and transform it into a shell. The area surrounding the main passage into the church invariably
*Fig. 1*    receives particular attention. Here rows of arcades soar over the entry;
*Fig. 11*    elsewhere concentric arches appear to descend around the doorway,

penetrating and eroding the mass of the western wall. These multiple arcades and the capitals that serve as their supports are in most instances the bearers of lushly carved ornamental detail. On many monuments animated and varied figures cavort with seemingly boundless energy in these zones; elsewhere similar creatures, along with vegetal motifs, appear instead as rigid, repetitive designs. Their potential for movement has been restricted, if not fully suppressed in these cases, by the architectural constraints of the frames within which they are carved.

*Fig. 10*
*Fig. 8*

The recurrent decorative elements of these churches are among the most conspicuous identifying features of European architecture of their time. Thousands of churches across the continent utilized arcades, vigorously carved voussoirs, and ornamental capitals in a variety of ways in their construction throughout the eleventh and twelfth centuries. Even so, the richly adorned monuments that proliferated in Aquitaine from approximately 1090 until the close of the twelfth century and after retain a striking identifiability among these structures. The particular uniform way in which the standard decorative elements were handled over a long period of time distinguishes these buildings from all others; the churches of Aquitaine persist to this day as tangible testimony, not just to an exceptional and widespread artistic vitality, but to the constancy of taste in a vast geographical area during nearly a dozen decades.

Yet scholarly attention has not been drawn to these monuments in proportion to their number. Instead interest in the architecture of this period has tended to seek out either those monuments that are differentiated from others because of unique qualities of form, content, and style or, somewhat ironically, lost churches, those that succumbed through the centuries to the whims of political fortune and the ravaging effects of passing time and changing taste. The destroyed abbey church at Cluny, for example, where major rebuilding was begun late in the eleventh century, and the pilgrimage shrine at Tours built to honor Saint Martin are more widely perceived as representatives of their age than are any of the surviving churches of Aquitaine. The archaeological information gleaned from lost buildings would seem to have contributed disproportionately to our knowledge of the period.

Indifference to the vast amount of architecture in Aquitaine may be attributed to certain features of the art itself. The sheer number of churches draws attention to the uniformity of their appearance. This lack of variety and the almost disarming inelegance of much of the carving vividly contrast with the exquisite and singular contemporary work at Autun, in Burgundy, and at Moissac, in nearby Languedoc. And scholars trained to scrutinize in detail the particular qualities of individual monuments have not dealt in the same way with the characteristics of large groups: while it is appropriate to search for and applaud the unique in the former, it seems more plausible to seek out and appraise the typical among the latter.

It is all the more unfortunate, therefore, that Aquitaine has neither a "unique" nor an obviously major "typical" monument on which attention can readily be focused. The only one that truly qualifies is the *Fig. 14* cathedral at Angoulême; it is larger and grander than all the other regional churches and, consequently, might have served as a model for the rest. Angoulême has, indeed, captured scholarly interest and been suggested as a source of inspiration for monuments throughout Aquitaine. But it is not easy to appreciate the church at Angoulême because of the radical restoration it underwent late in the nineteenth century. At that time, some of its authentic features were obscured by the addition of a gable, towers, and newly carved reliefs. Certainly much of its original effect vanished behind these elements: the church was transformed from a bona fide twelfth-century monument into a model of the nineteenth-century's impression of the ecclesiastical architecture of that distant century.[3]

Therein lies the key, I believe, to an understanding of much of the art of this region, or, I should say, to an appreciation of its misunderstanding. So many of the Aquitainian churches fail not merely to arouse but to sustain scholarly attention because, by and large, they seem to fall short in significant ways of the implicit "standards" set by scholars for the art of their time. Yet, if these unannounced and often highly arbitrary "norms" are openly identified and their genesis understood, it may be possible to become free of their limiting presumptions and to approach this art from a different perspective. In order to do that, it is necessary to define the expectations imposed on the sculpture of the Middle Ages by a succession of its alleged advocates.

In fact, round-headed arches and expressive sculptural ornament, the typical features of Aquitainian monumental art, were the very elements that led observers of such pre-Renaissance art to name it "Romanesque." The early nineteenth-century Norman and English archaeologists, who were among the first to look at such medieval churches appreciatively, noticed that the structures' most prominent architectural features were similar to certain salient aspects of late Roman work. They suggested that this ecclesiastical art, examples of which existed in virtually every European country, descended from decadent antique architecture that had survived from earlier centuries throughout the western regions of the former empire. One aspect of this association that particularly appealed to these early critics was the fact that the ancient imperial art had not been narrowly ethnic: it was not the art of a particular people but had been practiced all over Europe. Moreover, a well-studied phenomenon within late Roman culture

4

seemed, to these philologically oriented nineteenth-century critics, to provide an analogue to the presumed origins of this newly identified Romanesque art. Vernacular Romance languages, it was observed, had begun to emerge from a debased Latin tongue at about the same time that these visual modes of expression were developing from provincialized variants on Roman architecture. These could be seen as parallel and corroborating events. But the comparison with language ended abruptly: Romanesque, unlike Romance, was not perceived as having continued into contemporary forms. Rather, Romanesque art, to the early nineteenth-century *amateur*, stretched only from the fall of Rome up to the appearance of a modern, indigenous, and original type of architecture, known to them, as it is to us, as "Gothic." The appellation "Romanesque" served then to differentiate the work of earlier centuries from that of later ones. The term stressed continuity with the past by emphasizing what quite obviously seemed to be Romanesque's legitimate inheritance.[4]

However, the superficial architectural similarities to antique art that had inspired the name "Romanesque" remained unexplored. This is not surprising since the way in which the past is perceived at any time depends at least as much upon the needs of the moment as it does on the evidence available. The early "discoverers" of Romanesque buildings neither understood nor truly admired the medieval and antique monuments and generally felt detached from both. As "northerners," they experienced an honest distance from the localized Mediterranean art of the earliest centuries and had only incomplete access to its examples. In addition, antiquity presented more than one aspect to the early nineteenth-century eye. In part, the term implied magnificent and heroic structures, such as those that had been suitable for Napoleon's emulation. Of course, such imposing arches and temples showed little connection to the modest-sized, highly practical masonry buildings of the Middle Ages. Such architecture could, therefore, provide little incentive for an investigation of the development of the recently identified Roman-Romanesque association. Moreover, with the fall of the French emperor and the emergence of nationalistic governments, there was less sentiment for exploring connections with pompous, official art. Finally, Roman art was seen, in itself, as a late and decadent phase of an earlier and superior classical style.[5] It did not, in its own right, excite much attention.

Toward the middle of the century, the critic Quicherat suggested that Romance languages and Romanesque architecture had, in fact, different relationships to their parent Latin forms. If the former could be compared to a slightly overripe wine, the latter, he claimed, should rather be seen as vinegar: something materially altered and different in essence. He viewed Romanesque as an intermediary between Roman and Gothic and stressed that its definition should take both "framing" periods into account. Consequently Quicherat stressed the ways in which Romanesque architecture did *not* exclusively resemble Roman work. But interest in Romanesque in its own right never took shape; enthusiasm for its forms was overshadowed by the allure of the picturesque and seemingly original Gothic structures that loomed more prominent nearby. After 1830 especially, these edifices consumed the public's attention.[6] Romanesque was regarded as little more than its forerunner.

Curiosity about the reliance of Romanesque architecture on antiquity never really manifested itself; moreover, the evidence was elusive at best. Little enthusiasm was shown for Romanesque's ill-proportioned figural art either. Intellectual interest was stimulated, however, by the more general question of a *cultural* dependence in the Middle Ages on the classical past. Research in this area, pursued primarily in literary and linguistic circles, was developed in the first half of *this* century; it provided art historians interested in Romanesque art with a truely concrete, but, unfortunately, highly limited concept of the antique. Evidence of medieval familiarity with classical texts, uncovered by such studies, facilitated the identification of certain mythological depictions; it also provided explanations for countless iconographical themes in post-antique art. Preoccupation with illustrations of literary material distracted attention, however, from forms. Adhémar, in a lengthy study of antique influences on medieval art in France, emphasized the textual, humanistic basis of his investigation and proceeded to deal primarily with mythological themes. Burgundian Romanesque art, with its numerous references to pagan images, appeared to him to reveal perva-

*Fig. 8*

sive influence of the antique. But apart from the large reliefs of equestrians that adorn numerous church façades in Aquitaine, he found very little to attract his attention there. Roman remains did not seem to him to be particularly abundant in that region; moreover, he doubted that this category of object would have exerted more than a very limited influence on medieval man. And what had survived seemed to bear little specific resemblance to the neighboring, rather florid Romanesque structures. Virtually none of the small-scale carving that abounds on Aquitaine's churches exhibits the recognizable antique or pagan scenes Adhémar sought, such as Ganymede or sacrificial processions, like those found at Vézelay. The rider figures that populate numerous Aquitaine façades he found, however, to be an exception; he linked them directly to the bronze statue of Marcus Aurelius in Rome, as others before him had done, stressing the unusually deep impression he assumed this sculpture would have made on visitors to the holy city by virtue of its imposing isolation in the vicinity of the Lateran Palace and its supposed, though spurious, identification with Constantine.

The Romanesque rider figure was for him the clearest and most important example in Aquitaine of the study of antique works of art; it has remained so for more recent historians.[7]

The fundamentally romanizing aspects of the accompanying architecture, specifically the arcaded exteriors framing the riders that first attracted the attention of nineteenth-century archaeologists, were ignored by Adhémar. Indeed, these elements have received only sporadic and usually narrow attention in the literature on the field. They have been analyzed more for their idiosyncratic permutations of a motif, their "regional" variations, than for their sources or significance. Yet these elements vividly illustrate the noble lineage of the Romanesque; if one takes the etymology of the term at face value, the abundant and even redundant utilization of arcuated forms in Aquitaine would make the art of that region one of the more characteristic expressions of its period. Yet, if anything, the art of this region, particularly its monumental architectural decoration, has struck critics as being strangely atypical; it has, therefore, attracted relatively little attention.

The actual or assumed affinity of the Romanesque with the antique is but one of a number of issues that have affected attitudes toward the art since its "rediscovery." Walter Cahn, in an insightful essay, characterized the polarity of attitudes toward medieval art that flourished in the nineteenth century and noted the sense of historical estrangement that accompanied them. One might add "artistic estrangement" as well, for the qualities that attracted the attention of both partisans and disparagers of the post-Carolingian centuries were not initially aesthetic ones. The religious tenor of that time, as conceived by the Romantic imagination, provided the major paradigm through which the Middle Ages were apprehended. The monotony of much medieval art was alternately blamed on the restrictive constraint of religion *and* appreciated as a manifestation of the orderliness and comprehensiveness of the period's institutions. The fantastic figures that inhabit much of its carving were experienced primarily as un-Christian and either attributed to the irrational barbaric mentality that was the legacy of the "dark ages," or valued in a positive light and admired as symptoms of individual creativity and spontaneity. As Cahn noted, each of these contrasting viewpoints, in its way, profoundly affected the study of medieval art.[8]

Out of nineteenth-century philosophic ideas of orthodoxy and liberty emerged the perspectives within which research on twelfth-century sculpture has been pursued in the twentieth century. The idea of an all-powerful, encyclopedic, Christian intellectual atmosphere dominated Emile Mâle's analysis of religious iconography with its fixed categories and its emphasis on other-worldly eternal themes. Henri Focillon's enunciation of a series of immutable laws of composition,

7

which he invoked to check intimations of unpremeditated expression in art, emerged from his acceptance of an awesome force that guided creative impulses. Even the phenomenon of pilgrimage, which shaped Kingsley Porter's understanding of the transmission of manners and motifs, was primarily regarded as an outpouring of religious fervor and viewed as an organized instrument of the church. The concept of a burgeoning worldly element in medieval society that brought with it a "new art, on the margins of the religious work," and displayed a fondness for the unpredictable, thoroughly novel, and frankly materialistic was championed in brilliant but lonely fashion by Meyer Schapiro. He cited in support of this idea of creative, secular impulses Saint Bernard's own seeming condemnation of the inappropriateness, in a monastic milieu, of the "follies" of irreligious subjects.[9]

These positions regarding custom and innovation in the postmillennial Middle Ages readily intersect in relation to matters of both content and form. Either can be interpreted as proof of the venerability of earlier traditions or as evidence of substantial novelty. Sometimes the persistence of the old constitutes the very element of freshness; shape and subject can, at times, be fused or even confused as issues. Approaches to the study of medieval representational art from the eleventh century on have been profoundly influenced by the pioneering efforts made by Mâle earlier in this century. His ideas provide insight into the inadequacies and inconsistencies that exist in the handling of familiar and often related materials.

In Mâle's studies, Romanesque sculpture is perceived primarily through the abiding Christian themes that give the art coherence and continuity. These themes have their source in manuscripts, the "repository of tradition," according to Mâle; at the same time, he wrote, they reflect and reveal more contemporary institutional phenomena of the eleventh and twelfth centuries such as the pilgrimage and emerging church drama. Concern for thematic elements drew Mâle's attention to the expansive exterior surfaces of churches on which the biblical and historic events are carved; in other words, content preceded interest in form in his case. Mâle went on to observe that architectural sculpture of such magnitude in stone had not been seen since antiquity and hailed its reappearance in late eleventh-century southern French churches as a rebirth. Thus, in contrast to the *continuity with* the past that Mâle suggested for much of the content of the art, he proposed a *revival of* the antique in matters of material and style. While there is no obvious contradiction in this argument, the congruence of the observations is not apparent. Nor is it at all clear why the "rediscovery" of stonecarving should have occurred in the first place.

Stimulated, perhaps, by the concept of a renaissance of letters being espoused in academic circles at the same time, scholars such as Deschamps and Porter embraced the idea of a rebirth of monumental sculpture in the art of southern Europe at the turn of the twelfth century without fully explaining it. Romans, it was agreed, had been the last to utilize large-scale stone carving so prominently on their structures. But if the idea of its use was obviously old, the manner of its manifestation in the Middle Ages appeared highly novel. Figured capitals and decorated doorposts and jambs, the compelling features of twelfth-century sculpture that gave shape to religious iconography, were developed in the Romanesque period to a new level of expressive complexity and sophistication. Nothing quite like them had been seen in the west before. It is indeed understandable, therefore, that studies of form and content in Romanesque art focused on these provocative aspects of the sculpture, often to the exclusion of other equally fascinating, but seemingly less inventive, elements such as corbels and voussoirs. Most of the attention has been devoted to the single feature that is perceived as Romanesque art's most original (and un-Roman) aspect, the tympanum.

This monumental, semicircular carving, frequently dominated by an imposing, hieratic figure of Christ, was elevated above the main arched entry of many twelfth-century churches, particularly in France. Such overdoor reliefs at Moissac, Beaulieu, Vézelay, and Autun have been described as the most impressive innovations of Romanesque art and are celebrated as its most distinctive achievements. The immediate model for these carvings is thought by many to have been the arched relief that formerly surmounted the western entry into the great monastic church at Cluny. Carved sometime during the first quarter of the twelfth century and destroyed, along with most of the abbey, at the time of the French Revolution, the relief is known chiefly through picturesque sketches and excavated fragments. This tympanum is often identified as the premier example of the genre and is implicitly credited thereby with having provided the inspiration for churches elsewhere in France and throughout Europe.[10] Such a straightforward suggestion has had important and unappreciated implications and ramifications.

This particular presumption about the genesis of a significant original Romanesque form reinforces attitudes already held concerning content. Concentration on the tympanum as the seminal sculptural element of this period focused scholarly attention on monasteries; there the semicircular relief enjoyed its greatest popularity and there the origins and manuscript sources of the overdoor carving appear to lie. Monks and clergy, the representatives of feudal institutional religion, have consequently been assumed to be both the chief patrons and major clients of Romanesque art: its sponsors, consumers, and even its producers.[11] Though attention in the study of Romanesque sculpture may shift from content to form, and from elements of continuity to aspects of innovation, curiosity remains cloistered by the constraints of what has, until now, been traditionally perceived as the dominant element in Christian society of that era. The role of other social groups in the creation and utilization of church art has scarcely been given serious consideration, except by Meyer Schapiro.

But certainly all Romanesque churches were not monastic; neither were tympana uniformly used throughout Europe. They are distinctly less typical of contemporary art in Italy, Spain, Germany, and England; moreover, and most significant for this study, a tympanum of the "Cluniac" sort scarcely exists in Aquitaine. The façades of churches in the regions known by medievalists as the Saintonge, Poitou, and Angoumois dramatically depart, in this key respect, from an expected and currently highly valued norm for Romanesque doorways. Even when "subarch" sculpture does occur, for example, in the regions' numerous *Figs. 8, 14* celebrated equestrian figures or in Angoulême's series of apostle carvings, it is chiefly as a narrative insert into a preeminent, continuous arcaded field.

This vexingly anomalous absence of a tympanum has frustrated students of Aquitainian art and has usually prompted apologies for the Romanesque sculpture there. Mâle observed that "the round arch above the door is empty and opens onto darkness. . . . So the artists of western France could not make their churches express all that other churches did." Focillon suggested that the elaborate decoration of arch moldings throughout the Poitou might be compensation "for the absence of the tympanum over the doorways." Other scholars too, lamenting the lack of this feature, have linked its absence in Aquitaine to local technological or material deficiencies.[12] Yet a single innovation, no matter how remarkable, scarcely provides an appropriate mode of reference with which to view all of a given period's creations, particularly when that period can be so readily understood not by originality but by its dependence on traditional forms—those vestiges of the antique that first gave it its name. Indeed, one risks overlooking or, even worse, misrepresenting diverse or less striking arrangements if one inspects them from a formally and conceptually biased point of view or tries, for example, to demonstrate where the forms are headed in their development before establishing securely where they have come from. Such a situation had encouraged observers since the mid-nineteenth century to accept the construction of apostle reliefs in the Musée des Augustins, Toulouse, as an authentic medieval doorway. Appreciation of the imposing statued jambs at northern French cathedral portals had inspired *amateurs* to regard the Toulouse standing figures primarily as relatives, in fact ancestors, of those columnar forms in the Ile-de-France. The impressiveness and originality of Gothic entries had blinded these critics to other, less dramatic local relationships for the Toulouse carvings.

Certain conceptual aspects that the latter share with pier and wall reliefs at southern abbeys, for instance, were overlooked in favor of apparent correspondences of posture, clothing, and manner of carving that recall work at Saint-Denis and Chartres. On this basis, the imposing Gothic portal, much admired by nineteenth-century taste, came to be adopted by writers of the time as the framework within which to view, not just the Languedoc carvings, but much other twelfth-century sculpture as well.[13]

An analogous dilemma has, I believe, confounded the study of Aquitainian façades. Analysis of Romanesque sculpture in general and of western French work in particular has been directed, either explicitly or implicitly, by the idea of the tympanum and by attitudes concerning religious art formulated in connection with its study. Relief sculpture, when it appears, and voussoir arrangements, which abound, have been studied thematically as illustrations primarily of sacred texts or of theological issues. Occasionally, as in the case of warring images, a connection between a motif and a specific historic event has been evoked.[14] These carvings have been treated in isolation, as though each were an internally focused, self-sufficient composition, comparable in that sense to a tympanum. Students of iconography have searched monastic libraries for manuscript models rather than seeking alternative and more accessible sources for a public archivolt program. And the arcades into which figurative carvings are invariably incorporated have been viewed as detached designs as well, disassociated from the character and content of their constituent parts. In fact, many articles treating arcaded façades as independent entities unrelated to their iconographic programs have appeared in European journals since the 1950s. Much of this literature initially emphasized the variety of organizational ways in which arches are employed on the façades; distinctions in both number and arrangement of the arches were interpreted as support for the concept of regional diversity within Romanesque—the "school" theory. Attempts to provide other, more meaningful explanations for the variety of arrangements were scarcely undertaken. A few studies considered the possibility of influence from the antique, but most, using the Gothic façade as a model, viewed Aquitainian arrangements in terms of that ideal and sought to organize them as stages in a continuous development.[15]

In contrast to this body of material, recent papers by two scholars dealing with arcaded façades have sought to identify the source of the motif and to relate this to the meaning of the form. Thomas Lyman has studied the utilization and migration of the arcade both inside and outside churches throughout medieval Europe. He hypothesized a symbolic function in its use because of its recurrent intersection with the door and observed a possible desire to revive the memory of the triumphant age of the Christian emperors through the adoption of an ancient motif. Jacques Gardelles likewise noted the resemblances to ancient civic structures but found in manuscripts of the tenth and eleventh centuries, primarily of Mozarabic manufacture, the source and inspiration for the southwestern French monuments of the next century. His desire to explain the striking popularity of the Aquitainian arcaded façades directed him to apply to them the significance associated with the miniature painted buildings in the manuscripts. He interpreted the former thereby as constructed projections of the Holy Temple or celestial Jerusalem. Both of these studies, in different ways and using different methods, relate to and support my own conclusions.[16]

Aquitainian façades, which, for the reasons suggested, have not seemed to fit comfortably into the generally acknowledged mainstream of medieval sculpture, have frequently been discussed individually, from an archaeological perspective, in the context of the groups of buildings of which they form an integral part. Much of this scholarship, primarily descriptions of the multitude of churches in the area, has regularly appeared in regional journals; it was consolidated by René Crozet in pioneering studies on the architecture and sculpture of Saintonge and Poitou, two of the most distinctive geographical subdivisions within Aquitaine. Crozet's works are further complemented by the slightly older and solitary discussion in English by Elizabeth Mendell and, more recently, by the popularized surveys of the Zodiac series.[17] All of these investigations have provided an essential foundation for my own work; the reader will find in them the enumerations of monuments and detailed lists of iconographic subjects for which he or she will search in vain in this book. Such tabulations have been omitted precisely because they are so readily accessible in the sources just named and since my own work has, in fact, little to add to them. Concerning the thorny issue of dating in particular, I follow the imprecise but unrefuted association of most of the Aquitainian churches with the closing decades of the eleventh and the first half or three-quarters of the twelfth century. This chronology, acknowledged by Crozet and others and recently sustained by Rupprecht, is corroborated by the comparative formal and interpretive material I present.[18]

I have tried to do something quite different with the monumental art of Aquitaine from that either essayed or accomplished by most of my predecessors. Thus the issues of priority of construction and the development of style are not directly addressed in these pages since neither, in itself, sheds light on the meaning of the arcaded façade type— whenever it appeared in Aquitaine—the issue that has motivated my own research. Impressed throughout my reading and travels by the immediate and repeated impact made by the entire "tympanum-less" entry wall, I have sought in this study to define that complete mural program in terms of its function and its form, not simply to identify its content. The latter, in fact, as will become apparent, has already been done with reasonable accuracy. What the isolated iconographic studies lack, however, has been an awareness of the context within which to examine the interactions and implications of the diverse themes.

In the process of investigating one celebrated motif on these western French churches, the pseudo-tympanum horseman, I became persuaded that the idiosyncracies of any individual portion of the entry wall were transcended by the recurrent associations of the complete composition.[19] Thus, instead of isolating the components of the façades and tracing the origins and evolution of motifs individually, as had been done, for example, for the arcaded element and as I had set out to do for the rider, I have tried to perceive these features at all times as parts of a greater design. I have analyzed them throughout in terms of their relationships to one another in order to understand what each one brings to the whole entry-wall format. This concern for relationships led me not only to try to ascertain the sources for individual elements but to venture to suggest factors that might have motivated the utilization of particular models. The façade, as a deliberate and original union of specific forms and figures, not merely as a compendium of familiar Christian images, has always occupied the foreground of my research.

It was both surprising to realize and interesting to note that, proceeding in this way, I was led to recapitulate the major approaches to the study of Romanesque which emerged for other reasons and which had focused on other regions; these have been outlined earlier in this chapter. The concept of a survival or a revival of antiquity in the twelfth century, the activities of a highly structured Christian church and the nature of the latter's intimate relationship to both a new social group and a new vocabulary of images all constitute significant issues in the analysis of these façades. The venerable values of tradition, constraint, and freedom in Romanesque sculpture, revised and redefined though I believe them to be, are fundamentally affirmed in this study.

In attempting to define and demonstrate a comprehensive explanation for a group of monuments that number in the hundreds, I have been obliged to cast my net deliberately wide. Few works of such scope, it seemed to me, could expect to match breadth by depth without jeopardizing the readers' capacity for attention and energy. Thus no individual building is given the monographic treatment it may deserve and numerous churches may seem to have been ignored in my analysis of form and content. There are losses and dangers in this approach, but the rewards of such explorations in offering an overview of a period justify the risks and provide, I believe, sufficient recompense.[20] In many instances, I have tried to offset what might be deemed art-historical oversights by drawing analogies with developments in other disciplines, particularly literature and history. In writing this essay, my imagined ideal reader has been a medievalist who is well versed in multiple aspects of the period's culture and who struggles to find some unity in a potpourri of seemingly irreconcilable archaeological and documentary data. I hope therefore that this study will be equally comprehensible and illuminating for Romance philologists, historians, and theologians, to whose work I am so deeply indebted, as it is for colleagues and students in my own field.

My concern from the outset has been the integrity of the entire monument and the place and purpose of each element in regard to the whole. Efforts to understand individual motifs necessitate an analysis of their specific *and* relative situations; figures and frames accumulate and intersect to form the façade and constantly direct attention to it as an entity. Finally, façades, which dominate the landscape and determine the means of entry into the church, point beyond the structure to the environs, both physical and social. It has been necessary, therefore, to consider the monuments within the context of complex regional and historical traditions. A brief introduction to some of this seemingly extra-artistic background is in order at this point, though its importance will only be fully clarified in the last chapter.

The artistic decentralization of western France was noted by Crozet, who commented upon the multitude of little churches, carved like *châsses,* that dot the region.[21] A startling increase in numbers characterizes the geographical and political growth of Aquitaine as it does the architectural development. In the eleventh and early twelfth centuries, the nature of the countryside was fundamentally transformed by the establishment of new *bourgs* in the vicinity of strategically placed châteaux; Parthenay, which has been well studied from this demographic point of view, had two such settlements around its imposing castle and its sires were involved in the development of others. In order to attract residents, generous charters were granted offering privileges to settlers in return for military service and some revenue. The individuals responsible for these newly fortified foundations had been initially appointed by the dukes of Aquitaine (simultaneously counts of Poitou) to subordinate positions as their custodians and defenders. But these petty lords quickly grew in number and rose in importance, first as vicars and then castellans. Their diffusion of power from the hands of the nominal rulers can be related to the disarray that followed the destruction of the Carolingian political system late in the ninth century. Encouraged, perhaps justified by that precedent of decentralized rule, the twelfth-century lords were unrelenting in their pursuit of increased power and sought to establish for their families hereditary rights to their newly built castles.[22]

The Carolingian connections of this growing group of petty rulers have been emphasized in recent historical research.[23] Attempts to celebrate and perhaps perpetuate those genealogical lines are apparent in many ways, not the least of which is the persistence of the name *Carlus Rex* on Poitevin money in the eleventh and twelfth centuries. Continuity between later Carolingian and early Capetian societies has also been demonstrated in a study of the patterns of fortress customs: the obligations owed by the tenant of a fortress toward the collective defense of the region. In the religious sphere, the desire to revive an appreciation for past glories is readily acknowledged.[24] The important role played by the duke and his numerous deputies in the benefaction and building of churches in Aquitaine continued the impetus given to ecclesiastical art in the Poitou by the foundations of earlier nobles such as Count Roger of Limoges at Charroux, Charlemagne at Saint-Savin, and Pepin at Saint-Cyprien.[25] William V, the duke and count of Poitou, who died in 1030, was praised by the chronicler of Aquitaine, Adémar de Chabannes, as a model lay prince, builder of sanctuaries, and friend of churches; Adémar compared him favorably with Carolingian, early Christian, and Roman emperors of the past. He also stressed the familial ties between the contemporary Poitevin dynasty and the founder of Cluny, an early tenth-century descendant of one of Charlemagne's powerful military commanders in the southern provinces, the first William of Aquitaine, whose donation of rich Burgundian estates assured the Benedictine abbey's prosperity and, through it, his own posthumous celebrity.[26]

This secular patronage rivals to a significant degree the more popular and pervasive perception of the primacy of ecclesiastical patronage throughout the Middle Ages.[27] Crozet acknowledged that the spread of monastic architecture in Aquitaine was surprisingly weak and that Cluny's artistic influence there was insignificant.[28] The counts of Poitou frequently reserved to themselves and their heirs the abbeys they had founded or restored and many of the local lords intended to be buried in the churches whose construction they had initiated.[29] In general, the monastic movement in Aquitaine depended on the good will of the count for whatever success it enjoyed. Although many churches throughout the region were given to monasteries for their administration and became parish churches, the imprint of the lay founder survived. Crozet pointed out the close similarities between the abbey churches of Saint-Hilaire in Poitiers and Sainte-Marie-des-Dames in Saintes, which were founded within two years of one another by Agnes, widow of William le Grand of Poitiers and wife of the count of Anjou.[30]

This group of rulers and patrons has been called a warrior aristocracy.[31] The Peace of God, a document that attempted to contain fighting between local lords and protect the unarmed and which depended for its success on ducal power, was first drawn up in western France at the

15

Synod of Charroux in 989. Some three decades later the Truce of God extended regulations to include times at which arms might be borne.[32] Events of the later years of the eleventh and twelfth centuries mitigated the necessity for such restraints. With the blessings of the church, the lords were able to divert their aggressive energies to the fight against the Moors, both in Spain, along the pilgrimage roads, and in the Holy Land, on the Crusades. The foundation of many churches was directly related to these soldiers' departures and returns,[33] and, as I hope to show, the novel means to salvation extended to these *milites Christi* inspired, and is reflected in, the program of church façades throughout their lands.

One of the most active participants on these missions was the early twelfth-century libertine Count William VII, whose voyages to Spain and Jerusalem were meant to emulate the deeds of the great Christian warrior Charlemagne, with whose circle each duke of Aquitaine (or count of Poitou) could claim identification. The adventures of the Carolingian ruler were at this moment being amplified and commemorated in the celebrated vernacular epic, the *Song of Roland*. In this poem, the great Charles was glorified as the undisputed hero of the battle against the heathens, emphatically enhancing his position as the immediate model for contemporary rulers such as William. And when the early twelfth-century duke of Aquitaine was not engaged in new campaigns against the Moors, he wrote some of the earliest known troubadour poems, extraordinary lyrics, both erotic and ironic, which, like the *Chanson,* were composed in a new, expressive, and indigenous tongue.[34]

In what follows, I have tried to show how varied threads and themes, political, liturgical, militaristic, and poetic, richly entwined, have their counterpart in the abundant architectural monuments of Aquitaine. The actual physical proliferation of ecclesiastical buildings, like the multiplication of the lords, can be related to the emergence of an effective and admired "type." Likewise, the development of the church's material image can be understood in the light of complex, contemporary Mediterranean phenomena to which these same lords, the counts most notorious among them, were exposed. The visual legacy of Romanesque Aquitaine, like the vernacular, verbal one, intermingles a strong sense of the Carolingian past with a heightened awareness of the present;[35] an art at once lofty and colloquial, it is as absorbed in this world as it is concerned about the next.

T W O

# *Trophies*

## THE ARCHITECTURAL FRAME

THE ASTONISHINGLY CONSISTENT WESTERN WALL OF THE
Aquitainian Romanesque church guards the entry into a
surprisingly varied space. In most instances, the interior is
vaulted; yet a dome or even a timber roof is often employed instead as
a cover for the nave. Aisles, generally anticipated in basilican churches,
are not a constant feature of any of these structures but rather appear to
relate to and depend upon the overall size of the building. The logic of
an individual structure's internal arrangement seems at times to have
been deliberately disguised by the application to its west wall of a
lavishly decorated "stock" facade plan. The disposition of arcaded
forms on the western mural surface often occurs without regard for
internal spatial divisions, and the entry wall frequently towers above
the roof, even extending around or beyond the side walls. The formal
similarities relating the façade at the Abbaye-aux-Dames in Saintes to *Figs. 7, 8*
that at Parthenay-le-Vieux, for example, conceal fundamental differences between the original use of domes in the former church
and pointed barrel vaulting in the latter. Despite similarities in the
tripartite arcading on the lower façade levels at both Châtres and
Chadenac, neither building has aisles inside; the former is, in fact, *Fig. 1*
unexpectedly covered with domes.

The varied architectural systems employed in the interior of these
churches and their independence from the treatment of the façade have
been observed and discussed in all major studies on Aquitainian art;
examples for each typology are enumerated there. Kubach, for instance,
identifies the architectural types as the cupola church (he counts more
than sixty of them in southwestern France), the barrel-vaulted, aisleless
church, and the hall church.[1] Crozet noted that, of the more than one
hundred churches in the Saintonge with tripartite arcading on the
ground story of the façade, only about twenty have correspondingly
arranged interiors, whereas several aisled churches, such as Jarnac-
Champagne, do not reflect this disposition on the entry wall. In the
Poitou, Crozet counted forty such churches with tripartite façade arrangements, only twelve of which have aisles. Even then, however, the

façade grouping is not always aligned in strict fashion with the interior organization, as indicated in his plan of Notre-Dame-la-Grande in Poitiers.[2] Finally, Mendell observed that the aisleless church was common in the Angoumois, although the façade in that region customarily displays three arches on the main story, thereby suggesting an aisled interior.[3] The "discoordination"[4] between the inside and outside of buildings that results from such juxtapositions is made all the more perplexing by the use in both places of the same architectural motifs. Those elements used ornamentally on the exterior are the ones that are routinely encountered within the same buildings as functional spatial and structural agents. Thus, while the organization of the façades may obscure the logic of the interior, the very use of forms such as bundled shafts, arches, and niches on the outside explicitly announces the character of the inside.

Is it possible to identify a rationale for the coherent, systematic employment of such architectural units within the building and the obviously deliberate but structurally meaningless decorative application of the same forms on the outside? The effect created by the distinction between interior and exterior organization is a readily apparent and highly provocative one. The building's external skin, liberated from a slavish association with the definition of enclosed space, gains immeasurably in prominence by becoming something more than mere initiator to the interior. The everted appearance of the building—the projection of traditional interior elements against the exterior surface—further heightens the effect of the outside while successfully demystifying the building's inside. The façade is particularly transformed by such means: disassociated from the three-dimensional, space-containing fabric of the rest of the monument, it rises like a dramatic free-standing screen. By providing an introduction to the church, yet standing independent of it, the western wall defines and identifies itself, quite literally, as a frontispiece.[5]

Aquitainian façades are "detached" from the interior in another curious way. They do not rivet the worshiper's attention at the point of passage into the church as do the storied porches and tympanaed doors of Languedoc, Burgundy, and Lombardy. Instead, the entry commonly appears here almost diffidently, as one of a series of apertures in a multileveled, arcuated arrangement. Even when a single door is employed as the heart of the composition, either flamboyantly encased in cusps as at Celles-sur-Belle or powerfully reinforced as at Fenioux, the artistic attention is distributed between mural enframement and the lure of entry. Emphasis, in every case, is focused on the arcuated adornment. Variations of this scheme, such as the inclusion of a porch at Airvault and the modest groupings at Meursac and Cressac,[6] in no way contradict the fundamental pattern elaborated on the imposing

*Fig. 11*

churches of the region, such as Notre-Dame-la-Grande at Poitiers and *Figs. 5, 14* the cathedral at Angoulême.

Simple façades can readily be dismissed as reductions of impressive local "models"; indeed, the examples in which interiors of churches fail to correspond to the arrangement of the façade have been identified as simplifications of a grander plan in which the rhythm of the façade originally did echo the interior structure.[7] But the arcuated arrangement as a design idea is too common, in too vast an area, to be explained as the progeny of a single prototype. Moreover, the French buildings share certain characteristics with churches as far away as central Italy. At Arezzo, for example, the multiplication of colonnades and arcades across the quadrangular façade occurs even more extravagantly than in Aquitaine and results in a still greater reduction of the western wall into a layered, lacey screen. It is possible that a relationship exists between the Aquitainian and Tuscan monuments; if so, an analysis and interpretation of the French material could provide an introduction to the Italian monuments and even offer an example for their investigation.[8] But the theory that a church in one area provided a model for one in the other and that from these buildings the type was diffused appears not to offer an adequate explanation. Such an approach may be justifiable when the numbers and even situation of objects involved are well defined and relatively restricted. But when hundreds of monuments of apparently independent or local rather than centralized production are involved, the strict model method fails as an adequate paradigm. It is necessary, instead, to seek a more broad-based explanation than that offered by the concept of a unique and common model with its concomitant assumption of an individual designer and a specific patron.

The approach taken in medieval literary studies and recently summarized by Stephen Nichols is instructive in this regard. Here the acceptance of the notion of a prevailing set of concepts, which each artistic monument of a period seeks to a degree to express, precedes investigation of the "dialectic," or interplay between such generic form and individual manifestation. Combination of preexistent elements in a work takes precedence over either the specifics of a particular piece or the part played by an individual in its formation. Tradition, rather than an author's individuality, constitutes the referent of a work. And the idea of audience "collaboration," not just in the enjoyment but in the creation of the work, is acknowledged.[9]

The study of hundreds of Aquitainian Romanesque churches suggests that these structures should be considered as essentially "communal" creations, poetically elaborated around and interacting with a core of traditional, familiar elements. Seemingly contradictory phenomena of their originality and uniformity can be readily explained in this way. Highly concentrated use of relatively standard arcading constitutes the key element in the definition of the Aquitainian façade as a preeminent, self-contained, screenlike surface. This familiar motif establishes both the novelty of the façade and, ultimately, its monotonous effectiveness; it must form the focus of any investigation into the models for and meaning of the entry-wall surface. In order to explore both the possible sources of the arch as a decorative and expressive element and the significance of its prominent role in the monumental art of Aquitaine, it will be helpful to review the major patterns or sequences in which it appears in western French façade design.

### Arcading in Aquitaine and Antiquity

The west walls of Aquitainian churches can be divided into groups and their development traced on the basis of the disposition and number of arches used in the decorative scheme.[10] On several structures, such as those at Melle, Saintes, and Parthenay, a strong horizontal molding and engaged columns give special prominence to a triple-arched lower story; other churches, Chadenac and Châtres for example, are further distinguished by the multiplication of arcading and its vertical extension into upper registers. A few of the buildings present a large, solitary central door like the one seen at Fenioux. In addition, a gable at times crowns the rectangular, arcuated façade, and slender, conical turrets form lateral frames, as at Saint-Jouin-de-Marnes.

*Figs. 7, 8*

*Fig. 1*

*Fig. 11*

*Fig. 6*

Fascination with either the arch or arcading is certainly far from unique. Nothing in fact is more ubiquitous in European art of the Middle Ages, and in post-antique art in general, than the use of arcaded elements, either alone or in sequences, both inside and outside of buildings and also incorporated as decorative or expressive enclosures in painting and sculpture. From aqueducts, bridges, city gates, theaters, triumphal monuments, and ceremonial entries to the apsidal frame, canon table, *tribelon,* and blind arcading, Roman imperial antiquity bequeathed to early Christian art the round-headed, narrow, architectural form which both societies employed for functional reasons, symbolic purposes, and strictly topical ornamental uses.[11]

It has at times been suggested that the emphatic use of arcading on Aquitainian churches reflects a special attraction to the remnants of antiquity. Rupprecht, emphasizing the *Bedeutungsrahmen* of these façades, perceived a triumphal theme at Angoulême because of the use of columns and arches; he linked churches such as those of Corme-Royal and Notre-Dame-la-Grande less explicitly to imperial antiquity or to arcaded sarcophagi and screens.[12] Certainly monuments from the time of Gaul's colonization were numerous, having survived the "dark ages" intact,[13] and many were readily accessible throughout Aquitaine, which had, after all, been one of Gaul's chief provinces. At Bordeaux, for example, there was an amphitheater and a palace, at Sanxay near

*Figs. 5, 14*

Poitiers a complex of structures, at Saintes an arch, and at Poitiers another arch, to single out a few of the best-known remains. And there was a splendid array of commemorative monuments to the southeast in Provence. All could have provided examples of ancient architectural forms and techniques although it is not immediately obvious why the twelfth-century builders would have sought to imitate them.[14] What motivation might there have been for a medieval church to be draped in a self-consciously appropriated civic or utilitarian form of pagan origin, a question Baldwin Smith raised in his study of the city gate. Insufficient credit is given to patrons and craftsmen when models are hypothesized for their work on the basis of similarity alone without due consideration of either the availability or the significance of the models chosen.

The western French façades most nearly evoke Roman arch types which, though not known in the immediate region, exist in two imposing examples in Provence. The tripartite structure at Orange, dominated by a lofty attic story, presents a vigorous articulation of monumental pedestals, cornices, and salient fluted columns and displays a hierarchical distinction between central and lateral openings. Although it shares certain basic formal similarities with the triple-arched main stories of Aquitainian churches, such as the one at Parthenay-le-Vieux, the tense coordination of rigid arcaded frame and mural integrity that are encountered on Romanesque church façades cannot be found on either the arch at Orange or the smaller one at Saint-Rémy.[15] A direct relationship between these structures is difficult to maintain.

In his study of Aquitainian façades, Crozet had observed that the lack of antique spirit and detailing mitigated the probability of any direct relationship between these structures and seemingly similar Roman work. He called attention instead to the resemblance between the western French treatment and the eighth-century gatehouse at Lorsch Abbey in Germany but again hesitated to make any direct connection between them. Crozet viewed the German gatehouse as an inconvenient if not inaccessible model for the French. Moreover, he was reluctant to relegate the Aquitainian artist to the subordinate role of imitator or assimilator in the use of a motif, such as the arch, which was so widely disseminated in the Mediterranean area; he was concerned that the postulation of a precise model for the Aquitainian form would diminish its originality.[16]

*Fig. 15*

In contrast to this point of view, which regards inspiration primarily as an absorptive, sterile process, is one which values the assertive, fertile potential of assimilation. The theologian Chenu, for example, stressed the initiative and inventiveness that are often involved in what is too easily dismissed as imitation. André Grabar, throughout his work, has emphasized the important influence of remembered images in the creation of new forms. The role of the artist as an innovator contributing to the tradition from which he draws his ideas was discussed by Pickering in an ambitious analysis of relationships between medieval art and literature. The "deliberate" choice of models and the "astonishing understanding" with which particular qualities were perceived in sources are themes Hanns Swarzenski emphasized in his investigation of the role of copies in the Middle Ages.[17]

Historians have long observed how much of the novelty of the Middle Ages, as well as of the Renaissance, was generated in precisely this manner, through reuses, revivals, and transformations of the past. Percy Schramm focused on this "creative side of medieval culture"; studies by Kitzinger, Demus, and Weitzmann have, more recently, illuminated the ways in which venerable, at times untypical, models were sought out again and again and copied in both western and eastern Europe.[18] By the twelfth century, years of selective borrowing had endowed certain monuments and motifs with special and intense meaning. The use of a particular theme brought with it abundant associations; in fact motifs oftentimes appear to have been selected for the meanings they had accrued.

A prominent example of the creative reuse of venerable motifs is found in the art of the Carolingians, those unabashedly enthusiastic emulators, even imitators, of Roman antiquity. It will be profitable to examine their well-defined and well-described appropriation of antique forms for two reasons: it provides special insights into the motivation and significance of such a reuse and constitutes an important source through which a portion of the later Middle Ages gained access to the art of antiquity.

### The Carolingian Use of "Classical" Forms

The story has frequently been recounted of the way in which Charlemagne, separated in time, space, and lineage from the grandeurs of Mediterranean civilization, sought to evoke the heritage to which he considered himself the legitimate political successor by adopting antique imperial forms and style. The Frankish emperor's programmatic revival of fourth- and fifth-century antiquity was documented by Richard Krautheimer, who demonstrated how, in the early ninth-century ruler's circle, the massive architectural elements of selected Christian Roman monuments were reinterpreted and associated with the edifices of the new European Christian empire.[19] Among his examples, Krautheimer included the triple-arched Lorsch portico, which he viewed as an explicit imitation of the Arch of Constantine. Manuscripts illuminated in Charlemagne's palace and court scriptoria were adorned with painted imitations of carved cameos, luxuriant vines, and colored marbles; even the Gospel writers were pictured as pagan philosophers

*Figs. 15, 16*

at home in imposing theatrical settings or at ease in spacious land-scapes.[20]

These largely Roman elements provided the northern Europeans, recent and sometimes inconstant converts to Christianity, with an instant, imposing self-image that stressed the break with their own barbarous past. The eradication of pagan practices and beliefs was one of the greatest challenges to Frankish kings and priests and became one of the central goals of the Carolingian reform program.[21] One of the key elements in the cultural reorientation of the converts was the proclamation of orthodox Christianity and its ceremonial performance. The use of antique decorative motifs and the retention of Latin in the liturgy were ways of emphasizing an alignment with a venerable tradition that was distinct from and superior to the indigenous vernacular and barbarous one.

It can be argued that the antique architectural forms utilized in church building and painting represented a radical break with Frankish customs of design and decoration. But the greatest impact of these antique motifs was achieved through their application to the sumptuous metal vessels and shrines that were consecrated to the service of the church. It was here, on the forms that most resembled the splendid portable objects that the northerners had long cultivated as a personal artistic genre, that antique motifs made their most dramatic impact. The explicit use of specific architectural designs on a group of Christian liturgical objects invested the sacred vessels with a powerful didactic message, and, equally important, this use transformed the antique motifs in significant ways.

One unusual incorporation of architraves and acanthus capitals occurs on a precious piece of Carolingian ivory carving, the so-called Lebuinus Chalice in Utrecht. The use of architectural motifs in this case closely parallels the decorative scheme on the bronze grilles made for Charlemagne's church at Aachen; it has been said to transform the cup into a *tempietto* ("little temple") signifying a well of life or tomb-tower.[22] While some scholars have argued that this is merely a reflection of iconoclastic tendencies at the Carolingian court,[23] or a theological and philosophical reluctance to employ more representational themes, the persistent intrusion of antique architectural elements of a patently triumphal nature in the design of other liturgical objects suggests a highly programmatic and positive intent for the introduction of these nonfigurative motifs.

The silver reliquary for a piece of the Cross, which was presented by Charlemagne's biographer Einhard to the church of St. Servatius in Maastricht early in the second quarter of the ninth century, was actually a miniature Roman arch of triumph of the single passageway type. It is often compared with the late first-century arch erected in Rome by Titus

*Figs. 17, 18*  to celebrate the conquest of Jerusalem. Images of Christ enthroned, the apostles and evangelists, warrior saints and victorious mounted figures were hierarchically ordered and inserted in place of pagan pictorial representations around an inscription which celebrated the victorious jewelled cross that was originally supported above. This splendid votive gift was destroyed at the time of the French Revolution; its memory is preserved in a seventeenth-century drawing in Paris.[24]

A triumphal arch, this time of the triple or "Constantinian" type, appears again as the interior frame and main architectural motif on the central units of the ivory covers to the Lorsch Gospel Book, said to have been made at the court of Charlemagne early in the ninth century. On the portion now in the Vatican Museum, a standing Christ, flanked by angels, tramples the lion and dragon, demons of darkness and evil, at *Fig. 19*  the center of a tripartite arcaded setting. The companion panels, in the Victoria and Albert Museum in London, employ a similar, somewhat more ornate frame as the backdrop for an enthroned Virgin and Child accompanied by John the Baptist and Zacharias. The theme of victory, implicit in the manner of Christ's presentation treading beasts, is made explicit by the appearance, at the tops of both covers, of flying angels supporting a medallion. These figures assume the form and position of the triumphant genii or winged victories of Roman art who appear in analogous situations, although with different attributes, above the *Fig. 16*  central arch on Constantine's triumphal monument in Rome.[25]

The design of both of these Carolingian objects appears then to be either based on or derived from one of the most iconographically charged structural shapes of late antique architecture, the triumphal arch, monumental symbol of Roman military prowess. The significance of the choice is apparent: both the base for a cross and the cover to a set of Gospels have a precise function in ecclesiastical ceremony, identifying the locus or place in which the essential Christian event, the sacrifice of Christ, recurs—either through re-creation or recitation. In the church environment, the arch, originally a tribute to Roman victory over hostile forces in battle, becomes a witness to Christ's victory over the forces of death, the theme of Christ's appearance in the central arcade of the back cover of the Lorsch Gospels and the inherent subject of the symbolic jewelled cross that rose above Einhard's shrine.[26]

Panofsky, in his discussion of the Carolingian use of classical images, remarked that the borrowed forms did not alter their original nature.[27] His observation aptly applies to the triumphal arch motif. The arcaded liturgical reliefs of the early ninth century were remarkably similar in concept to the Roman monuments whose structure they so closely emulated: memorials raised on the field of battle (the site of Christ's reenacted sacrifice) and dedicated to the victorious divinity. Like so many of the Roman monuments, the diminutive Carolingian ones could also be perceived as supports for a trophy.

24

Trophies, symbolic forms of armored mannequins, are included in the relief carvings on the arch at Saint-Rémy; they are invariably seen at the summit of the triumphal arches that are depicted on imperial coins. In an important study of the antique concept of this particular victory motif, Charles-Picard suggested that the quadriga atop Titus's monument may also have been accompanied by such objects.[28] Although trophies no longer survive in situ, their memory has been preserved for posterity in miniature numismatic depictions.

*Fig. 20*

Christian familiarity with the idea and the term *trophy* appeared as early as the third century, when the word was used to describe the monument to Saint Peter's victory over death that marked his burial place on Vatican hill; by the middle of the fourth century, the concept of the trophy was fully appropriated by Christians and associated with the cross.[29] The identification of imperial forms with Christ grew rapidly in the art of the post-Constantinian church, where it expressed subtly at first, yet powerfully, the political support newly proclaimed by the Roman emperor for the Christian religion. Imperial prototypes produced in this milieu, largely of the fifth and sixth centuries, were emphasized by Schnitzler in his search for the iconographic and stylistic models of the ninth-century Lorsch Gospel cover panels. But the possible reasons for such explicit choices—the significance of the model—have infrequently been investigated. Yet it would seem that the Carolingians had specific issues in mind in the choice of imperial sources: it was firmly "in the Roman sense" that the very term *trophy* was employed in connection with the arch in Carolingian art. According to a prominently displayed inscription, Einhard's miniature arch of triumph was in fact dedicated to the new trophy of eternal victory, the cross that originally stood above it.

*Fig. 19*

The Carolingian adoption of the antique arch motif had transformed a Roman tribute to prowess in battle into a witness to Christian victory in a genuinely novel way. In addition to trophies, Roman arches were often decorated with depictions of booty and even captured soldiers. The arch of Titus, for example, with which Einhard's arch is frequently compared and which may even have served as its model, is decorated along the inner passageway with a relief that depicts the Roman army triumphantly bringing treasures from Solomon's temple, in particular the candelabra, to Rome: the spoils of war carried as a token of success. By employing the monumental symbol of Roman victory, the arch, as the very form with which to visualize their own religion's crucial triumph, the Franks utilized the Roman concept of the spoils of the fallen as the essence of their design.[30]

*Figs. 17, 18*

The idea of *spolia* functioned in another way, too, for the Carolingians, in the actual utilization of ancient remains. Although the evidence is slim because of the disappearance of many objects, it is persuasive in the relevant instances in which it exists. The altar shrine known

*Fig. 21*     as the *escrain* of Charlemagne was crowned by a splendid antique gem
carved with an image of Titus's daughter, and a piece of ivory from a
consular diptych was utilized in the manufacture of the Lorsch book
cover. C. R. Morey, the pioneer American medievalist, pointed out long
ago that the reverse of the Lorsch plaque with the scenes of the Magi,
*Fig. 19*     inserted beneath the standing Christ on the Vatican panel, shows traces
of an inscription identifying a consul of about 500 A.D. It is clearly a
reused piece of ivory: a treasure from the past with which the Carolingians wished to be associated, if not, in this case, a relic of plunder.[31]

The identification of Christ with imperial imagery may have been
routine by the seventh century in those Mediterranean areas that had
been fully Romanized before they were Christianized, but such an association constitutes a novel and highly charged aspect of the trans-
alpine Carolingian sculptures. Within the northern and newly imperial
court, where the Lorsch panels most likely were carved and with which
Einhard was intimately associated, the Gospel covers and the silver arch
would have been understood as dramatic illustrations of the victory of
officially supported, orthodox, Roman Christianity over the discordant
beliefs of diverse Frankish converts: in effect, the political program of
the Carolingian reform.[32]

### Miniature and Monumental

Such diminutive Carolingian sacred sculpture, which Elbern suggested
existed in profusion, offers far more than a mere model for understanding the appropriation of antique elements by the art of a subsequent period or culture. This Christian metalwork displays intimate
formal relationships with the façades of Romanesque Aquitaine and the
similarities suggest direct connection between miniature and monumental, interior and exterior ecclesiastical decoration. Such objects
would have been both more accessible and more pertinent to the
twelfth century than the monumental remains of Rome, which had, in
turn, provided a portion of the Carolingian inspiration.[33] The idea was
put forward in a somewhat different form by Paul Deschamps more
than half a century ago. In a classic article of 1925, he argued that the
rebirth of western sculpture after the year 1000 was, in a sense, an
imitation of the forms and techniques that had been developed during
the Carolingian and Ottonian periods in the minor arts, particularly
metalwork.[34] The argument was taken up a couple of decades later by
the French scholar Daras, who suggested that the reliquaries known to
have been donated to the Aquitainian cathedral of Angoulême by the
bishop under whom the building was begun, about 1120, may have
*Fig. 14*     inspired the complex program of that façade; and from Angoulême, the
author argued, variations on the formula spread throughout Saintonge
and up into Poitou.[35]

The search for precise, plausible sources for the Aquitainian façades, wherever the latter first appeared, leads to three celebrated precious Carolingian shrines which resemble the Romanesque west walls quite remarkably in their choice and arrangement of arcaded motifs. Certainly there once were others; unfortunately, none of the three actually survives. The first, Einhard's arch, brings to mind the single broad arched entries encountered in Aquitaine at Loupiac, Fenioux, and Rioux. The second Carolingian object shared the ultimate fate of Einhard's arch and, like it, survives by means of a drawing in the Bibliothèque Nationale. The splendid shrine known as Charlemagne's *escrain,* a casket or reliquary, was composed of three registers of jewelled arches ascending toward a tapered summit, about a meter in height. Pendant crowns beneath the arcades emphasized the concept of victory which, from the beginning, was probably also implied by the reliquary base above which the arcaded screen rose, although the lower part shown in the drawing dated only from the Gothic period. This shrine closely suggests the multiple overall arcading of façades such as those at Châtres, at Angoulême, and at Plassac.[36]

*Figs. 11, 17*

*Figs. 1–2, 14, 21*

The third piece of metalwork integrated the arcade with the tripartite triumphal arch. It was the exquisite golden altar frontal donated by Charles the Bald to the church of Saint-Denis and known from its representation above the altar, as a retable, in the anonymous Flemish painting in the National Gallery, London, depicting the Mass of Saint Giles. The surface of this wide, rectangular shrine was divided by three lofty, jewel-studded arches into a central opening framed by lateral arches within which a more mural effect was created by the tighter configuration of forms. The triple-arched altar frontal resembles the prominent lower-story façade type found at Parthenay-le-Vieux, the Abbaye-aux-Dames at Saintes, and at Civray.[37]

*Figs. 7, 8, 22*

An association of the entry walls of the western French churches with altar objects helps to explain, at least visually, the walls' self-containment and apparent detachment from the architectural structures over which they often tower. If then, as Deschamps provocatively proposed more than fifty years ago, the sculptors of the structures wished to make of this surface "the magnificently developed replica of a *parement d'autel,*" the question, of course, is why? Why were liturgical objects, with their highly abstract decoration, singled out in this region as the mode for expressing the idea of the triumph of Christianity, a concept that can be illustrated just as well, and indeed was elsewhere at the time, by any one of a number of representational themes such as Christ enthroned? Moreover, how did the twelfth-century designers know of the miniature metalwork? Did specific altar objects provide direct inspiration for the façades or was their impact more general—rather that of a type or group?

Considerable light can be shed on the questions of motive and of meaning when the possible "models" for the Romanesque façades are examined more closely for clues to the implications of their own sources. The arch initially meant triumph in battle, victory over enemy forces; it was a potent image for militant Christianity. But Carolingian liturgical objects were not solely dependent on triumphal arch formulas for their inspiration. Other types of Roman commemorative monuments also appear to have influenced the design of reliquary shrines in the ninth century. The significance of this antique category of frequently ostentatious constructions for the history of subsequent medieval forms, both Carolingian and later, has not been sufficiently emphasized.

*Fig. 21*

The *escrain* of Charlemagne, conceived as a new type of container for relics,[38] is, for example, startlingly close in conception to the multitiered arcaded forms that were occasionally used as funeral pyres in imperial Rome. The memory of such constructions is preserved and was popularized on commemorative coins of the middle empire; those of Antoninus Pius, Marcus Aurelius, and Septimius Severus (161–211 A.D.) often display on the reverse such four-storied, or sometimes five-storied, structures, which diminish toward the top and which were decorated on the outside, according to descriptions, with precious materials. Garlands and even reliefs of horsemen are known to have adorned the base while statues stood under arcades in the middle registers framing a door; these elements are visible on the coins along with a triumphant chariot group that often surmounted the entire structure. In actual practice, as fire consumed the construction and melted the wax effigy that was contained within, an eagle would be released from the

*Fig. 23*

summit to signify the survival and triumph of the dead emperor's soul.

The pyre may have been known to the Carolingians through the description of the structure and the ceremony preserved in Latin texts.[39] Even more plausibly, ancient coins may have served as the means of transmission. Alfred Frazer argued that such a numismatic souvenir very likely served as Michelangelo's inspiration in his initial design for the tomb of Julius II, a "fitting sepulcher . . . for a Christian Caesar."[40] It is known that small precious objects were studied and collected in Carolingian circles and painted "imitations" of Roman coins and cameos appear in the borders and illuminations of Carolingian manuscripts. The precise nature of this Roman material can be defined in several instances. Appropriation of specific imperial gems and coins and incorporation of these treasures into important Christian imperial projects suggests that the diminutive objects, as a group, enjoyed special significance at the Carolingian court.

For example, the image of Charlemagne that appears on coins minted early in his reign closely imitates the portrait type used on Diocletian's coins. An ancient gem, thought to represent Antoninus Pius, was employed as the emperor's seal; set in a ring and surrounded with an appropriate Latin inscription invoking Christ's protection, it demonstrates at once the availability of such material and the high regard the Carolingians had for it. Furthermore, it may indicate particular familiarity with issues of late second-century Roman emperors, the reverse of whose coinage displayed the unusual funeral pyres. Another ancient gem, more properly a rock crystal intaglio, was, in fact, incorporated into the *escrain*, the Carolingian interpretation of the pyre, crowning the summit of the arcaded registers. Tangible proof of ninth-century familiarity with such diminutive treasures, it is, ironically, all that survives to this day of the Carolingian metal shrine.[41]

Monumental attempts, such as the pyre, to defeat the transience of glory, fame, and obviously life were common in Roman society. Another traditional commemorative funerary form was the multilevel turret. J. Toynbee distinguished canopy-tombs with several stories and frequently composed of polygonal as well as cylindrical units from tower-tombs, usually square or rectangular shapes rising from a stepped base. The latter are generally provincial structures, occurring on the western and eastern fringes of the empire, most dramatically in the Syrian desert and near Tarragona in Spain. The most imposing example of the canopy type occurs outside the ancient Glanum in Gaul, near Saint-Rémy in southern France. It is a mausoleum for the Julii family *Fig. 24* more than fifty feet high and decorated on its square base with hunt and battle scenes. The use of a variant on this type for a military monument at nearby La Turbie suggested to Brilliant possible symbolic connections in Roman times between victory in war and victory over death.[42]

Medieval adaptations and fusions of both the Roman canopy and tower forms make explicit the idea of Christian victory over death. André Grabar long ago observed that Christian Gaul's use of a turreted canopy structure probably derived from its familiarity with impressive local pagan monuments such as the one at Saint-Rémy.[43] As far back as Merovingian times, receptacles in this shape were used in churches to carry bread to the altar; called Eucharistic turrets, they are said to be symbolic of the tomb in which Christ's body was believed to have been placed. Indeed, a stepped-tower form with a cylindrical upper story set on a quadrangular base, appears as Christ's tomb on early Christian representations of the visit of the holy women, for example, on ivories in Munich and Milan.[44] Similar but loftier and more complex constructions were frequently used in Carolingian narrative illustrations to represent Christ's sepulcher; a somewhat squatter form was also employed to represent the tombs from which resurrected figures are shown emerging on a group of contemporary Crucifixion plaques. The

*Fig. 25*

tomb that marked Christ's own site of burial is seen rising in several stages behind the angel who alerts the Marys to its emptiness on a late Carolingian ivory in the Walters Art Gallery.[45] Philippe Verdier suggested that the transformation of Christ's tomb in artistic imagination into a multistaged form occurred under the influence of the Carolingian westwork, the towered architectural structure often appended to the western entry of the church and which is known to have served funerary functions. It may not be possible to construct an exact chronology for the influences and priorities among these objects, but correspondences of form among a group of towerlike elements, including representations of Christ's tomb, Eucharistic containers, and actual architectural structures of both pagan and Carolingian usage, are compelling and suggest an inclusive filiation.[46] Each had something to do with death whether it marked the site of actual interment, commemorated burial, or functioned as a symbol of one or the other.

*Fig. 26*

*Figs. 5, 6*

The oldest preserved miniature example of the tower type of shrine is the reliquary of Saint Vincent, also called Bégon's Lantern, in the treasury at Sainte-Foy in Conques. Possibly a ninth-century piece of metalwork with twelfth-century additions to its square base, the container has a cylindrical shaft; its upper part is open and resembles a gallery with columns supporting a conical, imbricated roof.[47] It is far from surprising, in the context of what has already been observed, to find such a form intimately connected to a key Romanesque church element—the lantern turrets that frame several of the arcaded façades. Although the relationship of the miniature Eucharistic lanterns to the lofty paired towers is not instantly apparent and may not be initially convincing, the probability of an association between the two is made compelling, to my mind, by the existence in Aquitaine of provocative intermediary forms. Large, isolated masonry lanterns similar in shape to the reliquaries and close in conception to the paired turrets on neighboring contemporary churches rise in lonely splendor in several of the rural cemeteries that dot the region. Such monumental Romanesque lanterns consist of a cylindrical core which is crowned by a conical roof

*Fig. 27*

supported by a ring of engaged columns.[48] Crozet suggested that Roman mausolea introduced to the architectural landscape the *clocher* or tower design with its tall silhouette and pointed termination. Observing that a late eleventh-century tomb of Saint Front in Périgueux was apparently built in the round and covered with a pyramidal vault, he concluded that the formula of the ancient mausoleum seems to have inspired funerary monuments as well as the upper parts of towers. But he did not pursue the formal connections in the latter case and did not examine the implications of the relationship between "model" and "copy." Previously, George M. Forsyth, Jr., had suggested that the crossing tower at the Carolingian church of Saint Martin's in Angers "probably served as a funerary monument commemorating the treasured fragment of Saint Martin's body which was entombed at the altar beneath." He, too, expressed caution, however, in transferring any symbolic significance to other tower constructions. Yet the popularity of the cylindrical, Romanesque cemetery lantern does indeed seem to confirm the persistence since Roman times of the explicit funerary connotations of this particular vertical shape.[49]

Cellefrouin, Fenioux, Château-Larcher, and Pranzac still display such unique shafts, the memory of which, in the form of archaeological evidence or descriptions, lingers in other towns in Aquitaine and in neighboring regions of Limoges and Berry. These forms are unfamiliar elsewhere in Europe; a study by Fayolle shows them clustering particularly between the Loire and Dordogne rivers. The functions of these towers, according to a frequently cited text attributed to Peter the Venerable, was to honor the dead whose tombs they illuminated, to bring to them the light of the altar, and to carry their memory far off: in other words to extend to them the promise of the arch.[50] It has been suggested in the case of Aulnay, which borders an old cemetery, that the façade turrets there may actually have been provided with openings for lights and thus have served as actual lanterns of the dead. A more extensive use of such paired forms on Aquitainian churches than is indicated by extant construction is suggested by the presence of uncrowned bundled shafts at the corners of numerous façades throughout the region.[51]

*Fig. 13*

*Fig. 11*

Once again, nothing except perhaps the arch and the arcade seems to be more familiar in medieval European architecture than the tower framing the façade. The most imposing example, always cited, is of course the French Gothic composition. But by looking backward from this achievement to its prototypes, all the while seeking to identify prior stages in a development presumed to be continuous, the implications of earlier schemes, such as the Aquitainian one, with its arcaded wall and unconventional turrets have been ignored. Because the western French treatment juxtaposes individual elements in a two-dimensional, decorative manner, independent of the interior, it has not been viewed as the generator of a unified entry-wall scheme. The Aquitainian design does not appear to fit coherently into the sequence of stages that scholars hypothesize led to the Gothic façade; consequently its sources and significance have gone largely unexplored.[52]

In fact, the towered elements of the Aquitaine entry walls draw attention to a formal relationship between the Romanesque façades and the Carolingian *église-porche* or westwork, the two-storied, either single or two-towered structure that often preceded the western entry to the church. The existence of these building types in the region is well documented. Saint-Laurent in Parthenay is known to have had such a structure at its western entry; Maillezais and Charroux provide extant

31

evidence of the survival of the *église-porche* tradition, with its tall, western tower or towers, in Aquitaine. Various scholars have considered the possibility of a connection between the Carolingian form and Romanesque architecture. Reinhardt, for example, developed ideas on the relation between Carolingian and later medieval façades; Daras associated the tripartite arcaded façade of the Romanesque tower porch at Lesterps with both Carolingian porch churches and contemporary church entry walls.[53]

Do these connections have any relevance for the meaning of the Aquitainian façade as considered in these pages? Carolingian western entry forms have been analyzed in terms of imperial symbolism because of their use by the emperor and their occasional similarities to Roman civic structures. More recently, these architectural elements have been studied in relation to interments and to liturgical ceremonies believed to have been performed *in* the structures; consequently their funerary associations have been emphasized. Professor Krautheimer, in his brilliant overview of medieval architecture, explained the development of the Carolingian church as bringing together distinct elements, in particular the sanctuary of the Savior and the martyr's tomb. He interpreted this phenomenon as an expression of the fusion of the triumphant and funerary cults in Christianity. If it was the task of the Romanesque period to integrate these separately identifiable forms and functions in a meaningful way, as Francastel, among others, has suggested, then the Aquitainian façades, with their absorption and interpenetration of the symbols of both victory and death, assume a natural, even paradigmatic, position as the culmination of that development.[54]

### Romanesque Reformulation

The triumphal arch, the canopy tower, and the vertically arcaded screen all originated as pagan commemorative monuments; the design of each was applied during the Carolingian era to a new category of Eucharistic objects. In the Romanesque period each of these sacramentalized antique elements assumed a prominent role in the composition of Aquitainian entry walls. The lantern turret can be associated with the mortal passing of Christ's earthly followers; such a structure also commemorates the site of Christ's own burial. As liturgical containers, little towers provided the link between the worldly reality of physical death and the promise of eternal salvation assured by the Eucharist. The arcaded, multilevel structure, an emblem of deification and immortality in imperial times, inspired, in the Carolingian period, the design of a shrine for the relics of martyrs, "witnesses to Christ"; it served as a sign of the triumph over death through which all Christians are guaranteed eternal life.[55] The triumphal arch defined the locus of the victorious battle, Christ's own triumph on the Cross. The juxtaposition of either arcaded wall or arch and lantern reliquary tower at the monumental western entry to Aquitainian churches represents a proclamation of the essential truth of Christian dogma, triumph over death, and an advertisement of its availability to all.

And this, to my mind, must have been the intention of the Romanesque façade in western France; it explains why liturgical forms were utilized in its conception and why the type was ritualistically repeated throughout the land. The combination of forms on the Romanesque façades cannot have been fortuitous. Neither, I believe, was the twelfth-century attraction to Carolingian liturgical objects, which, in turn, had so carefully emulated antique models, at all serendipitous. It is not surprising that artists should have utilized material from an immediately preceding historical period to define their own, particularly when genealogical and political ties remained strong between ninth-century and late eleventh-century Aquitaine. The age of Charlemagne was the most proximate glorious moment to which one could look back, and it is no coincidence that it was being evoked simultaneously, in even more brilliant fashion, in contemporary vernacular poems such as the *Song of Roland*. Moreover, the considerable evidence of ecclesiastical strength and splendor that existed in treasuries in Aquitaine, in the form of jewels and reliquaries, evoked those earlier centuries in a tangible way.[56]

I find it difficult, however, to accept the idea that a single unique object or small, select group of objects directly constituted the model for the Romanesque façade design. Rather the category of religious "utensils," which like the liturgy itself had been thoroughly Romanized by the Carolingians, more likely provided the inspiration for the monumental architecture. In northern Europe during the post-Carolingian period the forms of altar art, with once-novel Latin elements fully absorbed, became synonymous with Christianity's promise of triumph over death. In this manner the arcaded shrine and the message of salvation were made equally and simultaneously available to successive generations throughout the continent. Why Aquitaine, more than other areas, chose to define its architecture in such liturgical terms is a question that demands attention and is one which constantly directed my research; an explanation will become increasingly apparent throughout this study and is directly addressed in the concluding pages.

Western French churches are seen then to have been profoundly dependent upon Roman architecture but not in the slavish way early nineteenth-century archaeologists implied. Nor was Panofsky's observation that the Romanesque "liberated . . . the latent grandeur" of the classical model particularly generous to the twelfth-century phenomenon (to criticize him by employing one of his own elegant observations).[57] Both the antique and earlier medieval uses of arches and towers were essential ingredients of a Romanesque reformulation. The Aquitainian inventions, in no way mere imitations of the antique, knowingly and energetically regenerated Roman-Carolingian forms, as Krautheimer had suggested they might have done,[58] investing them with new, richer, and more active spiritual lives.

*Fig. 22*

*Fig. 9*

Within an ecclesiastical environment, the new meaning given by the Carolingians to these forms and fragments of antiquity could be perceived both as superseding the old and as substituting for it. But the potential significance gained from Christian possession of venerable Roman imperial symbols remained elite and private so long as the objects on which they were employed were the small, intimate ones of courtly Eucharistic ceremony. The full irony inherent in the sacramentalization of the arch could not be totally appreciated until the form was applied to the accessible portion of actual structures. This was done in Romanesque Aquitaine. Here the arch motif recaptured its original propagandistic power; it could proclaim outwardly the church's internal truth, Christ's victory over death, while heralding the site of the ongoing struggle. And in this location, the arch motif could capitalize on its old associations—openly challenging the memory of its pagan predecessors while at the same time enjoying the reflected grandeur of those far-off rivals. The arch was returned to a public setting no longer as the bearer of trophies but as the trophy itself. Romanesque Aquitaine was able to "Out-Rome Rome," in a sense, by using triumphant antique forms in a truly triumphant manner.[59]

# Chronicles and Chansons

## THE SCULPTURAL PROGRAM

THE AQUITAINIAN FAÇADE LOOMS OVER THE LANDSCAPE AS IT SO often looms over the church: an eminent exterior emblem of the spiritual triumph available to Christians within the building through the reenactment of the Eucharistic sacrifice. Wherever one roams, the recurrent frontispiece serves as an invitation to participate in Christian ceremony; the replication of the arcaded screen at abbeys, in the environs of castles, or adjacent to cemeteries enhances the impact of each individual monument persuading the viewer—pedestrian or cavalier, pilgrim or knight—of its ceremonial, ritualistic message. The repetition of the liturgical form along the horizon acts as a visual litany affirming the universality of Christianity and proclaiming the immediacy of the Christian message.[1]

The austere, abstract, architectural frame with its limited repertoire of instantly recognizable elements is ideally conceived to be apprehended at a distance. Indeed, immediate visual accessibility of form would seem to have been a principle of design, inspiring the adaptation of a highly familiar motif, determining its development in a monumental manner, and motivating its physical and aesthetic profusion. Upon closer inspection, the frame comes alive with the activity of bustling figures, many of whom reinforce by their postures the unrelenting rhythms of the arcaded unit with which they are equated. In several instances, however, the figural motifs lack the instant legibility of the surfaces on which they flourish and seem to be constrained by the relentless order of the zones to which they are restricted. This highly decorative figure carving appears to be in conflict with the architectural form in one other significant way.

It has often been observed that a considerable portion of the façade *Figs. 28, 29* sculpture in Aquitaine represents a fascination with alternately violent and playful decorative motifs. These anecdotal and frequently fabulous themes are scarcely religious and hardly seem therefore to affirm the sacramental implications of the monumental frame. Scenes of combats and hunts, of musicians and monsters enjoy unparalleled reign in this art, although no claim for their statistical predominance over traditional

Christian themes can be made. Yet the energy with which these themes are presented infuses them with exceptional prominence, particularly when viewed within the measured sobriety of the surrounding arcades. Genre images, as so many of these scenes certainly seem to be, are the common partner of arcading throughout Aquitaine; with it, they constitute the most celebrated attributes of its Romanesque art.

*Figs. 30, 31*

No dichotomy between religious and secular need be postulated, however, in approaching this decoration. The collaborative association of worldly aspects along with timeless ceremonial ones is an essential characteristic of Aquitainian Romanesque art and has already been observed in the structural components of the entry wall. The particular turreted forms that enclose numerous façades were seen to have entered ecclesiastical service from popular pagan funerary tradition; the ubiquitous core of the façade conception, the tripartite, multitiered, arcaded screen, was absorbed into liturgical art from a victorious, imperial milieu. Juxtaposition of these forms on the façades provided all viewers with a compelling and concrete illustration of the intimate relationship promised by Christianity between worldly death and eternal life. Such an interdependence of the secular and sublime spheres is vigorously sustained by the sculptural motifs that adorn the schematic frame; but, as often as not, the idea is transformed and inverted in these carvings so that the emphasis appears to be equally on the glories of worldly life and the terror of eternal death.

Several of the decorative and iconographic motifs found on the façades have received extensive attention in the studies of Crozet, Deschamps, Eygun, Mendell, and Tonnellier. For the most part, religious and anecdotal themes have been differentiated and discussed independently. Although primacy of place is given to the former, as with Deschamps's study of virtue and vice imagery, it has been noted that there is really not a lot of religious sculpture on these churches, that what there is represents the repetition of a small number of subjects, and that there seems to be "little close didactic unity" among the carvings. Crozet and Mendell both emphasized the surprising popularity of such early Christian themes as the Temptation of Adam and Eve, Daniel

*Fig. 32*

with the lions, and angels adoring the Lamb. The Marys at the tomb was singled out as the New Testament subject that enjoyed a particularly lively success in the region. Attempts to identify representations of the Last Judgment, however, the theme Emile Mâle had suggested was a recurrent one in the art of the time, led—except in the case of the gable

*Fig. 6*

*Figs. 33, 34*

carvings at Saint-Jouin—to little more than isolated depictions of the weighing of the souls and the parable of the wise and foolish virgins. Nevertheless, Mendell saw in these vignettes allusions to the grander theme and accepted the Last Judgment as the inherent subject of the façades. Crozet, however, doubted that such spotty representations could illustrate collectively a single great religious event or moral lesson.[2]

At the same time, limited contemporary messages or worldly implications were acknowledged for certain anecdotal representations. A duel between two knights was conceded by Mendell to suggest the Truce of God; Crozet observed reflections of activities of the real world in numerous profane carvings, particularly the labors of the months. He *Fig. 35* also confessed that there was a surprising amount of torture and vio- *Fig. 36* lence in much of the sculpture; in connection with the recurrent representation of the Temptation of Adam and Eve, he interpreted this as a message to guard against one's passions. But he took particular exception to Canon Tonnellier's suggestion that a coherent catechismal program, a "sermon Saintongeais," inspired the carvings on a large group of façades; Crozet denied the very existence of a tradition of preaching sermons in the twelfth century and argued that since no such interpretation could be applied to the main church in the area, the Abbaye- *Fig. 7* aux-Dames at Saintes, it was unlikely that other nearby churches would present such a program in the absence of a distinguished prototype.[3]

Since there is little if any disagreement over the identification of subjects, the scholarship on this material will not be reviewed systematically. It is a question rather of context and of interpretation. Interest here resides in exploring ways, formal as well as iconographic, in which selected themes of both a "sacred" and "secular" nature extend and personalize the concepts of Christian triumph and commemoration that are established by the façades' structure. Many subjects, most but not all overtly religious, can be perceived as permutations on the idea of either triumph over death or heroic struggle against evil. Sources of their inspiration can be found in venerable religious objects and texts, as has customarily been done; they can be compared as well with developments in contemporary vernacular literature. Images with explicit Eucharistic content, some traditional, at other times unique, punctuate the architectural screen and underscore its essentially liturgical message. The suggestion that these richly carved screens lack a coherent program can be put to rest.[4]

### Triumph over Death

Diverse examples of death and posthumous glory can be identified on numerous façades. At Chadenac, the three Marys approach the sepulcher of Christ on the southern face of a capital placed at the right angle of the façade. Immediately adjacent to this scene, on the western *Fig. 32* face of the capital, is a second structure shown with a figure recently said to be Christ in a rare early representation of the Resurrection. The appearance of wings to either side of this twisting figure's head suggests that it is an angel. The depiction of either subject would seem at first almost too commonplace on a Christian structure to bear commentary; yet the significance of the theme in the context of these façades should not be overlooked. The discovery of the empty tomb by the three women constituted the first evidence of Christ's triumph over death. His Resurrection provided his followers with the promise of their own individual victory. The Marys' conversation with the angel proclaimed the news and provided the language for the reenactment of the drama at a key point in church liturgy.[5] The isolation of this event from the passion narrative and the elaboration and important location it is given at Chadenac emphasize with particular immediacy the theme of Christ's triumph over death.

This immediacy extends to details of the carving as well. For example, the sepulcher and its enclosure are presented as real and highly tangible structures. A ciborium or canopy opens over the tomb with broad arches that are supported on coupled columns; the miniature architecture represents a precise reduction of the monumental portal immediately adjacent to the capital carving. Above, a corbeled stringcourse, gable, and lantern turrets crown the miniature ciborium in imitation of the façade treatment known, for example, at Saint-Jouin-de-Marnes. The theme of the Marys appeared elsewhere in Saintonge, on the façade at Saint-Léger at Cognac, at Chalais, and on a deposed capital from Saujon, where the tomb is shown within another literally depicted structure: this one is represented by a triple arcade resting on two twisted columns. The scene of the Marys at the tomb is also seen on a capital on the bell tower of the Abbaye-aux-Dames at Saintes.[6]

Fig. 6
Fig. 9

The idea of Christ's triumph is associated with that of his followers in the spandrel zone above the main arcades on the Chadenac façade. At the left angle, a mutilated relief of a warrior with a sword, elevated on a pilaster, is often identified as Saint George; immediately to the right of the main entry stands a winged Saint Michael trampling a dragon underfoot: the martyred military saint is here coupled with the guardian of the dead.[7] George reappears at Pont-l'Abbé, Talmont, Varaize, Nuaillé-sur-Boutonne, and still again, with other martyrs, in an archivolt on the upper level of the façade at Corme-Royal. In the Poitevin region, George is a popular subject on capital and corbel carving both within and without churches. Airvault, Saint-Nicholas at Maillezais, Aulnay, and Civray among other buildings boast images drawn from his chivalric legend. The "fear of destruction" that is inherent in martyrdom and the promise of delivery connect these images to representations of Daniel in the lions' den which proliferate in and on many of the same churches in the region.[8]

Fig. 28

Fig. 37

Martyrdom implies a belief in instant salvation at death, a concept made manifest in certain settings by the presence of angels. Winged creatures flourish in the art of Aquitaine. They surround Christ at Douhet; at Pérignac and Angoulême they herald his Ascension; and at Fenioux, they acclaim his majesty. On numerous portals, such as Nuaillé, Fenioux, Notre-Dame-de-la-Couldre at Parthenay, Pont-l'Abbé and Aulnay, Argenton-Château and Fontaines-d'Ozillac, pairs of them form an arch of censing or adoring figures and frequently they are seen holding aloft a medallion with the Lamb or hand of God.

*Figs. 38–42*

The theme of winged victorious figures is older than Christianity; it traces its roots firmly into antique traditions of funerary, numismatic, and triumphant architectural art, where the creatures appeared both as male and female, seminude and robed. They are seen singly holding laurel wreaths and presenting trophies or paired and supporting circular frames enclosing portraits or inscriptions. Except for coins, such beings appeared most familiarly on sarcophagi and in the spandrels to either side of the central passageway on Roman imperial arches. From this latter category they may have made the transition to the mosaic surfaces and frames of Christian apses, as in the sixth-century church of San Vitale in Ravenna, although this is by no means a clearly perceived circuit. At the same time, angels holding a circular medallion with the bust or symbol of Christ emerged as an important element in the "minor arts," as the crowning motif on ivory book covers and diptychs, for example the celebrated Barberini panel in Paris.[9] This imposing group of private ceremonial objects added a new category to the Roman repertoire of forms on which the flying figures were frequently encountered. The appearance of this theme on the Lorsch Gospel covers, above a victorious Christ in a tripartite arcaded setting, has already been discussed as a prominent manifestation of the Carolingian revitalization of Roman antique and earlier Christian motifs.

*Figs. 50b, c*

*Figs. 16, 18*

*Fig. 19*

Different aspects of triumph could be attributed to the figures in particular settings; victory over death is manifest in their appearance on sepulchral and liturgical objects; political or ideological success over enemies is implied primarily in their use on architectural monuments and in their recurrent presence on official coins. All of these earlier usages of the winged victory figure provide clear precedents for the Romanesque sculptures, and yet the particular route by which the motif reached western Europe is insufficiently understood and inadequately addressed. Critical for the appreciation of the source and significance of flying figures in the art of the medieval West is consideration of the actual role they play in the carved programs. If one analyzes where they are located and what they actually do, one may perceive clues to the type of models that inspired them. Berefelt's recent study of the winged angel noted that the figures are most common in a time and place of Roman revival, suggesting that there may be a programmatic as well as aesthetic explanation for their adoption.

39

The appearance of paired angels holding a medallion on a marble altar table at Toulouse, just beyond Aquitaine in Languedoc, during the last quarter of the eleventh century, was linked to local Gallo-Roman funerary carvings by Gerke and to ecclesiastical metalwork by Deschamps.[10] There is, of course, a relationship between those categories; direct association with the Carolingian liturgical objects that have been discussed in this study should, specifically, be considered. This was a large and relatively varied group of objects of precious materials and of medium scale which had utilized Roman imperial themes in order to illustrate more forcefully the Christian notion of victory. But there are other possible and probable sources for the Romanesque figures of flying angels; identification of these may enhance our understanding of the significance of the medieval usage.

*Fig. 42*      Numerous winged figures adorn the façade at Angoulême, almost, but not completely, overwhelmed by an overlay of nineteenth-century restoration. An angelic archivolt, which once would have crowned the uppermost register of the façade but is now subordinated to a false gable, forms an arched frame above an ascending Christ; two more angels descend through layers of clouds as though to crown him. Some distance beneath Christ, and separated from him by a frieze of medallions that enclose busts of nimbed figures, are two striding angels standing to either side of a small sprouting tree trunk. The latter appears to be the source of the foliation that surrounds the lower part of the oval mandorla in which Christ is contained; its leaves seem to bear him aloft. This foliation, sometimes designated a "tree of life,"[11] clearly connects Christ with the panel of striding angels who are carefully aligned beneath him along the central axis of the façade.

The resemblance of these elements to a group of antique motifs is striking; they present both a conflation and explosion of Roman triumphal formulas. The trophy, as conceived in Roman times, was a tree trunk with a crosspiece on which was draped enemy armor. Sometimes it was shown supporting a medallion. Victories, singly but also in pairs, often accompanied the trophy in depictions on coins. A sestertius of Septimius Severus, struck in commemoration of a victorious campaign, displays on its reverse paired Victories erecting a trophy consisting of an oval shield on a palm tree support.[12] Such an emblematic, propagandistic design was early adapted to Christian purpose. It appears in a number of variations on small metal flasks of the sixth or seventh century acquired by travelers to the Holy Land and preserved from an early date in the treasuries at Bobbio and Monza in Italy. André Grabar studied these tiny containers, whose importance for western iconography has long been suggested, and noted that Roman representations of trophies very likely inspired some of the images found on them.[13] The decoration of one of these ampullae recalls both the Angoulême façade and Roman coins in particularly vivid manner; winged angels are shown to either side of a cross made of sprouting wood: above, an ellipsoidal mandorla that rests on the cross is held at the sides by two flying angels; it encloses a full-length figure of Christ seen seated.

The relation of the form of the trophy to Christ's cross had been noted already in Constantinian times when the identification of the Roman and Christian symbols was officially established.[14] In the Bobbio ampulla, the transformation is complete: the trophy has become the cross and the victorious shield bears Christ's triumphant image. At Angoulême, a flowering tree replaces the cut wood of both the Roman trophy and the cross on the Bobbio flask. Sprouting forms similar to it, in the shape of vine tendrils, were also known in similar contexts in Roman art; they are seen creeping beneath the Victories that stand to either side of the trophy in the decoration carved on the cuirass of a fragmentary marble statue in the Louvre. They appear as well in early Christian art; another flask, this one at Monza depicting the visit of the Marys, shows similar flowering shoots to either side of the cross atop Christ's tomb. The shoots, which emerge from the roof of the building that represents the Holy Sepulcher, were said by Grabar to evoke the garden locale of the event.[15]

In twelfth-century art, the sprouting vine has far richer connotations. Both the trophy-cross as a support for Christ and the living tree had been introduced into the triumphal programs of apsidal decoration in western Europe by that time. The genealogical and paradisiac associations of the growing wood, with its suggestion of Jesse's lineage and the moralizing implications of its potential withering, were particularly central to twelfth-century theology. Although representations of such ideas could have been apprehended by French artists and patrons in Italy, there was no need to travel to come in contact with such themes. The intellectual "imagery" would have been readily accessible and consequently more available than any single visual "image" in a far-off church.[16] Moreover, the tendril forms are handled in a fresher way at Angoulême, with more fidelity to the antique models and with less deference either to abstract forms or an emblematic compositional formula such as one finds in contemporary mosaics in Rome. Decisive for details of design in the French case seem then to have been precious, small-scale objects such as coins, exemplars of triumphant vocabulary known to have been hoarded throughout the Middle Ages.

Inherently Roman themes appear to have been experienced this time, not via Carolingian forms, but directly, through late antique objects. Moreover, the introduction of framed panels set into the Angoulême

41

*Fig. 18*

façade recalls with precision the treatment of reliefs on Roman arches, as, for example, those surrounding the inscription on Titus's monument. It suggests direct experience as well of monumental ancient architecture. Given the availability of Roman remains in the region, particularly around Bordeaux, but also throughout the vast territories of Europe and the Near East—areas to which mobile medieval Christians had access—the emulation of ancient architecture should come as no surprise. However, direct Romanesque "imitation" of Roman architectural material has not been proposed heretofore in this study. Rather, the importance of Christian intermediaries has, until now, been stressed particularly in the utilization of the arcaded and turreted forms. The motivation for borrowing from Roman material directly must be established. An attempt may now be made to offer a hypothetical and, at this point, partial explanation.

Aquitainian patrons and artists appear to have been drawn initially to antique material through the Carolingian intermediary of sacred objects. Ninth-century shrines and reliquaries would have familiarized Europeans with the forms of monumental Roman arches and towers that survived and were accessible throughout southern Europe. Such architectural forms constituted the most imposing group of indigenous structures around, for the intervening centuries had not produced equally large or attractive edifices. Thus, the prime, even sole, visible rivals to the emerging Romanesque buildings were the very ones whose forms these structures sought, for other urgent and important reasons, to emulate. Strong feelings of kinship as well as rivalry would have connected Roman and Romanesque art in the twelfth century. These would have provided, I believe, part of the context in which both an appropriation and an elaboration of particular motifs could easily occur. There are other reasons, and I shall come back to them.

Although the Angoulême façade is itself unparalleled in richness in Aquitaine, angels on other Romanesque façades in the region evoke other types of Roman examples in equally striking ways. Once again the sources appear not to have been just coins but, in several cases, monumental art itself. Winged figures are most frequently encountered on the innermost archivolt of the churches above the main entry; a central

*Figs. 39, 41*

pair generally supports the circular shield or *clipeus* as was so often done in Roman art. They can be seen in that location, for example, at Notre-Dame-de-la-Couldre and at Aulnay. Their introduction into Aquitainian sculpture at this specific juncture—above the central passageway of the arcaded entry wall—suggests a direct and intimate awareness of monumental Roman architectural models, not merely the

*Fig. 50b*

coincidental transfer of a motif encountered on portable objects or coins to a monumental entry. The Aquitainian use of the motif over the entry emphatically recombines the winged Victory with the arch. On Con-

stantine's monument in Rome, such paired figures fill the spandrels     *Fig. 16*
around the main passageway. The explicit association of these creatures
with Romanesque entry portals reasserts the material and military
tradition in which Victories had been publicly encountered in antiquity.

At Pont-l'Abbé, the elements are handled in a particularly dramatic     *Fig. 38*
way, one that calls attention to monumental Roman sources in yet
another significant detail. In addition to the full-length angels surrounding a circularly framed Lamb of God on the face of the inner
archivolt, half-length angels in medallions adorn the underside of the
deeply recessed archivolt immediately over the entry; they appear to
sustain another medallion with the hand of God. The ornamentation of
the soffit or "surface" of the actual passageway emulates the decoration
of the vaults of triumphal arches, most conspicuously Titus's arch with
its apotheosis panel on the summit of the coffered barrel. The adaptation and compression of a sequence of Roman monumental elements
into a somewhat more constrained Romanesque format injects a highly
expressive, almost aggressive aspect into the conception of the church
door's frame. Even Crozet noted that the presentation of the divine
hand in this manner here and at Varaize seemed to bless those who
passed through the portal.[17]

But the Christian winged figures assume other more colloquial roles
as well on the Romanesque portals; they are not always presented as
obvious heirs to the traditions of triumphal art. At Civray, angelic musicians form an archivolt around a horseman, promising immortality to     *Fig. 43*
the mounted combattant as they do in the contemporary *Song of Roland*.[18] In the poem, they gather the soul of the fallen hero and carry it to
heaven offering a "saint's reward for his efficacy as a killer."[19] The
angels are aided in the *Chanson*, actually led, by Saint Michael, who has
already been seen in the sculpture with Saint George at Chadenac. He
figures again in reliefs at the left of the center door at Chail, on the
tower at Chauvigny, at Chalais, Haimpc, Gensac-la-Pallue, and Marestay. "God's warfaring angel," as Michael has been called,[20] may also
appear as the winged rider who, like the saints at Chadenac, is elevated
on a column in the manner of a trophy, above the façade at Saint-
Jouin-de-Marnes. There he enters the highest zone, that dominated by     *Fig. 6*
the resurrected, triumphant Christ seen in the center of the gable dis-
playing his wounds.[21] The situation of the mounted warrior saint at this
location evokes the long tradition of military allegiance with God that
stretches back through the Carolingian period into early Christian art
when the symbol of Roman military success, the trophy, was initially
assimilated with the cross of Christ. It introduces the themes of warfare
and struggle to which I shall return below.

The weighing of souls, the activity with which Michael is so closely

*Fig. 33*

associated, is among the themes that recur in the sculptural decoration of Aquitainian churches. It can be seen on a corbel prominently placed on the north angle of the façade at Corme-Royal, where it dramatically appears to be in support of the entire upper structure, and on the façade at Cognac. Capitals at Saujon, the Abbaye-aux-Dames and Saint-Eutrope at Saintes, Colombiers, Arces, Aulnay, and Saint-Laurent at Parthenay display the scene, although not, in these cases, on the façade. The frequent association of this scene with the Last Judgment, as, for example, in the Romanesque tympana at Conques and at Autun, overwhelms the motif with allusions that obscure and distort the sense it projects when seen by itself. Rather than being interpreted as an abbreviated symbol of punishment at the final days, as Mendell inferred, in these instances of isolated appearance it should be read as a sign of the immediate reckoning for which Christians, like Roland, must always be prepared and which awaits them at death.[22]

### Implications of Form

Choice of subject matter, however, is but one aspect of content. The particular ways in which themes are arranged and portrayed constitute equally, if not more, compelling components of imagery. Compositional forms and spatial and illusory devices are special features that differentiate visual from verbal modes of expression and provide each with its own efficacy. And it is with varied optical means that the concepts of martyrdom and triumph are underscored, not simply illustrated, on the Aquitainian façades. The selection and emphatic reuse of venerable forms that has been seen in the architectural conception of the west wall contributes significantly, in itself, to the iconography of triumphant death. It evokes the union with the Christian past that is guaranteed to the individual through martyrdom. Repetition of the same composition and of the same form within a single composition, another characteristic of the façades, similarly confers upon specific motifs and shapes a distinctly ceremonial aspect.[23]

*Fig. 29*

Numerous Aquitainian archivolts are organized as radial compositions in which the axes of repeated figural motifs recreate the radii of the circle on which the arch is constructed. A great variety of subjects is presented in this form. Frequently they are purely vegetal or drawn from the bestiary; sometimes Christian themes, such as the elders, follow this organization; most commonly, perhaps a dozen or more times, the signs of the zodiac and the labors of the months are seen side by side in a paratactic arrangement. Such a scheme emphasizes the literalness of each unit of which the arch is composed; by restricting the height of each figure and limiting its lateral area to one or two voussoirs, this grouping further permits the incorporation of many figures or elements in its decoration. Although fifty-four is clearly more than twice the requisite number of elders, this radial voussoir disposition may well have been selected for their display at Saintes to emphasize both their number and the tangibility of their ceremonial role. *Fig. 45*

The same principle of organization is used on a lateral arch at the same church for a highly liturgical representation of the Last Supper. The scene is meticulously rendered with the lower extremities of the apostles doubling over onto the soffit of the arch so that they seem to serve as supports for the table—the edge of which is aligned with the angle of the actual archivolt. Christ, about to feed a small figure to his right, is symmetrically framed by an elevated chalice and Host, an arrangement that led Crozet to suggest that this sculpture depicted the institution of the Eucharist. At Saint-Symphorien-de-Broue, Crozet preferred to call the repeated figures a collective *acclamatio* instead of identifying them simply as elders: in both instances he responded to the ceremonially repetitious effect of the radial composition without directly acknowledging it.[24] *Fig. 44*

A particularly expressive use of the radial construction appears again at Saintes, at the Abbaye-aux-Dames, where the central archivolt around the center door is decorated with representations of executions. Two figures, one a man with a sword or whip and the other a woman, flank a central nude figure who either is about to be or is in the process of being struck. The triad of forms is repeated along the voussoirs more than a dozen times, creating a cumulative, yet static effect of brutality. Mendell described the scenes as a "wholesale martyrdom" and identified the subject as the Massacre of the Innocents.[25] The identification has generally been accepted, although its representation in the area is infrequent if not unknown; Crozet noted, for example, that the scene of the massacre "fait défaut" in the art of Poitou.[26] *Fig. 45*

Representations of the Massacre of the Innocents traditionally display a wholly violent "group activity" directed by Herod, as, for example, in the capital frieze on the west façade at Chartres. It is unusual to find the event depicted as a leaderless sequence of repetitious tortures, as seen here at Saintes. Indeed this interpretation of the event recalls, by virtue of its arrangement, the repetitious grouping of martyrdoms known in Byzantium as early as the late tenth-century, when collections of martyrologies, calendars in which a different saint's death was shown on each page, became popular. By the twelfth century, such sequences were presented as icons, portable panels on which twenty or thirty scenes of torture might be painted in small compartments. Comparable groupings of saints also appeared on chancel screens and from there probably influenced the design of church doors, as can be seen, for example, at San Marco in Venice. The monotonous, repetitive organization of the Saintes' archivolt is, like the Byzantine bronze doors and the icon, ritualistic; it could be perceived, in a sense, as a sculptural equivalent.[27]

But it is not necessary to argue that a visual model from the eastern

Mediterranean inspired the European representation. The metaphoric idea of the Innocents as martyrs pervades western medieval literature, as D. H. Green has recently emphasized in an important study of twelfth-century German literature. Various texts, he notes, view the Innocents as the first soldiers of Christ who sacrifice themselves in battle in the service of their leader. And as the earliest martyrs, the Innocents serve as examples in the contemporary world for the Crusaders.[28] It is this familiar intellectual association that helps to explain why the Saintes' figures appear as mature victims in individual scenes of torture on the archivolt. Because their massacre is conceived as a martyrdom, it is organized as one; the infants, consequently, are represented in the familiar contemporary physical guise of martyrs.

In fact, the nude victims on the archivolt recall most closely the three impaled martyrs who appear beneath the feet, or in front of, Christ in the Wolfenbüttel Liber Floridus, a contemporary European manuscript. Originally written and illustrated in the second quarter of the twelfth century, and copied soon thereafter, this text has been intimately related to post-Crusade militancy, the important ecclesiastical and political reality of the period to which these western French façades are also intimately allied.[29]

Mendell, in discussing the placement of this scene at Saintes, near archivolts carved with the apocalyptic beasts and elders, suggested that it related to the passage in Revelation 6:9 when John sees the "souls of them that were slain for the word of God," a broad allusion to martyrs. Her observation is confirmed by an analysis of the contemporary meaning of the massacre story. But the allusion should be understood as being explicit and concrete, not vague or universal, in keeping with the literalness of Romanesque imagery. Such tangibility is further underscored by the organizational format of the archivolt. The repetitive, radial arrangement of voussoirs is employed at the Abbaye-aux-Dames to emphasize the collective and continuous character of the Christian concept of martyrs: those who, dying for Christ, are joined with others who, before them, have likewise sacrificed their souls for him.[30]

One final example of the incorporation of explicit death references into the triumphant façade scheme occurs at several churches where recessed niches, apparently intended for actual sepulchral use, are introduced beneath the arcades. At Ségonzac, two such openings frame the central portal although the overall effect hardly departs from that of *Fig. 46* the standard triple-arched doorway.[31] At the hospice at Pons, sepulchral receptacles are understandably incorporated beneath the lateral arches of the multiple arcade. The form of ceremonial triumph here embraces mortal death in a manner that explicitly recalls the combination of forms and usage on Charlemagne's reliquary *escrain*.[32] Even at tiny La Rochette, the recessed arches flanking the central entry permit the insertion of sarcophagi beneath the reliefs of rider and lion fighter. Admittedly it is not clear that such was originally intended there, but it is known that numerous churches in Aquitaine were explicitly founded to house the remains of their benefactors, in other words, to function as material shrines commemorating the deceased.[33]

The Aquitainian churches stand in strong visual contrast to more conventionally pious monastic foundations, such as those found at Languedoc and Burgundy, which were served by Benedictines. In these churches, the salvation of the soul and the perpetuation of its memory were primarily assured by the spiritual activity that took place *within* the building: prayers and the elaborate celebration of a particularly commemorative liturgy.[34] The main portal into these churches frequently dramatized, through a focused arrangement of sculpural forms, the unique point of entry into that interior space. The visitor to abbeys such as Moissac and Vézelay would encounter above these doors an image of an enthroned, celestial Christ, a projection onto the tympanum of the theme traditionally localized in the sanctuary vault, above the altar inside.[35] It is a "distant" program, one that is eschatological in content, emphasizing as it does Christ's reappearance at the end of time. Moreover, an inherently judgmental tone is reinforced by the broad, and at times forbidding, forms of sculpture which, as at Moissac, bar or occlude the entry rather than encourage passage within.

In contrast, the reliquarylike forms of the Aquitainian screen façades, with their depictions of themes of triumphant death, suggest an attitude toward salvation that is at once more immediate and accessible than the one conveyed by the monastic doorway scheme. Frequent representations of Eucharistic themes, such as birds drinking from chalices on the portal voussoirs at Saintes and Corme-Ecluse and next to the scene of the weighing of the souls at Corme-Royal, provide reinforcement for the idea of liturgical imminence that pervades the Aquitainian entry walls. An unusual and almost shockingly beautiful image of a woman, holding or eating a cross-inscribed wafer—a highly tangible reference to communion—can be observed on prominent exterior capitals at Aulnay, Dampierre-sur-Boutonne, Fontenet, Civray, and Saint-Etienne-le-Cigogne.[36] And at Pont-l'Abbé, the angels over the main door carry a candle, a censer, and a chalice, instruments of the Mass, as they accompany and elevate an image of the Lamb of God, whose appearance, in this context, evokes the words of the celebrant.

*Fig. 33*

*Fig. 47*

*Fig. 38*

It cannot be denied that the Aquitainian façades emphatically thrust outward both utensils and images of the ceremony that lies at the heart of the daily Christian liturgy; in this way, they make concrete and tangible the mysteries of the interior of the church. It is important as well to note that Augustinian canons, whose religious life was of a relatively worldly orientation, served a disproportionate number of foundations in this region while Benedictine houses, with their more "introspective" focus, were less frequent in Aquitaine than in other parts of France.[37]

### The Struggle for Moral Perfection: Celestial

By far the largest number of subjects that adorn the façades relate in one way or another to the moral struggle for perfection with its promised triumphal reward for the victor, a theme which had been likened to martyrdom in the early church.[38] Representations of the virtues and vices were identified by Deschamps on more than two-dozen façades in western France, from Civray, Argenton-Château, Notre-Dame-de-la-Couldre at Parthenay, and Foussais in Poitou, to Aulnay, Corme-Royal, Chadenac, and Pont-l'Abbé in Saintonge, down to Blasimon below Angoumois. They were discussed by him in considerable detail.[39] Although Crozet was dissatisfied with the description of this scheme as the key to a visual sermon, the subject does appear throughout Aquitaine with unprecedented frequency and in an unusual format.

*Figs. 10, 11, 28, 35, 37–41*

In the Aquitainian sculpture, armed amazons or, more usually, tall graceful figures surmount monstrous little creatures to form static couples with little evidence of discomfort apart from the losers' grimaces. The victorious women and their victims create a repetitive, anthropomorphic counterpart to the arcaded frame; each couple is frozen in the midst of actions which, like the gestures of the executioners on the Saintes archivolt, evoke the memory of a dramatic confrontation, without, in themselves, being active. The moral battle, like martyrdom, is presented in these sculptures as a recurrent ritual.[40]

*Figs. 39, 40, 45*

But the arrangement of these figures along the archivolt is dramatically different. In contrast to the radial scheme employed for the scenes of martyrdom, a circumferential treatment, in which the axis of each archivolt figure bends to fit the curve of the arch, is used for the virtues. This alternative design has often been thought to represent a significant conceptual development in portal configuration because it becomes the arrangement of choice in Gothic doorway design. But no stylistic or chronological distinction is consistently apparent in the use of either the radial or circumferential treatment and frequently both are employed on the same monuments. At the Abbaye-aux-Dames at Saintes, both arrangements are employed around the main door; at Notre-Dame-de-la-Couldre at Parthenay, at Aulnay, and at Pont-l'Abbé, the differentiation of voussoir treatment distinguishes the side arches from the main entry. The choice of one or the other of the arrangements appears to be bound to the number of figures each allows and the degree of literalness or allusiveness desired in a given representation.[41]

*Figs. 10, 45, 48*

Katzenellenbogen, who traced the development of the virtue and vice theme from its earliest literary statement through the course of the Middle Ages, noted that it was in the archivolt decoration of western French Romanesque churches that the portrayal of the triumph of the virtues, rather than the struggle and illusory successes of the vices, was given its fullest and most striking expression.[42] The idea of feminine virtues, but little else, appears to be drawn from the celebrated early Christian epic poem that was written by the Spaniard Prudentius around 405, a few years before his death. In the *Psychomachia*, the struggle for the soul is depicted as a series of fights waged between the opposing human forces of desire, who actually do quite well in the confrontation, and duty, the ultimate victors. The original, possibly contemporary illustrations to this text were dynamic representations seemingly modeled in part after Roman imperial reliefs of armed encounters. These images have not survived but the illustrations that were repeated over and over in the numerous versions of the manuscript made late in the Carolingian period betray familiarity with such models. Modifications, such as the wearing of armor and the bestialization of the vices, were introduced at this time. Still, through the tenth and eleventh centuries, the illustrations remained highly narrative, very worldly and irregular, emphasizing the wiley actions of the vices to which Prudentius devoted so much of his poem.[43]

A major transformation in the theme is observable in the twelfth century when the virtues appear detached from the poem either as individual, stressless moral personifications or as ceremonial static groups of paired antagonists. The lusty scenes of moral turpitude seem to vanish from the context of the struggle between good and evil. Since paired antagonists are the type that proliferated almost exclusively on the Aquitainian archivolts, the significance of their transformation of Prudentian imagery is of particular interest to this study.

Again it is a Carolingian appropriation of a late antique motif that provides the closest analogy to the Aquitainian Romanesque formulation. A late Carolingian ivory, now in Florence, possibly still identifiable with palace workmanship, displays a pair of armored males standing on fallen victims. They rest spears on their conquests' heads in a manner similar to that in which the Romanesque virtues appear in the Aquitainian archivolts.[44] The tight, arched frame around each pair on *Fig. 49* the ivory is particularly reminiscent of the miniaturization of triumphant architectural imagery discussed above; it draws attention to the relationship between this diptych leaf and the Lorsch book cover, to *Fig. 19* which it is formally and thematically related. There the victorious Christ is shown trampling beasts, a posture derived from representations of Roman emperors, for example, Arcadius, who had been depicted in a similar pose, trampling a defeated figure, on late fourth-century coinage. Prudentius was most certainly familiar with such a contemporary image and one may even have inspired his own description of Faith, trampling her foe's head underfoot.[45]

*Fig. 50d*

The Carolingians popularized the association of this pose with Christ, emphasizing its triumphant connotations as an illustration of Psalm 90 by juxtaposing it with an explicitly victorious setting.[46] The Florence ivory, a variant on this theme, has been thought to depict either virtues or, more recently, conquering emperors[47]—triumphant good in either event. The victorious Aquitainian virtues seen trampling demonic forms within a triumphant frame appear to have been visually inspired by this familiar category of Carolingian liturgical reliefs, which includes the Lorsch covers; Prudentius's text provided only indirect, or very general thematic, guidance. The transformation of the theme of the virtues and the transmission of the image of the triumph of good over evil recapitulate the process observed in the adaptation of the architectural frame: from late Roman imperial to early Christian forms and through Carolingian objects to Romanesque monuments.[48]

*Fig. 39*

Two additional observations may be made at this juncture. First, the Carolingian reform program demonstrated an important concern for personal morality as an aspect of religious conversion. Priests were provided with texts from church fathers on the virtues and vices which sharply contrasted Christian ethics from pagan systems, both Germanic and Greco-Roman. There is apparently little evidence to link Prudentius's text with the compilation of such *florilegia,* and yet it is apparent that the copying of the *Psychomachia* during this time must be viewed in the context of this reform spirituality.[49]

Second, apart from Aquitainian façades, the other area in which representations of the virtues were most frequently encountered in eleventh- and twelfth-century sculpture was in the ornamentation of sacred objects, the category with which the Aquitainian façades are, I believe, overtly allied. Katzenellenbogen enumerated examples of fonts, shrines, reliquaries, and even chalices and patens, that were adorned with timeless, moral personifications rather than victorious depictions of temporal triumph. A celebrated piece of eleventh-century metalwork, the golden antependium from Basel, associated such representations of virtues with an arcaded relief that enclosed images of Christ shown treading the demons of darkness and surrounded by archangels, elements seen in related combinations on the Aquitainian façades.[50]

The development and proliferation of the the explicitly triumphant version of the allegory of the virtues in Aquitaine must be linked to the pronounced victorious imagery of the region's architecture. Katzenellenbogen pointed out that a crown carved in the hands of the two topmost figures in the "Psychomachia" archivolt at Argenton-Château, but now lost, was a tangible token of the prize promised to the victor over evil. At Aulnay the two top figures may still be seen holding a crown aloft, as they do at Parthenay and at Fontaines d'Ozillac. The crowns can also be associated with a passage from Tertullian, cited by Mâle, in which the fight of the virtues against the vices is likened to the contests in an arena in which the winners receive crowns. Deschamps linked these crowns to the one Tertullian elsewhere says Christ will give his faithful at death, an association, essentially, of the victory over vice with the triumph over death.[51] Indeed, the stepped staging of the voussoirs from the surface of the wall at the outermost arch to a deeply recessed level at the innermost one adds genuine dimension to each archivolt and makes the crowns appear to be suspended over or extended to the worshiper who enters the portal. Thus Tertullian's metaphor is made tangible by the placement of the form in relation to the visitor's experience.

*Figs. 41, 39*

Another metaphoric illustration of the reward for virtue is found in the parable of the wise and foolish virgins, which is illustrated alongside or nearby the virtues on numerous voussoirs in Aquitaine. Matthew 25 tells how the five watchful, sensible maidens, whose lamps were well filled, gained easy entry to Paradise while their lazy, thoughtless counterparts arrived empty handed and too late and were barred at the door. The story, dramatized in a contemporary church play and known in a Limoges manuscript, is illustrated alongside the triumph of the virtues on the façades at Aulnay, Chadenac, Corme-Royal, Fenioux, Pont-l'Abbé, and Pérignac, reiterating there the idea of a glorious eternal reward for the virtuous.[52]

*Figs. 28, 34, 35, 37, 38, 51*

In these depictions, the Gate of Paradise, where the wise virgins meet the bridegroom, is judiciously located at the apex or keystone of the archivolt. At Corme-Royal, the upper portion of the archivolt breaks through the stringcourse that encloses the richly ornamented second story; it rises loftily above the central portion of the façade. This overt identification of the celestial portal with a material one provides a visible analogue to the anagogical thinking that permeates religious literature of the time. In contemporary writing, allusions to heavenly life are repeatedly recognized within historic events; the realities of earthly experience are consistently perceived as "figures" or manifestations of a variety of future truths. Auerbach dwelt at length on the phenomenon of "figural interpretation" in secular literature; Lubac investigated varied stages in the process emphasizing the dynamic unity and reciprocity of the different levels of meaning that emerge from such thinking. This "symbolist mentality," in Chenu's words, is evident in the visual as well as verbal spheres.[53] The sculptures of the Aquitainian façades give concrete form to a variety of intelligible but essentially invisible Christian truths about the ultimate rewards of the virtuous.

*Fig. 37*

Heavenly ideas are revealed by being visualized as tangible, familiar forms.

On one level then, the archivolt on which the parable of the wise and foolish virgins is shown is a visual metaphor for the Gate of Paradise at which Christ welcomes the well-prepared souls. The story is not simply illustrated along this arcuated backdrop; the key feature of the drama, the heavenly door, is literally identified with the central element of the actual portal structure and transforms it, thereby, into something more imposing. The archivolt does not merely stand for the celestial gate; in this place, it becomes the very gate itself.

*Fig. 28*

The identification of the material Aquitainian façade with the celestial portal is suggested in another way on a second façade. At Chadenac, where the subject receives attention on one of the main archivolts around the center door, Christ is shown as at Corme-Royal, at the apex of the arch, emerging from behind a miniature arched opening. The characterization of the diminutive archway, with ornate columns and a decorated archivolt, resembles the arcades of the actual façade; the tiny pine-cone-like turrets that rise to either side of the small celestial gate appear to confirm an identification of this entry with the familiar façade

*Figs. 5, 6*

type of the region, best represented at Saint-Jouin.[54]

*Figs. 30, 31, 51*

A second typically medieval level of interpretation, the identification of moral values in sacred experience, is also realized on many of these façades. The virtues, as acknowledged figures of the perfect soul, are arranged so that they compose another of the central archivolts on numerous façades. Like the portal in the parable, these figures are not simply *equated* with the church—they literally constitute a crucial portion of its fabric and become one with the monument. In building a segment of the actual shrine, the triumphant militia replicates the activity of the victorious virtues in the last section of the *Psychomachia*; there they too build a holy city, each face of which is said to be adorned, like many of the façades, with three gates (lines 823f.).[55] Tropological or moral content, the identification of the perfect soul with the heavenly temple, is thus expressed on the façade through the interpenetration of architectural frame and sculptural form. The overlay of images creates an optical "allegorical chain"—like the intellectual one that led Alain de Lille, according to Chenu, to link together the house in which men worship, the heavenly city, and the temple of Christ's body as a single, all encompassing metaphoric temple.[56]

Jerusalem, itself, was very often central to such literary imagery in the twelfth century.[57] Baudri of Bourgeuil, writing shortly after the First Crusade, discussed the earthly holy city as the prefiguration of the celestial Jerusalem attacked by an invisible enemy against whom spiritual conflict was necessary.[58] The description of the holy places found in the Crusade tract, *Gesta Francorum,* begins with Jewish places and monuments and intersperses them with Christian ones. Identifications are not always correct by modern standards, as when the mount of Golgotha is called the place where Adam was buried, Abraham attempted to sacrifice Isaac, and Christ was crucified, but such an identification accurately reflects medieval understanding. The implication of the continuity and primacy of the city throughout history is apparent and, obviously, most important. When the anonymous writer declares that the navel of the world lies thirteen feet to the west of Calvary, he is making explicit his era's concept of the cosmic centrality of the city.[59]

It is possible that the representations of the labors of the months and the signs of the zodiac that form the outermost archivolt on several façades relate to and are intended to illustrate this geographical localization of Jerusalem. Such imagery had a long tradition in ancient *Fig. 35* and early Christian art as a symbol of the heavens. It does more here, however, than suggest either the worldly dimension within which the Christian message is enacted, the natural rhythms of the seasons into which the religious cycles were fitted, or the fruits of manual work.[60] The carved calendrical system assumes the shape of a circular map similar to the painted and drawn versions of the universe that were known in Roman times. In this location and form, as a circular band at the outermost level of the archivolts, the cosmological scheme can be understood to represent the universe enclosing both the perfect souls who are Christ's church and the celestial portal. It reinforces, thereby, the key notion of the time that the Holy City, for which both the souls and the church stand, is truly at the hub of the universe.[61]

An analogous but far simpler annular format, in which the Lamb is seen at the center of a stark series of concentric rings, represents the heavenly Jerusalem in Carolingian manuscripts of the Apocalypse. A contemporary circular map of heaven depicts the sun chariot surrounded by concentric rings filled with depictions of the months and the zodiac.[62] It is tempting to suggest such miniatures as the ultimate source for the sculptural concept. Emile Mâle endorsed the iconographic dependence of medieval sculpture on manuscript painting early in this century and the idea has proven to be extremely durable. All that can be said in these cases, however, as in fact in many instances, is that the painted and carved images reflect common and profound medieval intellectual beliefs in the circular and annular disposition of the universe and in the notion that God resides in the celestial center. Each image may well be an independent, individual visualization of that concept although that suggestion need not negate the possibility that the depictions are related.

On the central door of the west façade at Aulnay, the radial and *Fig. 51* frontal treatment of the busy zodiacal scenes on the central portion of the outermost archivolt affirms the flatness of the façade surface; in contrast, the circumferential arrangement of the taller, twisting figures on the inner triad of voussoirs enhances the effect of recession which is so pronounced on many of these central portals. A meaningful distinction between these modes of decoration can be developed on thematic grounds and seems to have been intended. At Aulnay, the literal, material voussoir rendering is applied to the fixed signs of the visible world; it emphasizes man's collective, repetitive, and consequently ritualistic relationship to his environment. The tangible, ceremonial effect of this treatment most closely echoes that of the arcaded façades themselves.

*Fig. 48*  Radially arranged voussoirs around the lateral, blind arches, here and at Pont-l'Abbé, in like manner appropriately enclose ritualistic, worldly—and often historic—scenes of martyrdom. In contrast to the treatment of such themes, intelligible but theoretically invisible entities, such as virtues and angels, and even martyrs and elders, are identified with the more abstract and structural, not merely constructional, elements of the building itself. These triumphant motifs at once give shape to each complete arch and are inseparable from it.[63]

A metaphoric reading of the archivolts is particularly, but in no way exclusively, applicable to the central west door at Aulnay, the richest and most subtle of the Aquitainian monuments. Indeed figural thinking here genuinely transforms the unit of stepped carvings from a seemingly disparate series of paratactically organized sacred stories into something that is dramatically and aggressively allusive. The archivolts provide a precise, material visualization of the triumphant Christian's reception in the heavenly city; the metaphor of salvation is made, thereby, remarkably tangible. At the outermost level, zodiacal signs are shown encircling the Holy City, localizing and fixing it at the center of the cosmos. The celestial gate, in the middle of which Christ is seen welcoming the wise and vigilant, encloses the temple made of virtuous souls. As one passes through this third level, which spatially is distinct from but coexists with the others, the visitor comes face to face with the Lamb of God: the central, the innermost, the key element in this triumphant, celestial hierarchy.[64]

A crucial portion of the façade carving on several Aquitainian churches is thus devoted to hierarchic examples of victorious activity; themes that restate and reinforce the triumphant testimony of the architectural form constitute the very fabric of the abstract frame and present themselves as figural extensions of it. These motifs identify the structure of the building with a number of intellectual concepts concerning the church as an institution. At the same time, the architectural scheme provides a ritualistic setting in which the ceremonial activities that celebrate the invisible truths can be appreciated. The repetitive figures that are assembled side by side along selected archivolts particularly reinforce this aspect. The shrine embraces both; and two organizational schemes—radial and circumferential—provide complementary modes of presentation: tangible forms and events are customarily perceived and visualized as ritual; intelligible ones can only be experienced as metaphors.

So abiding is the victorious frame that even demonic forms illustrating the rule of disorder, such as devouring figures consuming archivolts and grimacing heads swallowing capitals, cannot threaten its stability; rather they ironically reinforce it. Such images of discord and struggle are subdued by the permanence of the arcade which always survives intact, surpassing any threats from internal disorder. The intermingling of spheres of experience, the permanent and the transient, the intelligible and the palpable, is intimate and inextricable; traditional distinctions between the categories of sacred and secular appear repeatedly to be transgressed; Aquitainian façades, as will be seen, are simultaneously chronicle as well as trophy.[65]

*Fig. 36*

### The Struggle for Moral Perfection: Terrestrial

Moral struggle, like the theme of martyrdom, is another central issue dealt with in contemporary vernacular literature. The *Song of Roland* can be read as an armed fight of good and evil in which the Franks are personifications of Christian virtue and the Muslims are the embodiments of pride, greed, and treachery. Auerbach emphasized that the language of the *Chanson* exteriorizes moral dilemmas so that they can be perceived as tangible deeds, not unlike the manner in which abstract qualities are acted out in Prudentius's poem. Focillon, it would seem, had been sensitive to the same qualities but viewed them in a reverse relationship; he noted that the twelfth-century sculpture in Aquitaine transformed the *Psychomachia* into a *chanson de geste*. Recently the *Song of Roland* has been compared directly with the *Psychomachia* and the similarity between certain actions has been emphasized. Roland, first to face battle, can in a sense be likened to Faith whose followers, like his, are martyrs; the brutal punishments of devious Discord and treacherous Ganelon, with which the epics end, provide another strong parallel between the texts.[66]

In the chronicle of *Pseudo-Turpin*, a prose account of some of the same material included in the *Song*, the fight of the Carolingian army against the Moors is overtly likened to the general fight against evil.[67] Just as Charles's warriors readied their weapons before battle, so the reader is reminded to prepare his weapons, that is his virtues, before undertaking the struggle against vice. The Pauline notion that man must arm himself with spiritual weapons in order to conquer base impulses (Eph. 6:11–17) informs both Prudentius's epic and the twelfth-century literature. These texts promise celestial recompense to those who overcome wrongdoing in themselves and who, in other ways, conquer terrestrial evil. "Whoso puts virtue before vice, his spear shall sprout and his victor's soul shall be crowned in heaven."[68] The virtuous man is promised an honor like that accorded the soldier martyred in battle.

The idea of moral struggle as it developed in the Middle Ages appears to derive in part from Prudentius's epic, yet the ritualized representations of the virtues and vices on the archivolts of Aquitaine have little to do formally, as has been seen, with either the illustrations or the text of the *Psychomachia*. Several of the narrative situations ascribed in the poem to the misrule of certain vices do, however, appear to crop up in sculptural details elsewhere on the western French portals. They represent, I believe, a deliberate contemporization, like the *Song of Roland*, of Prudentius's struggle allegory. The text then, known in western Europe from its multiple Carolingian copies, would seem to have had a twofold influence on Romanesque art: its theme inspired the idea of hieratic groups of antagonists, such as those allied with Aquitainian façade structure, while its narrative content served more directly as a source for anecdotal reliefs that were embroidered within this frame.

Among the more recurrent figures in this latter group are riders and women; their actions can, in good measure, be identified with those of Superbia and Luxuria in the *Psychomachia*. And, if they act like Pride and Lust, it is possible that they were intended to convey a degree of the same moral import. In other words, with the form goes at least a portion of the content. Pride, for example, is depicted in the Prudentius manuscripts riding on a horse. In entreating the vices for their support, she appeals directly to their heroic virtues. Mounted figures have a long and highly distinguished history in art, having been popularized in Roman imperial times in connection with scenes of political victory. It can be argued in this case that the popular visual form actually inspired the poetic one. But what had been in Roman and early Christian times an essentially elite image—that of a man on horseback—came to enjoy an unprecedented popularity in the twelfth century, not just a greater frequency in appearance but a substantially broadened usage as well. And this cannot be explained on the basis of a readily available model alone. Knights on horseback (as opposed to pedestrians) had emerged as an increasingly important class in post-Carolingian society and, it has been observed, a particularly vain one too. Courage, pride of lineage, and manhood, the qualities Pride addresses in the poem, are precisely those that would have contributed to the twelfth-century knight's arrogant sense of social superiority. It has been suggested that the proliferation of rider representations in early twelfth-century art, particularly abundant in western France, might be seen as a deliberate caveat to this proud, flourishing group. Should they emulate Superbia too successfully, they might similarly be undone: the vice is ultimately punished by a nose dive off her horse, one of the more powerful illustrations in Prudentius.[69]

Such interpretations linking art and mores in the Middle Ages owe much to Meyer Schapiro's observation that Unchastity, along with Avarice represented sins of the new aggressive class of men who, because of their worldly deeds, were distracted from church guidance.[70] The frequency with which the images of riders and women appear in Aquitaine and the popularity of their combination suggest both a significant relationship between the two "evils" and an important association with either contemporary institutions or ideas. The historian Herlihy recently questioned whether "a woman's world" might not have been created in Europe as the by-product of the man's world of warfare abroad.[71]

It is impossible, and, in this context, not really necessary, to pinpoint when the rider was invented as a motif. It is an ancient formula known in Mesopotamia, Greece, and in the nomadic North and employed to signify sovereignty, strength in battle, and victorious passage into the next world. Rome celebrated its emperors' triumphs by erecting monumental statues of them shown astride a walking horse and greeting their troops; sometimes a personification of victory would support the animal's hoof. This posture, frequently imitated on coinage, was, by the middle of the fourth century, identified with Christ's triumphant entry into Jerusalem. An alternate representation, known originally in funerary art and subsequently in the imperial realm, showed the rider in action, his steed rearing, often over a fallen victim. This image, also popularized on coins, undoubtedly inspired the original representation of Superbia as a soldier in Prudentius's manuscripts and came to be associated ultimately in the eastern part of the empire with Christ's Byzantine militia, the warrior saints George, Theodore, and Demetrius. Fleeting reference to a rider relief as Saint Michael has already been made in discussion of the Saint-Jouin façade.[72]

*Fig. 50e*

The key developments for the western Romanesque image emerge, as they had for the arcaded frame, the turrets, and the victorious virtues, through a Carolingian processing of Roman material. The ninth-century, with its self-conscious reuse of antique motifs, had appropriated both equestrian forms. An ancient statue of a triumphant imperial rider was imported from Ravenna to stand in the precinct of Charlemagne's palace at Aachen; later in the century, a diminutive bronze horseman was cast, possibly in an imperial atelier, in imitation of the Roman model. This use of the majestic *adventus* theme was an attempt to make visible the dynastic connections and continuity fundamental to Carolingian political theory.[73] But the victorious mounted figure represented a category of limited relevance for the time being; moreover, the

Carolingian usage did not substantially transform the theme. From the vantage point of the twelfth century, the rider-soldier type received the more creative appropriation by the Carolingians; the appearance of the mounted warrior on the base of Einhard's arch endowed the figure with *Fig. 17* a triumphant religious function and, clearly, a subordinate one.

Intimate associations of arches with riders also had important antique precedents—independent of, although not unrelated to, the solitary equestrian theme. These must have been equally familiar to educated, historically-minded members of the Frankish court such as Einhard, for whom, if not by whom, the relationship between arch and rider was dramatically and momentously altered. In commemoration of important battles, coins of Augustus, Nero, and Commodus, among others, had been decorated with representations of triumphal arches crowned at the top by statues of a rider usually in the *adventus* pose; trophies made of cuirasses or armor and hung on a wooden support often were seen *Fig. 20* framing the equestrian. A coin struck for Septimius Severus shows on the reverse his triumphal arch surmounted by a horse-drawn chariot *Fig. 50a* flanked by an equestrian statue to either side.[74] The audacious silver reliquary arch Einhard had fashioned for his church at Maastricht, which, as has been seen, Christianized the concept of the triumphal arch, in addition, carefully and, it would seem knowingly, rearranged and reinterpreted the main decorative motifs appearing in numismatic depictions of those pagan monuments. Both the riders and the chariot, agents of victory, and the armored trophies, symbols of the prowess that brings success in battle, were replaced at the top of the arch by the jeweled cross, the new trophy proclaimed in Einhard's inscription. The mounted figures were removed to the lowest, interior surface of the arch where the historic, worldly activities of imperial armies, such as those of Titus, had been portrayed on earlier Roman monuments; and the rider was consequently shown in a modification of the active, rather than the triumphal, pose: the steed seemingly at rest, the struggle over, the demonic serpent quietly curled underfoot. The pairing of riders, one on either side of the passageway, emphasizes that the figures were probably not seen as the reigning emperor. On the Severan coin, paired riders accompanied the imperial chariot at the summit of the arch; like them, the Einhard equestrians appear to represent a category of defenders of power, but in this case, they serve the cross rather than the emperor. No longer exalted by their participation in the victorious battle and therefore elevated above the arch as they had been in Roman times, the riders were now perceived as the servants of Christ's victory. While the riders' militant activities were spiritualized by their association with the overtly Christian setting, they were at the same time made subordinate to it.[75]

As central "supports" for the cross, the riders are accompanied, even framed, in this register by armed standing figures posed against the uprights of the arch. The position and attire of these figures bring to mind the trophies of armor, symbols of prowess seen to either side of the central equestrian in many of the numismatic depictions of arches. Perhaps they too are intended to suggest, like the paired riders, the expanded group of defenders of the cross. The association of militant riders with the architecture of victory and the dedication of both themes to Christian triumph dramatically revitalized two venerable imperial motifs—updating them and recasting them in an immediately relevant guise. Rider representations per se were readily available to medieval Europe from a variety of sources—eastern as well as western, both ancient and contemporary, kingly and secular—and, as we shall see, the twelfth century borrowed a little from them all. But it was this victorious Christian context that made the equestrian such an inherently and essentially meaningful figure for successive centuries. For those blessed with the gift of hindsight, the suggestion that the combination of riders with the arch on the Einhard reliquary influenced the Aquitainian façades must be given greater and more widespread credibility than it has received.[76]

By the twelfth century, in addition to the elite historical, imperial, and even liturgical associations, there existed a series of more colloquial and contemporary connections that enriched the meaning of the equestrian figure and made it more mundane, thereby reasserting its status as an image of a "tribal hero."[77] It had become a mark of distinction since Carolingian times to own a horse and to offer services to one's *seigneur* as a cavalryman rather than a foot soldier. Even the pacifist pedestrian Saint Martin was elevated in late eleventh-century representations, such as the capital in the Moissac cloister, to a position astride a mount. Local lords throughout Europe decorated their seals with representations of riders engaged in a variety of pursuits; these were drawn undoubtedly from a repertoire of noble or courtly themes. A relationship between the equestrian tympana of churches at Parthenay and the mounted figures in contemporary seals of the lords of that town was long ago pointed out by the local sigillographer, Eygun. Certainly the references between the two cannot have been unknown at the time; they enable us to acknowledge the military and social connotations, perhaps even patronage, of the sculptured reliefs.[78]

These contemporary riders were not just soldiers; their elevated status in society had earned them the right to leisure, too: they were hunters and promenaders and appear as such both on seals and in the monumental carvings. In fact, the rider relief on the façade at Parthenay-le-Vieux often bewilders viewers precisely because it incorporates several different references into a single, rather eclectic, and somewhat crudely carved representation. The figure tramples someone

*Fig. 52*

*Fig. 53*

underfoot in his capacity as a warrior, raises a falcon on his wrist as a sign of participation in the chivalric as well as worldly pastime—the chase—and wears a heavy crown, neatly riveted in imitation of metal-work and gem carving. It is possible, though unlikely, that this last attribute is intended to memorialize the rider's perpetuation of imperial warfaring traditions: the appearance of a crown is such a specific kingly reference that it is avoided in rider images unless the figure is intended to represent explicitly a historical royal personage, such as Char-lemagne, a biblical one, such as David, or possibly a triumphant, allegorical one.[79]

The crown is presented as a particularly tangible object, a product of "luxury artisanship," and is represented in a medium—namely, monumental narrative sculpture—which, as Schapiro pointed out, in itself implies a degree of concreteness and verity. The prominence given to inset stones in its design calls to mind the well-documented medieval fascination with precious gems, often of antique workman-ship, which were collected in church treasuries, even hoarded, because of the permanence and stability, the "resistance to corrosion," in Heckscher's words, they represented. It was suggested in the study by Lesne that the preservation of crowns and jewels by churches may have been related not merely to the value of the objects: such splendid gifts also served as memorials to the persons who offered them. Precious stones were acknowledged symbols of power and glory, and ancient gems, in particular, were utilized as seals by a variety of rulers to con-vey their legitimate inheritance of authority. For the medieval aristoc-racy, visible signs of wealth, jewelry in particular, but also weapons and the trappings of horses, were symbols of social distinction and rank. Since the possession of such precious objects was readily per-ceived as a sign of personal power, the prominence of the crown helps to identify the Parthenay figure as an imposing individual.[80]

The bejewelled headpiece, which gives the rider the appearance of a proud man of means, may also suggest, less positively, the possibilities for self-aggrandizement through plunder that were often enjoyed by members of the rider's vainglorious class. Knights and crusaders were infamous for the booty they carried away from battle, much of which was worn as personal adornment. By the thirteenth century, such "cameo worship" inspired an unusual representation of idolatry on the central portal of Notre-Dame in Paris. The personification of the vice is seen there, not in the characteristic pose adoring an idol, but rather in a position of reverence in front of a profile bust in an oval frame, an imitation of an antique gem.[81] The Parthenay image, with its distinc-tive gem-studded coronet, suggests the growing acquisitiveness that could inspire such an interpretation of idolatry. It should not necessarily be read as offering approval for such behavior, however; the image may well be deliberately ambivalent on that point. Yet those prominent jewels help to make the essential connection between manifestations of material wealth and the more promising prospect of immaterial riches.

Precious stones and ancient gems were frequently and ostentatiously employed in the decoration of sacred objects of metalwork such as crosses, book covers, and shrines. In the twelfth century, Abbot Suger had ancient mineral relics incorporated into contemporary settings in the creation of the splendid porphyry "eagle" vase and agate cup, and he appears to have intended to imply in this usage the magical absorption by the church of the "power" of the ancient charms. He was not alone in this; the adaptation of ancient gems to ecclesiastical purposes illustrated "pagan powers submitting to the new glory" and was understood as standing for the triumph of faith over antecedent superstitions. In this spirit, very likely, Charlemagne's *escrain* had been crowned with an *Fig. 21* ancient cameo at its summit; a reliquary cross from the Grandmont treasury had incorporated into it two intaglio gems, one of which was an amethyst of early Persian workmanship which showed a heroic hunt on horseback.[82]

The splendid crown the Parthenay rider wears may well be understood as an allusion to the more desirable martyr's crown, which is itself *Fig. 41* incorporated into so many other local façade programs; in fact, at the very time these churches were being built, such "crowns" were being "promised" to the knight as a reward in the war against the enemies of Christ. The immediate impact of this Parthenay "tympanum" was felt at Brinsop in Herefordshire, England, where a relief figure of Saint *Fig. 54* George killing the dragon appears surprisingly embellished with cloak and falcons. The patron of this church, Oliver de Merlimond, is known to have made a pilgrimage to Compostela via France. Zarnecki suggested that artists in his retinue brought home sketches of monuments observed en route and, with these aides, were able to incorporate themes from contemporary sculpture into the decor of their lord's church. "English" emulation of the "French" figure, to use national distinctions inappropriate for that time, indicates widespread appreciation of and sympathy for the Romanesque motif. Like the rider at Parthenay-le-Vieux, the Brinsop one is shown conscientiously as both courtier and soldier; he is, like Roland, also a martyr.[83]

The self-image of the rising group of lords was an important issue in the twelfth century and is carefully addressed in contemporary literature. The epic hero's exalted appreciation of his own values and his low opinion of his enemies' can be seen in the depreciatory comparisons that are made in the *Chansons*.[84] The vaunting of accomplishments, often in an ironical manner, infuses many of the inventive, vernacular lyrics that emerged at this moment from the hand of William IX, Duke of Aquitaine (d. 1126), poet as well as patron, intrepid warrior, and celebrated bon-vivant. His popular poems, the meaning of which have at times confused critics, are frequently erotic, celebrating, as one scholar pointed out, aggressive masculine pursuits, among them the amorous tribulations and triumphs of cavaliers.[85] The imagery evokes riders in gardens and shady arbors, sporting with their beloved or enticed into dalliance by passers-by. Birds are used to suggest the awakening of nature in spring and of love; they are also winged messengers effecting communication between lovers.[86]

The horse plays a particularly important part in the erotic imagery. William, in one verse, employs the image of the rider asleep on his horse to evoke a dreamlike state; another time, he crudely refers to two women in one of his bolder escapades as *juments* or mares.[87] He also borrows conquest imagery from the hunt and warfare to express sensual desire.[88] Licentiousness' fleeting conquests in the lyrics emulate the illusory victories of Luxuria in Prudentius's poem. Many specific motifs are the same: in the earlier work, Unchastity is pictured holding foliate *Fig. 57* sprays, dining, dancing, riding behind horses in a cart. In the twelfth-century writings, the vice is concretized in women of voracious appetites who engage in sexual adventures while pursued by or pursuing cavaliers.[89] The depiction of women involved in comparable activities in contemporary sculpture may well be intended to serve as illustrations of the sorts of immoral behavior that result from unbridled passion.

Women are, in fact, one of the more popular motifs in Aquitainian sculpture. At the far left of the capital frieze on the façade of Notre-*Fig. 30* Dame-de-la-Couldre at Parthenay, one woman stands in the company of musicians; at Echillais another looks on at activities, arm akimbo. Clothed or nude, they watch men fight and linger beneath or amidst *Fig. 3* vines on the capitals in the upper arcaded level at Corme-Ecluse. At the *Fig. 55* Abbaye-aux-Dames at Saintes, two women framed by leafy sprays evoke the description in Prudentius of Luxuria scattering baskets of flowers over adversaries (lines 326–27).[90] Along the left arcade on *Fig. 53* the façade at Parthenay-le-Vieux, a curious representation of nude women sitting in baskets initially evokes a scene of purification similar to that of the young virgin on the capital frieze at Chartres, or of wine-making, like the one at Civray. It also shares, paradoxically it would seem, certain elements with the depiction of Luxuria riding in a chariot. In a Leyden manuscript of the *Psychomachia*, thought to have been made in the ninth century around Limoges or Angoulême, Luxuria is shown half-length and bare-headed, not much more of her body visible than appears in the Romanesque sculpture.[91]

Because of its context, the Romanesque carving can be more closely compared with the novel presentation of an undressed woman in a

*Fig. 56*

basket that is carried on horseback behind a cavalier in a thirteenth-century Persian ceramic painting of a siege. Since depictions of nudity in Islamic art are localized in harem quarters and in bathhouses, Ettinghausen suggested that the figure on the Freer plate, by association, probably represented a dancer or entertainer of low social or moral standing furnished for the amusement of the soldiers.[92] A kind of Islamic Luxuria, it was probably not a recent invention as a type, for it is encountered at an earlier date in Arabic literature. The motif of people hiding in barrels is common in Arab poetry from whence, it has been suggested, it found its way into the twelfth-century French epic, the *Charroi de Nîmes*. More specifically, the image of a woman riding in a litter is used in an early Arab epic as a metaphor for defeated forces, those who submit to humility and abasement and surrender to captivity. An analogous western image of punishment and degradation is found in a passage in Ordericus Vitalis, where a procession of women, "clearly guilty of various sexual abuses," is described as being mounted on steeds, the saddles of which are covered with nails.[93]

Islamic artists drew heavily on classical and antique sources, and these may have influenced figural representations such as the nude woman. The Romanesque artist utilized the same sources while enriching his own artistic vocabulary with Carolingian motifs. Because of the common body of source material shared by east and west in the twelfth century, it is difficult to say with certainty in every case whether contemporary French and Muslim artists borrowed directly from one another.[94] But it is evident from other examples that the western Romanesque artist deliberately combined diverse traditions in an eclectic search for a powerful, even ironic image.

The women at Parthenay form the archivolt that surrounds the equestrian figure in the left tympanum. It is not difficult to suggest a justification for the juxtaposition of temptresses with the proud rider. Cavaliers, as has been said, were explicitly associated with lecherous acts in contemporary poems. In another popular contemporary text, the *Pseudo-Turpin*, the massacre of Charlemagne's rear guard in the Pyrenees is attributed to his soldiers' illicit dalliance with Saracen women the night before the battle, a transitory triumph that results in defeat: the sinful warriors pay for their lust with their lives. At an earlier date, Byzantium had similarly attributed its defeat at the hands of Islam to sexual license: the Arab invasion of the seventh century was seen as a divinely sent punishment for Christian sins.[95] But, the twelfth-century chronicle hastens to explain, Roland's men were able to overcome their prior transgression and were rewarded as virtuous men since they died in the fight against the evil infidel. They were instantly crowned among the holy martyrs in heaven.[96] The rider at Parthenay-le-Vieux is surrounded by thirty-seven such women depicted explicitly, possibly even literally, as Saracen booty, a token perhaps of the thousand women who were allegedly sent to Charlemagne by the Moorish king in a treacherous tribute prior to the battle.

They may equally be intended to evoke the immorality of plundering in warfare, which is condemned throughout the *Psychomachia*. Samuel forbids touching any spoils taken from a rich foe (lines 388–89), and the proud kings, Lot's captors, are handily cut down by Abraham in the preface to the poem because they are "weighed down with booty." Among their treasures, in addition to gold, jewels, and vessels, are maidens and mares (lines 22–31), the standard pleasures of the world enumerated again in the Koran, sura iii, 14. In contrast to early Christianity, however, Muslim tradition sanctioned booty, acknowledging it as the reward of the soldier who is *not* killed in battle.[97] And in practice even Christians departed from the moral positions of their texts. In the Chronicle of Moissac, the triumphant return of Charles Martel from the Battle of Tours heavily laden with spoils is vividly recounted.[98] It was, in fact, common practice in early Carolingian times for rulers to take land and "movable wealth" from opponents and to distribute it to gain military support.[99] One of the descriptions of the First Crusade recounts the Christian display of spoils—silks, horses, and shields—after the siege of Antioch, suggesting that the practice was still enjoyed.[100]

Perhaps it is irony, an inherently Romanesque expressive device which exploits contrast, that is employed in the voussoir figures to set off good and bad bounty, and perhaps even Christian from Muslim plunder. Purely personal aggrandizement, a source of pride and often the product of lust, for which the Muslims were celebrated at the time, is condemned in figurative carving such as the voussoirs; in contrast, booty that serves symbolic ends and can be used propagandistically is celebrated in the arcaded trophy of the façade, as we have seen. The crown the rider wears is intermediary between the two and partakes of both attitudes: it is only a material manifestation of the greater spiritual reward promised the Christian soldier.

Contemporary religious evocations of the blessed Christian soul reinforce several of the motifs observed in the sculptures and add a liturgical significance to what has been discussed in these pages primarily as a worldly theme. By the twelfth century, the Office of the Dead contained a prayer for the journey of the soul in which the soul's reception in heaven was portrayed as a royal *adventus*, a jubilant entry into celestial Jerusalem. The text seems to reflect visual traditions both of Christ's entry into Jerusalem and of the emperors' acclamation at the gates of a city, themes which had very likely inspired the words of the prayer. What is significant here, as Kantorowicz noted, is that "imagery and liturgy speak, as it were, the same language."[101] Guided by Saint Michael on its long journey, the soul should be welcomed at the celestial portal, according to the prayer, by a host of angels and a triumphant army of martyrs, personages encountered in the milieu of the rider at Civray and at Chadenac and, on their own, framing countless doorways throughout Aquitaine. The rider can then be said to represent, at once and on different levels, the Christian knight in his worldly activities on behalf of the church and the Christian soul in its celestial encounter receiving its reward, themes that echo and resound in numerous permutations across the façade.

The literary portrait of the Muslim martyr as drawn in the hadith, the book of tradition that accompanies the Koran, provides remarkable points of contact with the Parthenay figure. He is said to receive six privileges with God. Among these are instant pardon with the shedding of blood and a reception in paradise, honors also awarded his Christian counterpart. Further, a crown of glory is placed on his head, "one jewel of which is worth more than the world and all therein," and he is married to seventy dark-eyed virgins.[102] The relationship of this description to the French rider relief, with its crown and surrounding thirty-seven nubile women, is undeniable. It is possible, even likely, that such literature became known in the 1140s in Europe, during the years in which Peter the Venerable undertook the translation of the Koran into Latin. In fact, in his summary of Muslim beliefs, written possibly for Saint Bernard, Peter included "the embrace and sensual satisfaction of the loveliest women and virgins" in his description of Muhammad's paradise.[103] Such texts may have contributed to the representation of the new breed of Christian martyr by providing instant formulae for his depiction. Women, wealth, and war were as much on the Frenchman's agenda as on the Muslim's, as one can see in the poems and chronicles. Each of the categories provided a superficial symbol of triumph, but to the Christian all three were also perceived in varying degrees as temptations and even taboo.

To return to the women, the significance of their proximity to the equestrian in the sculpture is twofold. First they evoke an aspect of the rider's prowess that was celebrated in the lyrics written by and for contemporary local lords. William, in one of his especially boastful poems, vaunts himself as a *maistre certa* in love and describes his revenge when taunted. His successors, Jaufre Rudel, Bernard de Ventadour, Raimbaut d'Orange, extended these themes to indulge their patrons, the petty nobles of the region, with exaltations of amorous escapades.[104] The image of the cavalier that emerges in vernacular poetry is of a man defined by success in love, grace in song, and courage in battle, levels of accomplishment that have analogues in the multiple references on the Parthenay relief.[105] The seventy virgins referred to in the hadith fit in with this aspect.

But, as in Prudentius's poem, the successes of Lust and the triumphs of Pride are momentary. Neither the texts nor the sculpture lack ethical overtones. The poet Marcabru, whose verse is likened to a "moral battlefield," equates the horseman with lust and with self-illusion—an error of pride—and portrays him as defeated.[106] In sculpture, the implications of physical indulgence are made explicit by references to conventional symbols of licentiousness. A traditional representation of

*Fig. 58*   Luxuria, a woman with serpents biting her breasts, appears on the capital immediately above and to the left of the rider at Parthenay;[107] a frieze of menacing cats' heads, another erotic motif, forms a decorative molding framing this section of the portal. The feline masks reappear in combination with Luxuria on the church at Vouvant. In William's lusty lyric "Farai un vers," the cat is used as a grotesque device in a scene of violent fantasy to inject pain into an episode of illicit erotic encounter.[108]

*Multiple Meanings*

In poetry and in art, then, the woman is presented both as conquest or reward and as caveat. The memory of the Saracen temptresses at Roncesvalles and of the evil they wrought lurks behind the images of women in the sculpture.[109] Although it may seem complicated or overly intellectual to imagine so much "going on" in one image, multiplicity of meaning is far from inappropriate. The coexistence of several levels of content in the sculptured rider figure is paralleled by deliberately multiple and even paradoxical meanings for the knight in Count William's poems. For example, the alert, aggressive knight suddenly becomes contemplative and mystical—an otherworldly chevalier—when described as being asleep on his horse. And two different writing styles, refined and "gross," are employed to evoke different effects in William's work. "Multi-layeredness," borrowing Auerbach's word for biblical epic, with its "simultaneous existence of various layers of consciousness," is equally a fundamental aspect of Romanesque epic art, both visual and verbal.[110] It is employed and can be analyzed in another carving in which the rider is associated with an unusual image of lust.

Joan Ferrante recently remarked that women appear in medieval literature not as "real people" but as symbols of "philosophical and psychological problems that trouble the male world."[111] So it would seem to be in art as well; even though Luxuria is personified as a female and oftentimes may be intended to recall specific anecdotes—such as those regarding the easy virtue of women and the nature of booty—the lust women refer to is essentially the cavalier's. The vivid descriptions of sexual activity provided by the lyrics and poems are closely rivaled in sculpture by graphic representations of men and women, most of which appear on the corbels that support moldings framing the arcades on

*Fig. 59*   the façade or that underscore the roofline around the apse.[112] Such sculptures are scarcely insignificant or inconspicuous in these positions; their presence has been "overlooked" chiefly by scholars. Occasionally frank depictions of sex if not sexuality appear in prominent positions lower down on the façades as well. There can be no question, for example, about the gender of the large equestrian mounts that are unmistakably identified as stallions. Châteauneuf-sur-Charente provides one example and both Parthenays display others.

*Fig. 53*

One unacknowledged depiction of what appears to be the punishment of male lust occurs at the tiny church of La Rochette. The relief of the rider in the left arcade at this church has been studied and equated with the moral allegory of virtue overcoming vice by Daras.[113] Yet certain explicit details of this presentation remain to be clarified. The rider is crowned, like the Parthenay equestrian, surely an allusion to triumphant allegory, as Daras suggested, and possibly even to the victorious Christian's reward. But the figure on whom the horse's foot rests is neither conquered barbarian nor demonic evil. Crudely carved and partially eroded, he is nude and displays grossly enlarged genitalia; he introduces a startling obscene element into the traditional victorious motif. The rider, quite obviously, has brought a figure of brutish sexuality to his knees. Perhaps it is a heathen whose enormous appetites were legendary in Europe until reliable information about the Muslim enemy began to filter into the West.[114] But this would be a merely literal identification. Viewed against a remembered tableau of traditional images—allegorical, historical, and triumphant—the relief can be seen as a conflation and interpenetration of these often isolated themes. The rider evokes the proud knight victorious in his spiritual struggle against lust. Like Marcabru's horseman, he is boastful of his lusty conquests; yet, at the same time, he is perceived as being capable of overcoming carnal sin and is portrayed as its conqueror. Perhaps the "grossness" of the carving is an expression of the basic earthliness of the content.

*Fig. 60*

The visual formula of the rider trampling a figure underfoot initially evoked political conquest over the heathen, as I have indicated earlier. The association of such a figure with virtue, like so many of the Aquitainian themes, had already been made in Roman times. A denarius of ca. 48 B.C. shows on its reverse a horseman dragging a captive while the obverse displays a head personifying faith.[115] The Romanesque representation, without necessarily knowing the ancient coin, essentially combines the narrative and personified depictions into one provocative, multilayered image. To be sure, there is no precise model for such a representation as the one at La Rochette. And the search for one might well be in vain. Here the correspondences between the visual form and the vernacular literary metaphors help to "authenticate" the sense of the sculpture.

Multiple meanings permeate almost all of the façade carvings. At La

*Figs. 8, 10*    Rochette and at both Parthenays, the rider is paired with a lion-killer who has usually been called Samson, although some scholars have thought the theme to be too commonplace and widespread to insist on any specific significance.[116] It is more than likely that the figure depicts David, the humble shepherd, musician, poet, and model Old Testament king whom rulers of Europe since Charlemagne took pride in emulating.[117] References to David pepper Prudentius's epic: Sobriety invokes his name to discipline her army by reminding them that the Old Testament king never rested from battle (line 386); Hope, cutting off the head of Pride, makes an example of David overcoming the arrogant Goliath (lines 284–304).[118] In Psalters of the twelfth century and later, David is often depicted alongside scenes of spiritual struggle, in particular scenes of warriors and representations of Adam and Eve, themes frequently seen in the sculptures of Aquitaine.[119] The ivory psalter cover, made in the second quarter of that century for Melisende, daughter of Baldwin II, Latin prince of Jerusalem, displays six medallions with scenes from the life of David against a field filled with fighting virtues and vices.[120] The lion-fighter, the warrior, and the musician, three of the scenes on the cover, are types that proliferate in the ornamental friezes of Aquitainian façades, where they appear often in

*Figs. 30, 31*    the entourage of the rider and in the vicinity of the virtues and vices. Capitals in Spain and Provence, areas in which rider imagery also flourished, intimately juxtapose a crowned musician, certain reference to the biblical harpist, alongside either the lion-killer or the rider, extending to them, thereby, a Davidic identity.[121]

It is possible that the sculptured lion fights were intended as allusions to the shepherd's encounter with the beast in the Old Testament. Representations of the lion-killer may also allude to a passage in the *Song of Roland* in which Charlemagne, the night before his meeting with the Muslim Emir Baligant, dreams he is struggling with a fierce lion.[122] Charlemagne, of course, had been called David by his court intimates and knowledge of this may have survived in the twelfth century. At the Baptistery at Parma, for example, a statue of King David is juxtaposed with one of the Carolingian ruler. Whether or not a Davidic identity is intended to connect the carved and dreamed lion fights with one another and with Charlemagne, the sculptured representations of lion-fighters on Aquitainian façades, like so many of the other images, can be perceived as symbols of the struggle between good and evil, the imprecise and ubiquitous theme that assumes so many shapes on the façades and in the epics.

In some contemporary illustrations, David's rescue of his flock was overtly equated with his other victory over evil, his murder of Goliath.[123] Lejeune and Stiennon demonstrated that twelfth-century representations of the youthful David shown pitted against a huge and hideous Philistine were intended to evoke, not only the Old Testament story, but also the more immediately relevant, legendary confrontation of Roland against Ferragut, of Christian against Moor. There are countless representations of combat on the Aquitaine churches from exalted, armored encounters to simple acts of angry beard-pulling. They parallel varied events in the *Song of Roland* where, for example, a mocking of the French knight's pride precedes his final battle.[124] The sculpture and the poems can be experienced on many levels then as evocations of historical, legendary, and contemporary situations, as allegories of both good and bad,[125] of aggression and humility.

The monumental frontispieces of Aquitainian churches can be seen simultaneously as celebrators of the sublime and as chronicles of the secular; they should be likened to contemporary vernacular literature, particularly the *Chansons de geste*, in which similar metaphoric language is employed in the service of similar goals. Poem and portal reinterpret historic themes and images according to present needs and intertwine them with contemporary motifs. Both recapitulate the past to make the present more fertile.[126] In each, triumphant virtue and its celestial reward transcend defeat, temptation, and illusion. A recent summary of the theme of the *Song* as the "triumph of man over his own weakness in the face of death," is equally applicable to the façades.[127]

Schapiro suggested that the terms descriptive of poetic entanglement were equally suitable for contemporary sculpture.[128] The entry walls, like the *Chansons*, weave together Christian, moral, and social themes into a dense, vibrant fabric; both emerge as popular, vernacular inventions in which the ideals of permanent order confront and mingle with the transient and sometimes chaotic forces of reality. But poem and portal make the ideas accessible in the opposing ways appropriate to their distinct disciplines or media. Whereas the lyrics introduce the listener to the actions of men via anecdotes that cumulatively build toward a triumphant conclusion, the façades present the viewer at once with a permanent schematization of the victorious, timeless message. If the poems are Songs of Deeds, then the façades can truly be called Songs of Glory.[129]

# F O U R

# Soldiers of Christ and Men of Means

## THE PATRONS AND PURVEYORS

IN THE CLOSING DECADES OF THE ELEVENTH CENTURY, CHRISTIANITY openly began to stress an intimate relationship between the individual's struggle for his own soul and the greater fight for God and country. The association of personal salvation with the defense of the worldly church emerged as one of the fundamental principles of twelfth-century religious thought.[1]

In earlier centuries, especially the immediately preceeding one, the only sanctioned Christian battle had been the one waged against the devil for men's souls. In that confrontation, Benedictine monks, specifically Cluniacs, acted as Christ's militia. The Cluniacs were "Christian knights in the sphere of the supernatural," in one scholar's felicitous description.[2] The extensive liturgy that resounded throughout their splendid structures has been likened to vicarious warfare; prayers fought the battle for spiritual rewards in behalf of those who supported the monasteries with gifts of money and land.

It was the upper classes, the nobility, and the pretenders to hereditary rank, for whom the Benedictine path to salvation promised to be most efficacious. The penitential needs of this wealthy, acquisitive group were directly related to their acknowledged proclivity for warfare. Since lay violence was forbidden by the Church, repentance for such transgressions was needed. It could be and indeed was "attained" with the assistance of Benedictine intermediaries in exchange for donations: practically speaking, it was bought from them. The vast increase in Cluny's size and wealth during the eleventh century testifies to the popularity this relationship enjoyed.

At no time, however, did the fighting itself really cease. On numerous occasions it interfered with the tranquility of individual churches by threatening or disrupting their own holdings and, in these instances, the Church found it opportune to support agreements which carefully regulated rather than outlawed eruptions of fighting between lay powers. Moral approval was offered through truces to those campaigns that were directed against the particularly unruly knights who threatened ecclesiastical power. Duby noted that the aggression of the knightly class was initially contained by the Peace of God and then condemned and disciplined by the Truce of God; ultimately, the potential for violence was diverted.[3] The attempt to control the rivalries of lay princes was not truly successful in the long run since the knights were not easily thwarted in their energies and ambitions. Moreover, the Church saw its own need for broad-based military support in terrestrial disputes dramatically increase.

### Spiritual Rewards of the Crusades

Thus, in the third quarter of the eleventh century, Pope Alexander II found it useful to commute penance for those who took up arms on the Church's side in Spain; subsequently, in a theological decision occasioned by political reality, Gregory VII ordered lay princes to seek salvation in the world, rather than in the monastery, by bearing arms for Christ's vicar in Rome. Precedent for such activity was found in the Bible: "For God still lives who sanctioned such action through the arms of David."[4] Secular warriors were instantly elevated over spiritual ones; liturgical blessings now prepared knights for battle and sanctioned their bloodshed; those who died defending Christianity were described as martyrs and absolved of their sins. Knights were free to earn their own salvation, as Guibert de Nogent, observed; no longer did they need to buy it from the Benedictines in the form of prayer.[5]

The Pope enticed European knights into battle by evoking for them Charlemagne's legendary triumphs over the Moors; in the speech at Clermont-Ferrand in which he preached the First Crusade, he presented that imperial example as a model for their own activities.[6] The Duke of Aquitaine, who had been active in the reconquest of Spain, assisting the courts of Léon, Castille, and Aragon into which members of his family had married, enjoyed retrospective praise for those involvements and eagerly embarked, as did other European princes, on the new course.[7] Even after the successful First Crusade, propaganda in the West continued to be directed toward additional recruits who were urgently needed to maintain the position of the Latin princes in the Holy Land. Bohemond, prince of Antioch, visiting Poitiers in 1106 to seek support for his cause, was reportedly received there with enthusiasm, evidence that literature or information about him had been circulated in advance of his trip to stimulate interest.[8] One of the eyewitness accounts of the First Crusade, the *Historia de Hierosolymitano Itinere,* was written about this time by Peter Tudebode, a priest of nearby Civray.[9]

The preaching of the Crusade had emphasized the deliverance of the holy places, and literature produced in the aftermath of the event likewise focused on the centrality of Jerusalem in that quest. The liberation of the church in Jerusalem was identified with the salvation of the knights' own souls. As time went on, the necessity for the knight to express appropriate moral discipline even before embarking on the journey became increasingly emphasized in Crusade literature. In the writings of Saint Bernard concerning the Second Crusade, Jerusalem is at the heart of a mission aimed specifically at individual regeneration. What had been loosely expounded among the emotional goals of the First Crusade became tightly knit in the program of the next.[10]

It has been suggested that lay enthusiasm for the Crusade reflected a popularly felt need for self-justification and for divine approval of the nobles' naturally bellicose inclinations and values.[11] In other words, the knights were happy to have the chance once again to do what they most liked doing. In addition, being a crusader was now an attractive social obligation, something of a status symbol, which gained stature by virtue of its Carolingian association and its acceptability to the Church as a worthwhile act of devotion.

This spirit, and spirituality, I believe, shaped the Aquitainian façades and determined their sculptural programs. This statement goes beyond the frequently made suggestion that the Crusades influenced themes in art and provided the opportunity for exchanges of style.[12] The relationship is more profound and pervasive. Romanesque art in western France emerged alongside the worldly orientation of the crusading Church.[13] It visualized and popularized the promise of immediate salvation newly extended to the band of warring nobles and petty princes who were sanctioned in their aggressive activities by the papacy. Ostensibly direct access to the heavenly kingdom was available to knights and soldiers through their armed service in behalf of Christendom. And this was made manifest to and for them in the external forms and decoration of their churches. The architectural shapes of arcaded screen *Figs. 5, 6,* and lantern turret and the decorative vocabulary of victorious figures *14, 48* that form the visual language of church after church throughout Aquitaine were drawn from a venerable tradition of triumphal motifs. These had been associated in more private and interior ways with the militant aspects of Christianity since the days of Constantine; their use had increased in importance and frequency in Carolingian times. The new visibility and monumentality afforded these forms in the twelfth century did more than acknowledge the availability of salvation; in their new location, they evoked publicly the splendors and triumphs of the past and, in doing so, invoked its support. The figural language of forms was doing exactly what the pope had done when he used Charlemagne's example to stir the knights to battle: each legitimized the campaign and incorporated it into a victorious tradition.

In addition to the biblical and Carolingian examples that were put before the knights, part of the Crusade *excitatoria* summoned up memories of the Roman past for comparison as well. In particular, an encyclical attributed to the eleventh-century pope Sergius IV, but more recently thought to have been forged early in the twelfth century in the vicinity of Moissac, avows that "the battle for Jerusalem would be as victorious as Titus and Vespasian were when they destroyed Jerusalem to avenge the Savior." A poem describing the raid by Pisans on Muslims in North Africa in 1087 similarly made comparisons with the wars of Rome.[14] It may well be that the pervasive element of Romanism perceived, not just indirectly in the forms of these façades but more immediately and specifically, in the arrangement of particular motifs used in their decoration may represent a deliberate attempt to effect an association with Rome, the previous victor over heathens in the Holy Land.

Were these forms put there to admonish the knights to fulfill their pledge to the Church or to reiterate the Church's promise to them? The imagery of Aquitaine seems to have worked both ways; Christianity depended upon the armed force of the knights to carry out the papal program in the East and individual churches relied on that same group to provide defense and support at home; the donations of the knights built the local ecclesiastical structures which, it is often forgotten, were intended to commemorate the donors and thus to serve personal needs for expiation and glorification.

The armed struggle was bound up with the moral one for these men; conquest of the earthly Jerusalem was but a metaphor for entry into the heavenly one for which, more and more, the state of their souls was called into question. The promised prize for a victory in either "arena"—the military or the spiritual one—was the martyr's crown. The central role played by a moral program in the formulation of plans for a Second Crusade, and in the justification for its failure, is paralleled by the key position enjoyed by virtue and vice imagery on the Aquitainian portals. The emphasis on spiritual perfection in both life and art may provide support for the dating of much of the sculpture in the 1140s and 1150s, the years immediately surrounding the Second Crusade. It also helps to explain the particular patronage and function of these monuments which have appeared to be so eccentric among French Romanesque monastic churches.

The attitudes just described, toward warfare, penitence, and eternal reward, conflict in fundamental ways with the monastically sponsored path to salvation that was epitomized by Cluny and is believed to have been so firmly rooted in much of France. It is not surprising to find this Cluniac spirituality underrepresented in Aquitaine, where the crusading spirit thrived. Urban's voyage through France to drum up support for the Crusades in 1095 has been called Cluniac, not because the goal of the Crusade directly served Cluny's interest—in fact, in one sense, it did the opposite—but because the pope, a former Cluniac monk, lodged with his brothers en route and spent much of his time at Cluniac foundations.[15] Yet in the Poitou, Urban spent a month with scant mention of papal favors accorded religious communities; presumably there was little to report about his stay in these parts because there were few Cluniac foundations either to visit or consecrate. Openly anti-Cluniac attitudes are particularly apparent in the unwillingness of Abbot Rainaud of Saint-Cyprien to submit to Cluny. The pope's voyage toward Saintonge was not much better; it was reported that the abbot of Saint-Maixent also lacked any special attachment to the Burgundian abbey. Only in Saintes, Crozet reported in his discussion of the trip, did the pope recapture the "Cluniac" atmosphere. It is probably more accurate to suggest, as one scholar has, that Cluny capitalized on the Crusade whenever and wherever it could than to say that the Crusade was outright Cluniac.[16] Although the Benedictines acknowledged that the monastic life was not suitable for everyone, they stood to lose a substantial constituency to the newly authorized pathway to salvation.

### The European Knight and Islam

The Crusade was viewed as a holy war by Fulcher of Chartres in his *History of the First Crusade,* which he wrote to encourage others to take up the cause. Building on Augustine's notion of a just war, he compared the campaign with the ancient wars of the Maccabees and Israelites, just as Gregory VII's supporters had done in the 1080s in seeking to justify pre-Crusade Church-sponsored aggression.[17] Some have said that the emergence in Christianity of the concept of divinely sanctioned warfare was influenced by knowledge of the Muslim fight for the faith, the *jihad;*[18] it is also possible that both East and West derived their militant stands independently from biblical precedents.[19] The Old Testament, full of righteous warfare, was esteemed as a prophetic text by Muslims as well as Christians; Abraham was considered a prophet to both religions and from his first-born Ishmael, Muslims claimed descent.[20] Isaac, Abraham's preferred son, was, of course, seen by Christians as a prefiguration of Christ. Islam revered the New Testament, too, and probably derived from it their acceptance of Gabriel as Muhammad's helper and a host of other angels as fighters for the Faithful.

The West, however, did not share a comparable familiarity with Islam's religious texts. In theological matters, Europe remained sadly ill-informed about its Muslim rival until the 1140s, when Peter the Venerable commissioned a translation of the Koran hoping to educate Christians about the religion he called "the greatest of all heresies." Until this time, unfounded myths about the Moors and Muhammad's faith circulated in Europe, a tribute to what has been described as the "ignorance of the triumphant imagination."[21] But these often malicious fables that were spread about the habits and abilities of the enemy[22] may have been intended primarily to enhance the luster of the conquering army back home and to urge them on. The West was genuinely fascinated by the highly developed culture it encountered at Muslim courts as it pursued the policy of the Crusade and paid the rival society, which seemed to return so little practical curiosity, the supreme compliment of emulation.[23]

"Oriental influence" on the forms, themes, and style of French Romanesque art has long been observed and disputed. It constitutes one of the most imposing examples of the tribute of imitation paid by the Christians.[24] Mâle pointed to motifs of Islamic origin in Burgundy, Auvergne, and the Midi as well as in Aquitaine. Lacey foliate carving on church voussoirs, fantastic animals on archivolts, cusping and polychromy of arches, all observable and studied at the churches of Le Puy, have been discussed as evidence of the impact made by Mozarabic architecture on French pilgrims traveling the roads to Santiago de Compostela. Such elements were sporadically incorporated into monuments back home where they were employed seemingly as spoils. Multilobed arches, like those visible in Mozarabic Spain, form the primary adornment of church entries at Châtres, Aubeterre, and Chalais, among others, in Aquitaine; the cusped archivolts are integrated emblematically into the characteristic triple-arched portal scheme like elegant souvenirs of conquest: the tangible fruits of victory framed by the borrowed symbol of triumph.[25]

*Figs. 1, 4, 9*

Controversy over the preponderance and chronology of influence in the relationship between Christian and Islamic, western and eastern exists. It is argued that the proliferation in Romanesque art of certain typically "oriental" motifs, such as stylized flora and fauna, has nothing to do with Islam but rather represents the timely fruition of an earlier exposure to such forms via the Byzantine textiles that were valued at the Carolingian court.[26] In his studies of Languedocian portals and domed churches, Schapiro recommended an association with Islam more intimate than that obtainable in Spain and suggested direct contact with both Islamic and Byzantine art in the Near East to explain particular characteristics he observed in the architecture and sculpture of southern France; these he provocatively interpreted in terms of the social needs of the interacting groups.[27]

The question is complicated by the fact that it is not at all easy to distinguish Byzantine and Islamic influence. Both shared the legacy of Sassanian Persian ceremonial forms, both borrowed as well from Roman imperial art, and, by the twelfth-century, each had influenced the other's life-style. Islamic aesthetic, with its curtainlike surfaces that have been described as taking "revenge on architecture,"[28] seems to have affected dramatically the ornamental treatment of exteriors in mid-Byzantine churches.[29] Byzantium, in turn, was often the immediate source through which Muslims encountered the forms of the more remote past; failing to find adequate inspiration in their own Arab heritage, they were forced to borrow themes of power from the Christian protector of classical vocabulary.[30] The Europeans' exposure to the forms of the Byzantine intermediary, their Christian brothers and hosts as they traversed Greek territory to the Holy Land, would have reduced the exoticism of the Islamic variants and nullified any taint or taboo for them in assimilating motifs from a heathen art. Would the crusaders then have bothered to differentiate between Byzantine and Islamic elements since they sprang from a common source and often resembled one another?[31]

The answer, I believe, is yes. The European Christians and Muslims possessed a remarkable number of affinities in social structure and outlook that distinguished them from the Byzantines, the former's eastern kin and the latter's neighbors; both were recently described by Daniel as courtly societies valuing similar principles of largesse and prowess.[32] In place of the imperial model that organized life in the eastern lands of the Church, European and Islamic societies were dominated by a group of militaristic upstarts who acted independently of institutions and relied primarily upon their own accomplishments for recognition in life. The pope, in promulgating the Crusade, had established a counterpart to the Muslim fight against the infidel; the *jihad*, like the Christian campaign, was viewed within its own society as a moral struggle against the self, a sentiment expressed in the hadith, where the greatest *jihad* is said to be the fight against one's evil passions. Thus, salvation through individual attainment, one of the principles of Muhammad's faith, was established as a precept of Christianity with the endorsement of the Crusade. The European knight, freed from reliance on spiritual intervention, was very much like the Muslim prince who had never learned to depend on a monastic class; both, in a sense, were their own holy men. Apart from the names of their gods, the two groups are portrayed in similar manner, down to minor details as Auerbach notes, in the *Song of Roland*.[33]

Yet these similarities, which may not even have been conscious knowledge, did not result in a uniform attraction to Islamic models all over Europe. Some further distinction between Aquitainian Christians and most of their continental cousins seems to have sensitized the former to the structures and designs then dominating the non-Christian art and architecture of the Mediterranean. Certainly proximity and the near abandon with which the western French knights crossed the Pyrenees to fight in Al-Andalus, the Arab name for Spain, must have provided the occasion and stimulated the exchange. But a more fundamental similarity between the societies made the moment ripe. It was in

Aquitaine that this new group of Christian knights most nearly resembled its Muslim counterparts; each experienced life on the fringes of hostile territory, neither felt itself subservient to a local ecclesiastical or secular power, and both were aggressive and ambitious, eager to enhance their station in life.

Dreams of martyrdom and self-glorification inspired buildings in both territories. Along the frontiers of Islam, in Egypt and Iran, a new form of commemorative, sometimes funerary, monument appeared in the tenth and eleventh centuries, representing the desire for self-glorification of the emerging acquisitive class.[34] These structures, though secular, evoke the commemorative churches and shrines along the Christian frontier not merely in their form, usually either a domed chamber with a monumental gateway or a tomb-tower with rich surface ornamentation, but in their patronage and function as well. The western French buildings of the late eleventh and first half of the twelfth century integrated archway and turret into a highly developed façade program that perpetuated the memory of the knights who defended the faith and who sometimes chose to be buried within. Like the interest in epic poetry observed in both groups, such commemorative structures are further suggestions of the common tastes shared by "a young and warlike society engaged in territorial expansion." The content of vernacular Muslim poetry complements and parallels that of the western French troubadours which it predates. In both cultures composers sing of prostitutes and dancing girls by whom they are sometimes tricked; they brag of their conquests. Other songs encourage Arab fighters in battle.[35] These similarities help to explain why certain figural motifs, particularly ones describing daily life, with their implicit allusions to social status and self-image, could be lifted by Europeans from the rival, heathen Muslim culture and successfully absorbed into their own art; there the motifs thrived compatibly, even indistinguishably, alongside more characteristic local and Christian forms.

Many of the figural themes were, to be sure, familiar as well in Byzantine court art, whence they had come from the same ancient Near Eastern princely sources available to Islam. For example, a broad-faced, long-haired nude figure, probably a woman, depicted playing a lute on an eleventh-century Byzantine casket in Darmstadt recalls the ample dancer on an Iranian silver urn of the ninth century now in Leningrad;[36] both, in turn, resemble the female busts that surround the rider at Parthenay. Likewise, equestrians, warriors, and hunters were popular motifs on the ivory boxes that were produced in both Byzantium and in Moorish Spain; such coffers made their way into Christian Europe along the trade routes or as gifts and ultimately found their way into church treasuries.[37] In Byzantium, these motifs remained associated with an elite court group and informed the representation of religious

*Fig. 61*

themes, for example, the depiction of soldier-saints. But in Muslim society, "princely" imagery received rare and "democratic" diffusion. Oleg Grabar has studied its early development in the stuccos and frescos of Islamic palace art, tracing its absorption by Muslim princes from the ceremonial art they encountered in conquered lands through its transposition by them into a personal iconography of power. By the late eleventh century, images of elegantly dressed men hunting or feasting and surrounded by musicians, riders, or women dancing proliferated on the portable luxury objects and pottery produced in Egyptian and Syrian shops for obviously commercial consumption. The motifs were employed on utilitarian objects designed for middle class Muslim taste and were intended, according to Grabar, to reflect the aspirations of this new, rising social group.[38] This art of pleasurable pastimes and intricate surfaces, known to European knights through the commerce of the Mediterranean and so intriguing to them, in no way expressed religious sentiments. It was a vernacular, at times unrefined, art, and that may explain why it could be plucked out of the Levant and integrated so well into a cosmopolitan and fluid European setting.

The distinguished scholar of Islam, H. A. R. Gibb, in a paper on Muslim-Christian exchanges in the Middle Ages, emphasized that the elements taken over by western culture from Islamic tradition either had a European origin to begin with or were closely related to aspects of western culture.[39] He went on to observe that the elements were usually of limited range and conformed to the adapter's temperament and psychic structure. More recently, Sylvia Thrupp demonstrated that the West perceived Islam as a superior civilization and openly envied it.[40] So it was that the art of an increasingly independent, confident class that portrayed itself as it longed to be perceived could be borrowed to fulfill the same role for an analogous aspiring group in the West.

The worldly images of hunters, musicians, dancers, and riders that punctuate the foliate or geometric fields on utilitarian and luxury items of Islamic metalwork and ceramics are permitted to invade, unselfconsciously, the capitals and vegetal friezes carved across

*Figs. 3, 7, 14,*
*30, 31*

Aquitainian façades. The treatment has been likened to the way in which Islamic decoration covered "structurally impotent" architecture with a decoration that "ignored the solidity and stability of its members."[41] Notre-Dame-de-la-Couldre provides one striking example; Angoulême and Saintes offer others. In contrast to the rigidly architectonic ways in which sacred themes were utilized for the most part, these elements were generally afforded less constraining fields in which to be displayed. There is no apparent stress in the Romanesque interpretation of the assimilated motifs. The figures are neither savored as exotic trophies nor introduced as alien quotations. Infused with the irresistible energy of the West, they are transformed into Christian examples of the good and tempting terrestrial life enjoyed by the valiant knight and are completely absorbed into the decorative formulae of the monumental shrines he served.

It is plausible to assume that the Islamic objects that provided models for the Aquitainian carving were collected by western lords, the patrons and users of the churches. At Saint-Antonin, not far from Cahors in southern France, a mid-twelfth-century townhouse survives, unusual *Fig. 62* testimony to domestic architectural taste. Imbedded into the façade at the time of construction was a series of ceramic lustreware plates, of either Syrian or Spanish manufacture, fragments of which are on display inside the building. Immediately below the disclike indentations for the plates is an open gallery decorated with sculptures in contemporary Languedocian style. The themes of some of these carvings, particularly the representation of a pair of harpies, further suggest knowledge of Islamic portable objects, such as ceramics, on which this subject in particular, received important illustration.[42] The new aristocracy of the West, in seeking to project a proper upper class image, appropriated motifs available on the "mass-produced" products that emanated from the circle of their Muslim peers and applied them to their own public monuments. The riders at Parthenay and at Brinsop succeed in re- *Figs. 53,* sembling to a surprising degree the mounted hunter who appears on a *54, 63* tympanum-shaped stone relief from an aristocratic house in the Caucasus.[43] Each was probably intended to evoke similar societal associations. Such prosaic themes persisted in the art of the West evolving into a secular, courtly iconography that flourished in the Gothic period. In the early thirteenth century, these motifs were employed to decorate copper washbasins made in Limoges in apparent imitation of objects seen or collected in the East.[44] One such container, in the Detroit Institute of Art, displays a central medallion with a falconer on a prancing steed surrounded by six lobes which frame female dancers, themes familiar by now from the church façades of Aquitaine as well as from the pottery of Egypt and Persia.[45]

Christians traveling in the hinterlands had succumbed to the showy tastes of their heathen counterparts and brought home manners and styles of dress as well as an artistic mode that provided them with the vocabulary in which they could portray themselves as they wished to be seen. Usama, a cultivated, twelfth-century Syrian gentleman, recorded impressions in his autobiography of the Franks in the Holy Land noting, on a particular occasion, the clothes, trinkets, jewels, and swords that were taken from a Muslim family. The Aquitainians were described in a contemporary text as being full of life, courageous in battle, able soldiers, nimble hunters, elegant in dress, handsome in face, generous, and hospitable; that is how they chose to have themselves portrayed.[46] The "oriental" influence so often described in the Romanesque art of western France went far beyond the polylobed portals and arabesques usually cited as evidence of postpilgrimage contact, "reminiscences of Muslim art that Christians couldn't forget."[47]

The mobile Christian nobility identified profoundly with the luxurious themes that had most recently been recovered by the Muslim middle class from the melting pot of courtly motifs to which all of the Mediterranean, especially the eastern portion, was heir. Spread over the ceramics, silks, and carved coffers that migrated from Africa to Europe as barter and as booty, these secular elements were readily incorporated into the art of which these new Christian knights were the patrons. The recent suggestion that scenes of the hunt in Islamic art depict not just royal pleasures and pastimes but apotheosis as well, that they "represent or at least remind one of the rewards of the afterlife," suggests another level of similarity in the imagery of East and West.[48]

The sculpture of Aquitaine offers scant opportunity to appreciate style or subtlety of artistic definition. A few forms, such as the voussoir figures, are particularly languid and rhythmic and many of the delicate veil-like friezes bristle with energy and inventive metamorphoses of motifs. But the art remains one of form primarily in which the dominance of a single pervasive scheme defines the whole and overwhelms the individual elements that it frames and of which it is composed. The sculpture of this entire region, with its hundreds of monuments, lacks the refinement of style displayed in the art of the fewer churches of Languedoc; it is expressive of turbulent and ultimately transient moods and movement and is deliberately eclectic in its selection of forms and modes. It is clearly an art, like a region, that is boldly in search of its own definition; its style is oft-times unashamedly impetuous and imitative. Even the remarkable synthesis that is made cannot conceal the upstart and impulsive roots. The Romanesque art of Aquitaine is an exquisitely popular art—in content, patronage, distribution, and also style; until the former are observed, the latter cannot be appreciated.

# F I V E

# *Conclusion*

ARTISTIC PIRACY WAS A RECURRENT AND REWARDING PHENOMENON in the Middle Ages. In the Dome of the Rock, A.D. 690, Islam had usurped courtly Byzantine motifs of crowns and jewels to demonstrate the subjugation of the local unbeliever and to declare its own religious supremacy.[1] In the Carolingian emperor's circle one hundred years later, pagan imperial forms were identified with the liturgical celebration of Christian victory in order to dramatize for the Franks the break with persistent barbarous cultural forms. And when Europeans, especially Aquitainians, appropriated their Muslim foes' favorite motifs sometime after the year 1100, they too may have been trying both to put down their rivals and to mitigate some of their power by possessing their forms. But the fluid, inconspicuous ways in which the images were integrated into Romanesque design suggest that little intellectual hostility was intended. Rather Christians seem to have utilized a readily available vocabulary of forms in an attempt to identify with, not to differentiate themselves from, a particular peer group. In this way, they could advertise their own real sense of rising social status.

Though the confrontation with Islam was the immediate stimulus for the imagery of the churches along the western Christian frontier, Muslims were not necessarily perceived as the exclusive enemy. They were seen as Christian deviants rather than pagans even though they may have been portrayed as the latter in contemporary literature. In part they were subjected to ridicule in order to enhance the prestige and valor of the Christians; in part it helped to make a good story. Such exaggeration ought not to be perceived as an objective or profound reflection of European attitudes.[2] Islam was, to be sure, the latest in a long series of threats to Christianity, but it was in a sense a "familiar" one: even Peter the Venerable had called it the last and greatest of heresies at a time when heresy needed to be confronted.[3] Thus the challenge Islam presented to the Christian West in the twelfth century was viewed as an outward manifestation of a basic, ongoing, inner struggle, one that Christianity had fought since the time of Paul. Since that time there had developed a verbal and visual vocabulary that addressed this issue. And in such fundamental theological matters, Christians preferred to emphasize, as they always had, continuity with the past. This was expressed, in twelfth-century literature, by the celebration of the deeds of Carolingian heroes and, in contemporary art, by the adoption and revitalization of a related group of sacred forms and themes. Islam, the ostensible antagonist in this affair, provided only a limited and curiously neutral influence, one that was both transient and colloquial—in a very real sense, superficial.[4]

The western walls of Aquitainian Romanesque churches emerge thus as a remarkably coherent group of structures, astonishingly expressive of the age in which they were constructed. They survive en masse, testimony to a crucial and provocative event in European and Christian history, and demonstrate, through the selective arrangement of their forms, the power of the figurative and historical thinking that permeated the age.

Three artistic aspects of the façades have been considered in this study; the significance of the monuments may be summarized according to these perspectives now.[5] I have suggested that the abstract, architectural forms of Romanesque façades in Aquitaine deliberately utilized a group of triumphal and commemorative motifs of Roman imperial invention that had been transformed into a sacred Christian vocabulary in Carolingian times. In their new location, these liturgical shapes monumentalized and publicized the Church-sponsored concept of salvation and triumph through death to which each knight possessed direct access and which he was urged to exercise in the struggle against the Moors. Second, the explicitly venerable vocabulary of hierarchic themes that is bound up with the triumphant façade-frame derives from a similar repertoire of essentially imperial forms. It invokes an association with previous victories over heathen forces and stresses spiritual struggle. It also expresses Christian continuity with the past, Carolingian, early Christian, and, in some cases, even Roman, emphasizing the ongoing revitalization of victorious faith. This confrontation with forms of the past acted as a visual analogue of martyrdom which the knight, in his pursuit, was prepared to encounter. Finally, the supplementary small-scale sculpture that was used to embellish the skin of the ecclesiastical structure reflected the images found in contemporary luxury objects that circulated throughout the Mediterranean area in the entourage of the pilgrims and crusaders. The subjects on these precious plates, fabrics, and containers represented the pleasurable pastimes to which Muslim princes aspired both in this world and in the next. Back home, on the monumental shrines Christian soldiers built and served, similar animated depictions evoked for them the moral exigencies of their worldly battles; at the same time, they celebrated the perquisites of the knight's new-found social status.

# Notes

## Chapter One

1. The predominant sense in which the terms "foreground" and "background" are employed in the title of this chapter and further along in the text is borrowed from Erich Auerbach, *Mimesis: The Representation of Reality in Western Literature*, trans. W. R. Trask (Princeton, N.J., 1953). There the words are used to differentiate "fully externalized description" from "suggestive influence of the unexpressed," in a contrast between Homeric and biblical epic. See esp. pp. 11–12 and 23.

Ilustrations, unless otherwise acknowledged, are my own.

2. The region around Parthenay was studied in detail by George T. Beech, *A Rural Society in Medieval France: The Gâtine of Poitou in the Eleventh and Twelfth Centuries* (Baltimore, 1964), pp. 32, 59, 127. See also, for the churches, *Dictionnaire des églises de France*, vol. 3 (Tours, 1967), section C 122; Michel Dillange, *Vendée romane: Bas-Poitou roman* (La-Pierre-qui-Vire, 1976), pp. 113–15, 151; Bélisaire Ledain, *Histoire de la ville de Parthenay* (Paris, 1858), pp. 25–26, 71; Maurice Poignat, *Parthenay et le quartier Saint-Jacques* (Niort, 1976), p. 11.

3. On Angoulême and its restoration see the monograph by Charles Daras, *La Cathédrale d'Angoulême: Chef-d'oeuvre monumental de Girard II* (Angoulême, 1942).

4. For the use of the term *roman(e)* in connection with both architecture and language see the papers by Arcisse de Caumont, "Essai sur l'architecture religieuse du moyen âge," *Mémoires de la Société des antiquaires de Normandie* 1 (1824): 539, and *Histoire sommaire de l'architecture religieuse, civile et militaire au moyen âge*, 2d ed. (Caen, 1838), pp. 25–26. Enumeration of the antique characteristics of the style without descriptive use of the term *Romanesque* has been documented in the previous century in the writings of English poets and architects. Carol H. Krinsky, "Romanesque Architecture and Some Eighteenth-Century Critics," *Gesta* 1, no. 2 (1964): n.p.; Thomas H. Cocke, "Pre-Nineteenth-Century Attitudes in England to Romanesque Architecture," *Journal of the British Archaeological Society*, 3d ser., 36 (1973): 72–97. Analogies between Romanesque art and contemporary languages have recently been developed by Roberto Salvini, *Medieval Sculpture*, History of Western Sculpture (New York, 1969), pp. 20–21, and idem, "Pre-Romanesque Ottonian and Romanesque," *Journal of the British Archaeological Association*, 3d ser., 33 (1970): 1–20. Meyer Schapiro earlier touched on such aspects in his essay "On the Aesthetic Attitude in Romanesque Art," reprinted in his *Romanesque Art* (New York, 1977), pp. 1–27.

5. See Robert Rosenblum's helpful characterization of the early nineteenth-century attitude toward classical monuments in *Transformations in Late Eighteenth Century Art* (Princeton, N.J., 1967), pp. 107–45. Attitudes toward Roman art were surveyed by Otto J. Brendel in his newly reissued *Prolegomena to the Study of Roman Art* (New Haven, Conn., 1979), pp. 15–24.

6. Jules Quicherat, "De l'architecture romane," *Revue archéologique* 8 (1851): 145–58.

7. The evidence for a cultural revival is studied in the classic work by Charles Homer Haskins, *The Renaissance of the Twelfth Century* (Cambridge, Mass., 1927), and the recent, more popular survey by Christopher Brooke, *The Twelfth Century Renaissance* (New York, 1970), where the equestrian carvings are featured on pp. 15–17. The standard point of departure for students in these matters is Erwin Panofsky, *Renaissance and Renascences in Western Art,* Icon Edition (Stockholm, 1960), chap. 2. The study by Jean Adhémar is *Influences antiques dans l'art du moyen âge français,* Studies of the Warburg Institute 7 (London, 1939), pp. 52–53, 207–16 and 241–48 for material discussed here. Harry Bober deals with the literary focus of nineteenth-century research on medieval art in his foreword to Emile Mâle, *Religious Art in France, the Twelfth Century: A Study of the Origins of Medieval Iconography,* ed. Harry Bober, trans. Marthiel Mathews, Bollingen Series 90:1 (Princeton, N.J., 1978), pp. xiv–xvii. Willibald Sauerländer, for example, stressed that the twelfth-century monuments were "linked to Antiquity only in a general sense . . . ; in a strict sense of the word there was not and there could not have been a renaissance of the twelfth-century in the field of figurative sculpture" ("Sculpture on Early Gothic Churches: The State of Research and Open Questions," *Gesta* 9, no. 2 [1970]: 32–48, esp. p. 32).

8. Cahn's informative paper, "The Artist as Outlaw and *Apparatchik*: Freedom and Constraint in the Interpretation of Medieval Art," appeared in Stephen K. Scher, *The Renaissance of the Twelfth Century* (Providence, R.I., 1969), pp. 10–14. I am indebted to it for its succinct evaluation of some of the material treated here. See also Morton W. Bloomfield's perspectives on related issues, "Continuities and Discontinuities," *New Literary History* 10 (1979): 409–16, and the earlier paper by Brian Stock, "The Middle Ages as Subject and Object: Romantic Attitudes and Academic Medievalism," ibid., 5 (1974): 527–47.

9. Mâle, *Religious Art in France, the Twelfth Century,* esp. chap. 9; Henri Focillon, *The Art of the West in the Middle Ages,* ed. Jean Bony, trans. Donald King (2 vols.; London, 1963), vol. 1, *Romanesque Art,* esp. chap. 3; A. Kingsley Porter, *Romanesque Sculpture of the Pilgrimage Roads* (10 vols.; Boston, 1923; reprinted New York, 1966), 1:171–79; Schapiro, *Romanesque Art,* pp. 1–2, 6–7.

10. See Mâle, *Religious Art in France, the Twelfth Century,* p. 6, fig. 1, and chap. 11, pp. 377–444. A detailed account of the meaning of the tympanaed doorway as a projection of interior apsidal decoration is found in Yves Christe, *Les Grand portails romans* (Geneva, 1969), esp. p. 10; the idea was earlier proposed by Joseph Sauer, *Symbolik der Kirchengebäudes und seiner Ausstattung in der Auffassung des Mittelalters* (Freiburg, 1924; reprinted Münster, 1964), pp. 310ff. The tympanum and the figured capital were isolated as the most important challenges of Romanesque sculpture in France most recently by Bernhard Rupprecht, *Romanische Skulptur in Frankreich* (Munich, 1975), p. 24. Moissac's doorway is presented as the unidentified exemplar of the Romanesque portal in the *fiche supplément* on that subject that appeared in *Archéologia* 126 (1979); the Aquitainian "portails sans tympans" are described as a regional variation.

Cluny has been brought to light primarily through Kenneth Conant's half-century of labor. His excavation reports, which began to appear in *Speculum* in 1929, have been reshaped in his volume on the abbey, *Cluny: Les Eglises et la maison du chef d'ordre* (Cambridge, Mass., 1968). The old prints were also collected and published by Conant, "Five Old Prints of the Abbey Church of

Cluny," *Speculum* 3 (1928): 401–4. Additional documentary and interpretive materials have been put forward by Francis Salet and Alain Erlande-Brandenburg in articles entitled "Cluny III," and "Iconographie de Cluny III," *Bulletin monumental* 126 (1968): 235–92 and 293–322.

Controversy has long surrounded the dating of Cluny's sculpture but recent scholarship tends to support the early date put forward initially by Kingsley Porter and Conant. Willibald Sauerländer, in a short survey of medieval sculpture, emphasized that the Cluny portal, conceived and erected before 1113, was to be of "unforeseeable significance for the art of the twelfth century in France" (*Skulptur des Mittelalters*, Ullstein Kunstgeschichte [Berlin, 1963], pp. 57–58). These ideas concerning the preeminence and priority of the Cluny project were developed in his article, "Über die Komposition des Weltgerichts-Tympanons in Autun," *Zeitschrift für Kunstgeschichte* 29 (1966): 261–94. The dependence of Moissac, Autun, and Vézelay on Cluny is assumed as well by Salvini, *Medieval Sculpture*, pp. 26–27. Conant, in a recent review of H. E. Kubach's book on *Romanesque Architecture*, remarked that the Cluny portal "actually triggered the fabulous series of portals at Moissac, Vézelay, Autun and the rest" (*Journal of the Society of Architectural Historians* 36 [1977]: 44).

11. Such an attitude underlies much of the literature in the field. In addition to Mâle's *Religious Art in France, the Twelfth Century*, see Joan Evans, *Cluniac Art of the Romanesque Period* (Cambridge, 1950); Wolfgang Braunfels, *Monasteries of Western Europe: The Architecture of the Orders*, 3d ed. (Princeton, N.J., 1972); George Zarnecki, *The Monastic Achievement* (New York, [1972]).

12. Mâle, *Religious Art in France, the Twelfth Century*, p. 440. Focillon, *Art of the West: Romanesque*, p. 107; see also his remarks on tympana, p. 103, and on technical factors related to carving, p. 131. A brief but precise analysis of this latter aspect is provided by George Zarnecki, *Romanesque Art* (New York, 1971), p. 82. Earlier support for such an explanation is found in F. Deshoulières, "La Théorie d'Eugène Lefèvre-Pontalis sur les écoles romanes: Ecole du sud-ouest," *Bulletin monumental* 85 (1926): 5–22, and Elizabeth L. Mendell, *Romanesque Sculpture in Saintonge* (New Haven, Conn., 1940), pp. 130–31.

13. See my study of this matter, "A Romantic Forgery: The Romanesque 'Portal' from Saint-Etienne in Toulouse," *Art Bulletin* 50 (1968): 33–42. Despite initial criticism of this suggestion that the apostles were not originally conceived as a doorway, the French have introduced the term "pseudo-portal" in recent discussions of the construction (*Le Petit journal des grands expositions*, n.s., 66 [July–November 1978]). Marcel Durliat's latest book, in which there is extensive commentary on the Saint-Etienne cloister project, adds nothing substantially new to the matter (*Haut-Languedoc roman* [La Pierre-qui-Vire, 1978], pp. 196–205).

14. See, for example, the article by René Crozet on equestrian reliefs, "Le Thème du cavalier victorieux dans l'art roman de France et d'Espagne," *Principe de Viana* 32 (1971): 125–43; that by Paul Deschamps on the virtue and vice theme on archivolts "Le Combat des vertus et des vices sur les portails romans de la Saintonge et de Poitou," *Congrès archéologique* 79, no. 2 (1912): 309–24; and the remarks on contemporary history and a lintel on the façade at Angoulême in Rita Lejeune and Jacques Stiennon, *La Légende de Roland dans l'art du moyen-âge*, 2 vols. (Brussels, 1966), 1:29–42. All of this material is considered at length in chap. 3, below.

15. Among the major articles are the following: L. Schürenberg, "Die romanischen Kirchenfassaden Aquitaniens," *Das Münster* 4 (1951): 257–68; Pierre Héliot, "Sur la façade des églises romanes d'Aquitaine à propos d'une

étude récente," *Bulletin de la Société archéologique de l'Ouest,* 4th ser., 2 (1952): 243–71, and "Observations sur les façades décorées d'arcades aveugles dans les églises romanes," ibid., 4th ser., 4 (1958): 367–99, 419–58; Charles Daras, "L'Evolution de l'architecture aux façades des églises romanes ornées d'arcatures en Charente: leur origine, leur filiation," *Bulletin monumental* 119 (1961): 121–38; Richard Hamann McLean, "Les Origines des portails et façades sculptés gothiques," *Cahiers de civilisation médiévale* 2 (1959): 157–75; R. Chappuis, "Utilisation du trace ovale dans l'architecture des églises romanes," *Bulletin monumental* 134 (1976): 7–36. Focillon's ideas about the sources and importance of arcaded forms are summarized in his *Art of the West: Romanesque,* pp. 48–49.

16. I am grateful to Professor Lyman for having provided me with a copy of his paper, "L'Intégration du portail dans la façade méridionale," *Les Cahiers de Saint-Michel de Cuxa* 8 (1977): 55–68, and for many generous and illuminating conversations as we have pursued related problems from complementary perspectives. See also the article by Gardelles, "Recherches sur les origines des façades à étages d'arcatures des églises médiévales," *Bulletin monumental* 136 (1978): 113–33. In connection with this latter study see the earlier work of Henri Stern, "Nouvelles recherches sur les images des Conciles dans l'Eglise de la Nativité à Bethlehem," *Cahiers archéologiques* 3 (1948): 82–105.

17. *Congrès archéologique de France: Poitiers* 70 (1903); *Angoulême* 79 (1912); *Bordeaux, Bayonne* 102 (1939); *Poitiers* 109 (1951); *La Rochelle* 114 (1956). René Crozet, *L'Art roman en Poitou* (Paris, 1948) and *L'Art roman en Saintonge* (Paris, 1971). Mendell's study is *Romanesque Sculpture in Saintonge.* Relevant volumes in the Zodiac series include Charles Daras, *Angoumois roman* (La-Pierre-qui-Vire, 1961); Michel Dillange, *Vendée romane;* Pierre Dubourg-Noves, *Guyenne romane* (La-Pierre-qui-Vire, 1969); François Eygun, *Saintonge roman* (La-Pierre-qui-Vire, 1970); Yvonne Labande-Mailfert, *Poitou roman* (La-Pierre-qui-Vire, 1957); Raymond Oursel, *Haut-Poitou roman* (La-Pierre-qui-Vire, 1975). See also François Eygun's study *Art des pays d'Ouest* (Paris, 1965).

18. Rupprecht, *Romanische Skulptur,* pp. 88ff., where Aulnay and Angoulême are placed in the first half of the twelfth century and Saintes, Civray, and Marignac, among others, in the second half.

19. "Holy Warriors: The Romanesque Rider and the Fight against Islam," in Thomas P. Murphy, ed., *The Holy War* (Columbus, Ohio, 1976), pp. 33–77. The explanation of purpose in what follows comes very close to paraphrasing Claude Lévi-Strauss's recent, succinct definition of his structuralist approach as "the quest for the . . . invariant elements among superficial differences" (*Myth and Meaning* [New York, 1979], p. 8).

20. I have profited from the remarks of M.-D. Chenu on the importance of identifying procedures and perspectives in an analysis of a historical period. See his introduction to *Nature, Man and Society in the Twelfth Century,* ed. and trans. Jerome Taylor and Lester K. Little (Chicago, 1968), pp. xv–xx, and the prefatory comments of Etienne Gilson, pp. ix–xiii. Christopher Dawson's *Medieval Essays* (London, 1953), with its emphasis on the fundamental importance of religious institutions and sanctions in the formation of culture and social activities in the Middle Ages, addresses many of the issues touched upon in these pages, although it does not concern itself with the art of the time. It provides a helpful introduction to elements of Christian culture often, and incorrectly I believe, considered aspects of "secular" society.

21. In Marcel Aubert, ed., *L'Art roman en France* (Paris, 1961), p. 168.

22. There is much fascinating new research in this area, of which only a selection can be included here. In addition to the work by Beech, *A Rural Society in Medieval France,* I have found these studies to be particularly helpful: Marcel

Garaud, *Les Châtelains de Poitou et l'avènement du règime féodale, XI^e et XII^e siècle* (Poitiers, 1967) and "Recherches sur les défrichements dans la Gâtine poitevine aux XI^e et XII^e siècles," *Bulletin de la Société des antiquaires de l'Ouest*, 4th ser., 9 (1967): 11–27; Roland Sanfaçon, *Défrichements, peuplement et institutions seigneuriales en Haut-Poitou du X^e au XIII^e siècle* (Quebec, 1967); and A. R. Lewis, *The Development of Southern French and Catalan Society, 718–1050* (Austin, 1965); also Sidney Painter, "Castellans of the Plain of the Poitou in the Eleventh and Twelfth Centuries," in Fred A. Cazel, Jr., ed., *Feudalism and Liberty* (Baltimore, 1961), pp. 17–40; J. R. Strayer, "The Two Levels of Feudalism," in Robert S. Hoyt, ed., *Life and Thought in the Early Middle Ages* (Minneapolis, 1967), pp. 51–65; Charles Higounet, "Le Groupe aristocratique en Aquitaine et en Gascogne, fin X^e–début XII^e siècle," in *Les Structures sociales de l'Aquitaine, du Languedoc et de l'Espagne au premier âge féodal*, Colloques internationales du Centre nationale de la recherche scientifique (Paris, 1969), pp. 221–37; Léopold Genicot, "The Nobility in Medieval *Francia*: Continuity, Break or Evolution?" in F. L. Cheyette, ed., *Lordship and Community in Medieval Europe* (New York, 1968), pp. 128–36; Jane Martindale, "Conventum inter Guillelmum Aquitanorum comes et Hugonem Chiliarchum," *English Historical Review* 84 (1969): 528–48; René Crozet, "Recherches sur les sites de châteaux et de lieux fortifiés en Haut-Poitou au moyen-âge," *Bulletin de la Société des antiquaires de l'Ouest*, 4th ser., 11 (1971): 187–217; Bernard S. Bachrach, "A Study in Feudal Politics: Relations between Fulk Nerra and William the Great, 995–1030," *Viator* 7 (1976): 111–22; also Joseph di Corcia, "*Bourg, Bourgeois, Bourgeois de Paris* from the Eleventh to the Eighteenth Century," *Journal of Modern History* 50 (1978): 207–33; Fredric Cheyette, "The Castles of the Trencavels: A Preliminary Aerial Survey," in W. C. Jordan, B. McNab, and T. F. Ruiz, eds., *Order and Innovation in the Middle Ages: Essays in Honor of Joseph R. Strayer* (Princeton, N.J., 1976), pp. 255–72. The situation in the Poitou has been characterized most recently by Robert Hajdu, "Family and Feudal Ties in Poitou, 1100–1300," *Journal of Interdisciplinary Studies* 8 (1977): 117–39, and "Castles, Castellans and the Structure of Politics in Poitou, 1152–1271," *Journal of Medieval History* 4 (1978): 27–53.

23. See, in particular, the review of current material by Jane Martindale, "The French Aristocracy in the Early Middle Ages: A Reappraisal," *Past and Present* 75 (1977): 5–45, as well as the earlier book by Léonce Auzias, *L'Aquitaine carolingienne* (Toulouse and Paris, 1937), and the papers by Marcel Garaud, "L'Aquitaine carolingienne et l'histoire du Poitou à propos d'un livre récent," *Revue historique* 186 (1939): 78–84, and Philippe Wolff, "L'Aquitaine et ses marges," *Karl der Grosse: Lebenswerk und Nachleben*, vol. 1, *Personlichkeit und Geschichte* (Düsseldorf, 1965), pp. 269–306. Valuable also are the studies by George T. Beech, "The Origins of the Family of the Viscounts of Thouars," in *Etudes de civilisation médiévale* (Poitiers, 1974), pp. 25–31; idem, "A Feudal Document of Early Eleventh Century Poitou," *Mélanges offerts à René Crozet*, 1:203–13; and idem, "Prosopography," in James M. Powell, ed., *Medieval Studies: An Introduction* (Syracuse, N.Y., 1976), pp. 151–84.

24. Faustin Poey d'Avant, *Monnaies féodales de France*, 3 vols. (Paris, 1858–62); Graz, 1961), 2:1–41; C. H. Coulson, "Fortresses and Social Responsibility in Late Carolingian France," *Zeitschrift für Archäologie des Mittelalters* 4 (1976): 29–36; Theodore Evergates, "Historiography and Sociology in Early Feudal Society: The Case of Hariulf and the 'Milites' of St-Riquier," *Viator* 6 (1975): 35–49.

25. René Crozet, "Aspects sociaux de l'art du moyen-âge en Poitou," *Bulletin de la Société des antiquaires de l'Ouest*, 4th ser., 3 (1955): 8; idem, *L'Art roman en Poitou*, pp. 12–13; and G. Chapeau, "Un pèlerinage noble à Charroux au XI^e

siècle," *Bulletin de la Société des antiquaires de l'Ouest,* 3d ser., 13 (1943): 264; a special treasure of the old emperor, a phylactery containing a relic of the true cross, was said to have been preserved at Charroux.

26. See the articles by F. Brisset, "Guillaume le Grand et l'église," *Bulletin de la Société des antiquaires de l'Ouest,* 4th ser., 11 (1972): 441–60, and Martindale, "French Aristocracy," p. 32. The text of Adémar's chronicle was published by Jules Chavanon, *Adémar de Chabannes: Chronique* (Paris, 1897); the foundation of Cluny is mentioned in chap. 21 (p. 140); William the Great is portrayed sympathetically in chaps. 41 and 54 (pp. 163–65 and 176–77). The extent and effectiveness of William's real power was recently reevaluated by Bernard S. Bachrach, who emphasized his military reverses and the extent to which "castellans usurped comital prerogatives" during his reign ("Toward a Reappraisal of William the Great, Duke of Aquitaine [995–1030]," *Journal of Medieval History* 5 [1979]: 19).

Adémar's chronicle was known and used by the author of another contemporary history. See the study by Jean Verdon, "La chronique du Saint-Maixent et l'histoire du Poitou au IX$^e$–XII$^e$ siècles," *Bulletin de la Société des antiquaires de l'Ouest,* 4th ser., 13 (1976): 437–72, in which the important passages on the counts and the churches in the region from the time of Charlemagne up to 1141 are translated and commented upon.

27. For remarks on church patronage, see H. E. J. Cowdrey, *The Cluniacs and the Gregorian Reform* (Oxford, 1970), pp. 87–88, 103; Giles Constable, "Monastic Possession of Churches and 'Spiritualia' in the Age of Reform," in *Il Monachesimo e la Riforma Ecclesiastica, 1049–1122,* Atti della quarta Settimana internazionale di studio, Mendola, 1968 (Milan, 1971), pp. 304–31; G. Fournier, "Rural Churches and Rural Communities in Early Medieval Auvergne," in Cheyette, ed., *Lordship and Community,* pp. 320–30; Crozet, "Aspects sociaux," p. 10; see also the remarks in L. Bruhat, *Le Monachisme en Saintonge* (La Rochelle, 1907), p. 182, and of course, Adémar's chronicle. Documentation on the churches is discussed by E. R. Labande, "L'Historiographie de la France de l'Ouest au X$^e$ et XI$^e$ siècles," *La Storiografia Altomedievale,* 2 vols. Settimane di Studio del Centro Italiano di Studi sull'alto Medioevo 17 (Spoleto, 1970), 2:751–91. Related observations on the churches of Anjou appear in Olivier Guillot, *Le Comte d'Anjou et son entourage au XI$^e$ siècle,* 2 vols. (Paris, 1972), 1:129ff. and, for the south, Elisabeth Magnou-Nortier, *La Société laïque et l'église dans la province ecclésiastique de Narbonne de la fin du VIII$^e$ à la fin du XI$^e$ siècle* (Toulouse, 1974). She emphasizes, among other matters, the social diversity of the rural region and the importance of Charlemagne. For a study of lay and ecclesiastical activity at a monastery see C. van de Kieft, "La Seigneurie de l'abbaye de Saint-Jean d'Angély au milieu du XI$^e$ siècle," *Miscellanea Mediaevalia in memoriam Jan Frederik Niermeyer* (Groningen, 1967), pp. 167–75.

28. For the influence, or lack thereof, of Cluny in western France, see René Crozet, "Les Etablissements clunisiens en Saintonge," *Annales du Midi* 75 (1963): 575–81; Oursel, *Haut-Poitou roman,* pp. 62–63. See B. Guillemain, "Les Moines sur les sièges épiscopaux du sud-ouest de la France aux XI$^e$ et XII$^e$ siècles," *Etudes de civilisation médiévale,* pp. 377–84, on the importance of aristocratic and familial ties, and Charles Daras, "Les Eglises au onzième siècle en Charente," *Bulletin de la Société archéologique de l'Ouest,* 4th ser., 5 (1959): 177–213. Political rather than religious motivation for the reform of religious houses is considered in F. X. Hartigan, "Reform of the Collegiate Clergy in the Eleventh Century: The Case of St-Nicholas at Poitiers," *Studies in Medieval Culture* 11 (1977): 55–62. See also the series of related articles in *La Vita comune del clero nei secoli XI e XII,* Miscellanea del centro di studi mediovali 3, Atti della prima

Settimana internazionale de studio, Mendola, 1959, 2 vols. (Milan, 1962), vol. 1. The surprising prominence of the (nonmonastic) regular canons in parts of this region in the eleventh century is discussed by J. C. Dickinson, *The Origins of the Austin Canons and Their Introduction into England* (London, 1950), p. 47.

Interest in the importance of the canons regular in Aquitaine has emerged in recent writings. See, in particular, the paper by Georges Pon, "L'Apparition des chanoines réguliers en Poitou: Saint-Nicolas de Poitiers," *Bulletin de la Société des antiquaires de l'Ouest*, 4th ser., 13 (1975): 55–70, where a sense of scorn against the Benedictines is suggested in the foundation documents; see pp. 59–60 and 69. Yves-Jean Riou has studied a little-known and largely destroyed Augustinian foundation in his paper, "Le prieuré Notre-Dame d'Oulmes (Charente-Maritime)," ibid., 4th ser., 13 (1975): 165–87. The basic study is by Charles Dereine, "Vie commune, règle de Saint Augustin et chanoines réguliers au XI^e siècle," *Revue d'histoire écclesiastique* 41 (1946): 365–406.

29. Marcel Garaud, "Observations sur les vicissitudes de la propriété écclesiastique dans le diocèse de Poitiers du IX^e au XIII^e siècle," *Bulletin de la Société des antiquaires de l'Ouest*, 4th ser., 5 (1960): 368, and Jean Becquet, "La Paroisse en France aux XI^e et XII^e siècles," *Le Istituzioni ecclesiastiche della "Societas Christiana" dei secoli XI–XII: Diocesi, pievi e parrocchie*, Miscellanea del centro di studi medioevali, 8, Atti della sesta Settimana internazionale de studio, Mendola, 1974 (Milan, 1977), pp. 199–229, esp. 202. Crozet commented on the donations to the churches of Maillezais, Vouvant, and Talmont (*L'Art roman en Poitou*, pp. 45–46, 49), and Daras remarked on those to Montierneuf and St-Cybard ("Les Eglises au onzième siècle," pp. 181–82). For the churches in Parthenay, see Beech, *A Rural Society in Medieval France*, p. 32.

30. Crozet, *L'Art roman en Poitou*, pp. 51–56. More recently, on Agnes of Burgundy and her patronage of churches, see Jean Verdon, "La Femme en Poitou aux X^e et XI^e siècles," *Bulletin de la Société des antiquaires de l'Ouest*, 4th ser., 14 (1977): 91–102, and Jean Michaud, "Dédicaces en Poitou: Faste des cérémonies (ca. 800–1050)," ibid., pp. 143–63.

31. The literature on this subject has also grown considerably in the last few years and only a few of the studies that I have found to be particularly helpful are cited here: H. E. J. Cowdrey, *The Cluniacs and the Gregorian Reform* and "The Genesis of the Crusades: The Springs of Western Ideas of Holy War," in Murphy, ed., *The Holy War*, pp. 9–32; Paul Rousset, "Les Laïcs dans la croisade," and George Duby, "Les Laïcs et la Paix de Dieu," *I Laici nella "Societas Christiana" dei secoli XI e XII*, Miscellanea del centro di studi medioevali, 5, Atti della terza Settimana internazionale de studio, Mendola, 1965 (Milan, 1968), pp. 428–43 and 448–61. The latter paper has been translated as "Laity and the Peace of God," in Duby's collected papers, *The Chivalrous Society*, trans. Cynthia Postan (Berkeley and Los Angeles, 1977), pp. 123–33. Both the Carolingian and Aquitainian situations are well summarized in John Beeler, *Warfare in Feudal Europe* (Ithaca, N.Y., 1971), pp. 9–17 and 151–58.

32. Roger Bonnaud-Delamare, "Les Institutions de paix en Aquitaine au XI^e siècle," *Recueils de la Société Jean Bodin pour l'histoire comparative des institutions* 14 (1962): 415–87.

33. See, for example, the charters of Hugh of Lusignan's and Pierre Abruitit's donations to Nouaillé before going off to fight the Saracens in Spain in 1087 (*Archives historiques du Poitou*, vol. 49, nos. 157, 158). Likewise, the viscount of Thouars, who was in the Holy Land in 1098, expressed the desire to be buried at one of the churches he endowed (Hugues Imbert, *Histoire de Thouars* [Niort, 1870; reprint, Marseilles, 1976], p. 63).

34. Again, only a selection of key works on these vast topics is possible; see,

e.g., Robert Folz, *Le Souvenir et la légende de Charlemagne dans l'empire germanique médiévale*, Publications de l'Université de Dijon, n.s., 7 (Paris, 1950), for the importance of Charlemagne in the later Middle Ages; Alfred G. Richard, *Histoire des comtes de Poitou, 778–1204* (Paris, 1903), pp. 496–97 for a biography of the counts; Pierre Le Gentil's study, *La Chanson de Roland*, trans. Frances F. Beer (Cambridge, Mass., 1969), for the text in English and commentary on the historic position of the poem; *La Chanson de Roland: Reproduction phototypique du manuscrit Digby 23*, ed. Alexandre de Laborde (Paris, 1933), for the "original" version of the epic; and W. T. H. Jackson, *The Literature of the Middle Ages* (New York, 1960), for general comments on the troubadour poems. The standard edition of William's poems is outdated and has recently been replaced by a new study. See both *Les Chansons de Guillaume IX, duc d'Aquitaine*, ed. Alfred Jeanroy (Paris, 1913), and Nicolò Pasero, *Poesie Guglielmo IX: edizione critica* (Modena, 1973). For a detailed account of some of William's independent ways, see F. Villard, "Guillaume IX d'Aquitaine et le concile de Reims 1119," *CCM* 16 (1973): 295–302, and the earlier study by James Lea Cate, "A Gay Crusader," *Byzantion* 16 (1942–43): 503–26.

35. Consider and compare Lynn White's cautionary and helpful remarks on a *word*-bound historical orientation in "Cultural Climates and Technological Advance in the Middle Ages," *Viator* 2 (1971): 171–201, esp. 181.

### Chapter Two

1. H. Erich Kubach, *Romanesque Architecture* (New York, 1975), pp. 215–27.

2. Crozet, *L'Art roman en Saintonge*, pp. 98–106, and *L'Art roman en Poitou*, p. 153 and the plan on p. 113.

3. Mendell, *Romanesque Sculpture in Saintonge*, pp. 34–35 and 40–41.

4. The term is borrowed from Meyer Schapiro, who employed it forty years ago to identify the "discrepant relationship of corresponding parts" ("The Sculptures of Souillac," reprinted in *Romanesque Art*, p. 104).

5. Similar terminology has often been used to describe the façades of Aquitaine: e.g., Mendell refers to them as "screen façades" (*Romanesque Sculpture in Saintonge*, p. 34), as does George Zarnecki, *Art of the Medieval World* (New York, 1975), p. 288; *Schauwand* is used by Erich Kubach and Peter Bloch, *Kunst der Welt: Früh und Hochromanik* (Baden-Baden, 1964), p. 186.

6. For illustrations of these structures see Crozet, *L'Art roman en Poitou*, pl. 16-2 (Celles-sur-Belle), pl. 32 (Airvault), and *L'Art roman en Saintonge*, pl. 34-C (Meursac), pl. 35-D (Cressac).

7. See, for example Zygmunt Swiechowski, "La Formation de l'oeuvre architecturale au cours du haut moyen âge," *Cahiers de civilisation médiévale* 1 (1958): 371–78.

8. Salvini briefly discusses the possibility of a common Armenian influence in both areas (*Medieval Sculpture*, pp. 28–29). For the Arezzo façade, see pl. 266 in Kubach, *Romanesque Architecture*.

9. Stephen G. Nichols, Jr., "A Poetics of Historicism? Recent Trends in Medieval Literary Studies," *Medievalia et Humanistica*, n.s., 8 (1977): 77–101. Compare also the related remarks of Edward B. Henning, "Patronage and Style in the Arts: A Suggestion concerning Their Relations," in *The Sociology of Art and Literature*, ed. Milton C. Albrecht, James A. Barnett, and Mason Griff (New York, 1970), pp. 353–62, esp. p. 361, and those of Peter Dronke, "Learned Lyric and Popular Ballad in the Early Middle Ages," *Studi Medievali*, 3d ser., 17 (1976): 5, where he observes that the most "authentic poetry of the Latin Middle Ages," combines classical and biblical elements with motifs drawn from the poet's own vernacular tradition. There are useful observations on methodology in poetic

interpretation, particularly in the utility of "genre as an internal substitute for context," in J. A. Burrow, "Poems without Contexts," *Essays in Criticism* 29 (1979): 6–32.

10. Oursel, in particular, gives a careful definition of this in *Haut-Poitou*, pp. 373–80, with schematic renderings of the basic types. See also the studies cited in chap. 1, n. 15. The gable, which I do not consider here in depth, has been discussed by Pierre Dubourg-Noves, "Remarques sur les portails romans à fronton de l'ouest de la France," *Cahiers de civilisation médiévale* 17 (1974): 25–39.

11. Useful consideration of some of these aspects can be found in E. Baldwin Smith, *Architectural Symbolism of Imperial Rome and the Middle Ages* (Princeton, N. J., 1956), although his conclusions are not acceptable in every case.

12. Rupprecht, *Romanische Skulptur*, p. 52. See also the studies cited in chap. 1, n. 16.

13. Dubourg-Noves noted that it would be impossible to reconstruct what might have been perceived at the time from ruins; fortunately, since so much survived intact, this was not necessary ("Remarques sur les portails romans à fronton," p. 38). There is a map of Gallo-Roman remains in France known in the twelfth century in Marie Durand-Lefebvre, *Art Gallo-romain et sculpture romane* (Paris, 1937), opp. p. 307 and Répertoire, pp. 309ff. Additional insight into the importance of the Roman foundations in Gaul is provided by Paul-Albert Février in his review of recent excavations ("The Origin and Growth of the Cities of Southern Gaul to the Third Century A.D." *Journal of Roman Studies* 63 [1973]: 1–28). The substantial ancient fortifications of Poitiers have been studied by Gérard Jarousseau, "Essai de localisation de la Porte-le-Comte et de la Porte Mainard dans l'enceinte du bas empire à Poitiers," *Bulletin de la Société des antiquaires de l'Ouest*, 4th ser., 13 (1975): 143–53.

14. On the relationship to the antique, see René Crozet, "Survivances antiques dans le décor roman de Poitou, de l'Angoumois et de la Saintonge," *Bulletin monumental* 114 (1956): 7–33, in addition to the study by Adhémar, *Influences antiques dans l'art du moyen âge français*. A splendid pictorial presentation of the riches of Roman Gaul is available in Henri-Paul Eydoux, *La France antique* (Paris, 1962).

15. A comparison of Aquitainian façades with triumphal arches was made by Chan. Tonnellier, "L'Art roman en Saintonge," *Richesses de France: La Charente-Maritime* 75 (1968): 56–69. My own consideration of symbolic relationships is found below, after the discussion of formal correspondences. Concerning the arch at Saintes, E. Espérandieu noted that it was not a victory monument but "a witness to the people's attachment to a prince whose virtues announce a good future" ("L'Arc de Triomphe de Saintes," *Revue poitevine et saintongeaise* 46 [1887]: 289–307). For the arches at Orange and at Saint-Rémy, which were *not* triumphal monuments in a true sense, see the supplements to the journal *Gallia:* R. Amy et al., *L'Arc d'Orange, Gallia*, supplement 15 (1962), p. 12, where the arch is described as having defined the sacred earth beyond which there could be no burials, and Henri Rolland, *L'Arc de Glanum, Gallia*, supplement 31 (1977).

16. Crozet, *L'Art roman en Saintonge*, pp. 105–6.

17. Chenu, *Nature, Man, and Society*, p. 3; André Grabar, *Christian Iconography: A Study of Its Origins*, Bollingen Series 35.10 (Princeton, N.J., 1968), p. xliii; F. P. Pickering, *Literature and Art in the Middle Ages* (Coral Gables, 1970), p. 77; Hanns Swarzenski, "The Role of Copies in the Formation of the Styles of the Eleventh Century," *Studies in Western Art*, vol. 1, *Romanesque and Gothic Art*, Acts of the Twentieth International Congress of the History of Art, New York, 1961 (Princeton, N.J., 1963), pp. 7–18, esp. p. 12.

18. The studies that have illustrated this point to me most forcefully are those by Percy E. Schramm, whose work is discussed in a useful article by J. M. Bak, "Medieval Symbology of the State: Percy E. Schramm's Contribution," *Viator* 4 (1973): 33–63; Ernst Kitzinger, "The Role of Miniature Painting in Mural Decoration," *The Place of Book Illumination in Byzantine Art* (Princeton, N.J., 1975), pp. 99ff.; Otto Demus, *The Church of San Marco in Venice: History, Architecture, Sculpture* (Washington, D.C., 1960); Kurt Weitzmann, "The Mosaics of San Marco and the Cotton Genesis," *Venezia e l'Europa*, Atti del XVIII Congresso internazionale di storia dell'arte, Venezia, 1955 (Venice, 1956), pp. 152ff., and "The Classical in Byzantine Art as a Mode of Individual Expression," *Byzantine Art: An European Art* (Athens, 1966), pp. 151–77. Richard Krautheimer's article, "Introduction to an 'Iconography of Medieval Architecture,'" *Journal of the Warburg and Courtauld Institutes* 5 (1942): 1–33, presents a particularly valuable examination of the use and transformation of architectural models and has wide relevance to many of the points I make.

19. Krautheimer, "The Carolingian Revival of Early Christian Architecture," *Studies in Early Christian, Medieval and Renaissance Art*, ed. Elizabeth MacDougall (New York, 1969), pp. 203–256, reprinted, with additional comments from *Art Bulletin* 24 (1942): 1–38.

20. The manuscripts have been strikingly illustrated most recently in Florentine Mütherich and Joachim Gaehde, *Carolingian Painting* (New York, 1976), e.g., the Gospels of Saint Médard of Soissons, pls. 4–7, for the cameos and architecture, and Coronation Gospels, pls. 8, 10, for the landscape. See also Mütherich's article, "Die Buchmalerei am Hofe Karls des Grossen," in *Karl der Grosse* 3:9–53.

21. R. McKitterick, *The Frankish Church and the Carolingian Reforms, 789–895* (London, 1977), esp. pp. xvii–xviii, 8–9, 115–54. See also Cyrille Vogel, "La Réforme liturgique sous Charlemagne," in *Karl der Grosse* 2:217–32. Donald A. Bullough, in a recent paper, has emphasized that Rome was thought about first as a model for religious revival and only subsequently as the source for a *renovatio imperii* ("Roman Books and Carolingian *Renovatio*," in *Renaissance and Renewal in Christian History*, ed. Derek Baker, Studies in Church History 14 [Cambridge, 1977], pp. 23–50). The essays of F. L. Ganshof, "Einhard, Biographer of Charlemagne," and "The Impact of Charlemagne on the Institutions of the Frankish Realm," are also valuable in this context (*The Carolingians and the Frankish Monarchy*, trans. Janet Sondheimer [Ithaca, N.Y., 1971], pp. 1–16 and 143–61).

22. Werner Meyer-Barkhausen, "Ein karolingisches Bronzegitter als Schmuckmotiv des Elfenbeinkelches von Deventer," *Zeitschrift für bildende Kunst* 64 (1930–31): 244–48, and Victor Elbern, "Der eucharistische Kelch im frühen Mittelalter," *Zeitschrift des deutschen Vereins für Kunstwissenschaft* 17 (1963): 1–76 and 117–88, esp. 75 and 128–29.

23. For example, Jean Hubert, "Introïbo ad altare," *Revue de l'art* 24 (1974): 9–21, and Donald Bullough, "'Imagines Regum' and Their Significance in the Early Medieval West," in *Studies in Memory of David Talbot Rice*, ed. Giles Robertson and George Henderson (Edinburgh, 1975), p. 242. On the important subject of iconoclasm in the Carolingian period, see the articles by Ann Freeman, "Theodulf of Orleans and the *Libri Carolini*," *Speculum* 32 (1957): 663–705, esp. pp. 695–703, and Hermann Schnitzler, "Das karolingische Kuppelmosaik der Aachener Pfalzkapelle," *Aachener Kunstblätter* 29 (1964): 17–44.

24. To the initial articles by B. de Montesquiou-Fézensac, "L'Arc de triomphe d'Einhardus," *Cahiers archéologiques* 4 (1949): 79–103, and "L'arc Eginhard," ibid. 8 (1956): 147–74, add now the detailed papers in Karl Hauck, ed., *Das*

*Einhardkreuz*, Abhandlungen der Akademie der Wissenschaften in Göttingen, philologisch-historische Klasse, 3d ser., 87 (Göttingen, 1974). I am grateful to Florentine Mütherich for first making this volume available to me. Interesting remarks on Einhard as patron of other objects appear in Roswitha Zeilinger, "Eginhard et la sculpture carolingienne," *Dossiers de l'archéologie* 30 (1978): 104–12.

25. The Lorsch covers are discussed in detail in several studies: M. H. Longhurst and C. R. Morey, "The Covers of the Lorsch Gospels," *Speculum* 3 (1928): 64–74; H. Schnitzler, "Die Komposition der Lorscher Elfenbeintafeln," *Münchner Jahrbuch der bildenden Kunst*, 3d ser., 1 (1950): 26–42; H. Fillitz, "Die Elfenbeinreliefs zur Zeit Kaiser Karls des Grossen," *Aachener Kunstblätter* 32 (1966): 14–45. Schnitzler searched for stylistic and iconographic sources for the ivories emphasizing the imperial, but not emphatically triumphal, associations of the architectural frame. He cited the gateway on the Missorium of Theodosius in Madrid and the palace façade in Ravenna as prototypes for the gateways on the Lorsch covers (pp. 34–40). Such tripartite schemes appear as architectural frames or backdrops in numerous manuscript illuminations from the ninth century on. Consideration of this material has, however, been omitted from this essay because of the discrete problems posed by manuscript studies concerning texts, hands, and copies and because of the formal and thematic coherence of the sculptural material. John of Salisbury's admiration of the Arch of Constantine is noted by James Bruce Ross in "A Study of Twelfth-Century Interest in the Antiquities of Rome," *Medieval and Historiographical Essays in Honor of James Westfall Thompson*, ed. James Lea Cate and Eugene N. Anderson (Chicago, 1938), p. 312.

26. An article by Massey H. Shepherd, Jr., was initially helpful in formulating these and subsequent remarks ("Liturgical Expression of the Constantinian Triumph," *Dumbarton Oaks Papers* 21 [1967]: 59–78). See also the comments of Chenu on the mass as triumph and as battle against the devil (*Nature, Man, and Society*, p. 152). For the sense of a "reactualization of a sacred event," I am dependent upon *Myths, Rites, Symbols: A Mircea Eliade Reader*, ed. Wendell E. Beane and William G. Doty, 2 vols. (New York, 1976), 1:33. My perception of the meaning of Einhard's arch both here and below parallels in many ways the interpretation offered by Hans Belting, "Der Einhardsbogen," *Zeitschrift für Kunstgeschichte* 36 (1973): 93–121, esp. pp. 107–9. The centrality of Carolingian creativity in the emergence of splendid book covers was remarked upon by Philippe Verdier in his review of Frauke Steenbock, *Die Kirchliche Prachteinband im frühen Mittelalter* (Berlin, 1965) in *Speculum* 46 (1971): 186–87.

27. *Renaissance and Renascences*, pp. 50–51.

28. On the arch as a trophy bearer, see H. Kähler, "Triumphbogen," *Realencyclopädie der classischen Altertumswissenschaft*, ed. A. F. von Pauly (Stuttgart, 1939), 13:371–491, esp. p. 476. Especially valuable and relevant material is presented by Gilbert Charles-Picard, *Les Trophées romains: Contribution à l'histoire de la religion et de l'art triomphal de Rome*, Bibliothèque des écoles françaises d'Athènes et de Rome, vol. 187 (Paris, 1957), pp. 196, 346, 496–97 and the chapter "Tropaeum Fidei," pp. 494–508. For the coins see Max Bernhart, *Handbuch zur Münzkunde der römischen Kaiserzeit* (Halle, 1926), vol. 2, pl. 94, nos. 4–6.

29. Charles-Picard, *Les Trophées romains*, pp. 497–500, and R. H. Storch, "The Trophy and the Cross: Pagan and Christian Symbolism in the Fourth and Fifth Centuries," *Byzantion* 40 (1970): 111–12. Also J. M. C. Toynbee, "The Shrine of St. Peter and Its Setting," *Journal of Roman Studies* 43 (1953): 23–24, and Richard Krautheimer, *Early Christian and Byzantine Architecture* (Baltimore, 1967), pp. 34

and 66, where the term *trophy* is also used to describe the shrine at the Holy Sepulcher.

30. For a related interpretation of Einhard's arch see Karl Hauck, "Versuch einer Gesamtdeutung des Einhard-Kreuzes," in *Das Einhardkreuz*, pp. 143–205, esp. p. 202 and pls. 2, 3.

31. Longhurst and Morey, "Lorsch Gospels," p. 68. Jan van der Meulen has commented on the reuse of old elements or *spolia* in twelfth-century architecture ("Sculpture and Its Architectural Context at Chartres around 1200," *The Year 1200: A Symposium* [New York, 1975], pp. 511–12). For the *escrain* see below and n. 36.

32. Belting reflected on the possibility that the political message he attributed to the silver base of a cross had originally been conceived for a court object where it would have been more suitable than on the private donation to a monastery, which Einhard's arch, in fact, was ("Der Einhardsbogen," p. 113). The most recent interpretation of Einhard's arch, written by André Grabar as a critical commentary on the symposium volume devoted to the object, emphasizes the importance of Constantine's arch as a model for the Carolingian shrine. Grabar stressed this particular Roman monument's significance as a glorification of the triumph of the cross—specifically, Constantine's victory over Maxentius at the Milvian Bridge accomplished under the sign of the cross. In his opinion, the theme of Einhard's arch, and of other Carolingian works of art, is the same: proclamation of the triumph of Christianity via the triumph of the cross. It is for this reason, he suggests, that the Constantinian material was so heavily drawn upon by the Carolingians in their search for meaningful models ("Observations sur l'arc de triomphe de la Croix dit Arc d'Eginhard, et sur d'autres bases de la Croix," *Cahiers archéologiques* 27 [1978]: 61–83).

33. Victor Elbern, "L'Orfèvrerie," *Charlemagne: Oeuvre, Rayonnement et Survivances*, Dixième Exposition sous les auspices du Conseil de l'Europe (Aix-la-Chapelle, 1965), pp. 357–62, esp. 358–59. Close relations between western France and Germany especially in the Carolingian period are discussed by E. Ewig in "L'Aquitaine et les Pays Rhénans au haut moyen âge," *Cahiers de civilisation médiévale* (1958): 37–54. The amount of precious metal in secular hands was emphasized by Jane Martindale, who noted that liturgical treasures generally derived from gifts of gold from the laity ("French Aristocracy," p. 26). Miniature architectural objects of both a sacred and a secular nature may have been more common than is usually supposed. Einhard appears to have been involved in the creation of other such precious constructions in addition to the arch, and a wax model of some sort was said to have been employed in the renovation of Saint-Germain in Auxerre (Bullough, "'Imagines Regum,'" p. 249, n. 117, and René Louis, *Les Eglises d'Auxerre des origines au XI$^e$ siècle* [Paris, 1952], p. 38).

The significance of the so-called minor arts, not merely as sources of inspiration for works on a monumental scale or as reflections of them, was stressed by Hanns Swarzenski in his brief but important introductory essay to *Monuments of Romanesque Art* (Chicago, 1954), pp. 11–36. He commented on the allusive meaning, particularly in young cultures, of precious materials and remarked on the role of such objects as unifying symbols of both spiritual and secular life (pp. 13–14).

34. Deschamps, "Etude sur la naissance de la sculpture en France à l'époque romane," *Bulletin monumental* 84 (1925): 5–98; see also Pierre Héliot, "Observations," pp. 441–42.

35. Charles Daras, "L'Evolution de l'architecture aux façades des églises romanes ornées d'arcatures en Charente: leur origine, leur filiation," *Bulletin*

NOTES TO PAGES 27–28

*monumental* 119 (1961): 121–38, esp. 123, 136, and "La Cathédrale d'Angoulême," *Bulletins et mémoires de la Société archéologique et historique de la Charente,* 1941, p. 127. The church at Cellefrouin appears to be earlier in date than Angoulême and has been suggested recently to be the original example of the arcaded design (Daras, "Les Eglises au onzième siècle," pp. 190–91). Jean Hubert has reasserted the connection between altar table and reliquary motifs and façades in western France; see the brief remarks in "Introïbo ad Altare," p. 17. A somewhat different but not unrelated approach to the question of relationships between metalwork and stonemasonry is pursued in a stimulating paper by Thomas Lyman, "Arts somptuaires et art monumental: Bilan des influences auliques pré-romanes sur la sculpture romane dans le sud-ouest de la France et en Espagne," *Les Cahiers de Saint-Michel de Cuxa* 9 (1978): 115–27. His observations on the availability of materials and the technical ability of craftsmen offer new insights into the artistic creativity of the period. A discussion of the migration of sanctuary imagery to the portal area in the Byzantine world can be found in M. E. Frazer, "Church Doors and the Gates of Paradise: Byzantine Bronze Doors in Italy," *Dumbarton Oaks Papers* 27 (1973): 145–62.

36. The basic discussion of the object is by Jean Hubert, "L'Escrain dit de Charlemagne," *Cahiers archéologiques* 4 (1949): 71–77, where the author commented on possible architectural relationships, for example, with the façade of Milan Cathedral, but noted that they all postdate the reliquary. More recently, the shrine has been studied by Peter Lasko, *Ars Sacra, 800–1200* (Harmondsworth, 1972), pp. 24–26, and "The *Escrain de Charlemagne,*" *Beiträge zur Kunst des Mittelalters* (Berlin, 1975), pp. 127–34, on its restorations. Elbern, in the catalog for the Charlemagne exhibition, remarked on the *escrain's* "ideal architecture," as an immediate representation of celestial Jerusalem; he suggested the probable influence of Byzantium on its composition ("L'Orfèvrerie," *Charlemagne: Oeuvre, rayonnement et survivances,* pp. 359–60).

37. Hubert commented on similarities between the *escrain* and the altar frontal and suggested that both were gifts of Charles the Bald early in the 860s ("L'Escrain," pp. 76–77); the surviving jewel from the *escrain* is here attributed to Diocletian. For both objects, see also Percy E. Schramm and Florentine Mütherich, *Denkmale der deutschen Könige und Kaiser* (Munich, 1962), pp. 132–33, nos. 47–48. All three pieces of metalwork are discussed, with earlier bibliography, in Victor Elbern, "Liturgisches Gerät in edlen Materialien zur Zeit Karls des Grossen," *Karl der Grosse* 3:115–67. For descriptions and the earliest documentation of the *escrain* and the altar frontal, see Blaise de Montesquiou-Fézensac, *Le Trésor de Saint-Denis,* 3 vols. (Paris, 1973–77) 1:89–110, 207–12, and 2:20–29, 292–303; for the jewels, see the article by B. de Montesquiou-Fézensac and Danielle Gaborit-Chopin, "Camées et intailles du Trésor de Saint-Denis," *Cahiers archéologiques* 24 (1975): 137–62. There are additional comments on the drawing of the *escrain* by Danielle Gaborit-Chopin, "Les arts précieux au IX<sup>e</sup> siècle," *Dossiers de l'archéologie* 30 (1978): 61–63.

38. On the emergence of containers for relics from the mid-ninth century on, including the *escrain,* see the article by Edmond Barbier, "Les Images, les reliques et la face supérieure de l'autel avant le XI<sup>e</sup> siècle," *Synthronon,* Bibliothèque des Cahiers Archéologiques 2 (Paris, 1968), pp. 199–207.

39. The availability of ancient texts in Charlemagne's court library is remarked upon by Bullough ("Roman Books," p. 42). The ancient funerary custom and Herodian's description of the ceremony for Septimius Severus are recounted by J. M. C. Toynbee in *Death and Burial in the Roman World* (London, 1971), pp. 60–61. A description of the funeral ceremony prepared by Septimius Severus for Pertinax, in which a three-tiered pyre in the form of a tower is

vividly described, is found in J. J. Pollitt, *The Art of Rome*, Sources and Documents in the History of Art Series (Englewood Cliffs, N. J., 1966), pp. 192–93, from Dio Cassius LXXIV, 4.

40. Coins with pyres are illustrated in Harold Mattingly, *Coins of the Roman Empire in the British Museum* (London, 1940), p. 4, pl. 54, and p. 393, pl. 71:8, and p. 525, pl. 101:10–11. For additional illustrations, see Anne S. Robertson, *Roman Imperial Coins in the Hunter Coin Cabinet* 3 (Oxford, 1977): 39, nos. 4 and 5, and pl. 13 with illustrations of Severus deified, and idem, 4 (Oxford, 1978): 32, no. 6 and pl. 9, a depiction of Valerian II standing frontally in a *biga* above his funeral pyre. The pyres are handily illustrated on a single plate in Bernhart, *Handbuch*, pl. 55. A. Frazer's article, "A Numismatic Source for Michelangelo's First Design for the Tomb of Julius II," *Art Bulletin* 57 (1975): 53–57, discussed medieval familiarity with quasi-related, surviving structures. The quote is from page 57 of his paper.

41. For the Prüm Gospels, with depictions of ancient coins in the illuminations, see George Henderson, *Early Medieval*, Style and Civilisation (Harmondsworth, 1972), pp. 107, 110–11, fig. 64. On Charlemagne's coins, see Jean Lafaurie, "Les monnaies impériales de Charlemagne," *Académie des Inscriptions et belles-lettres: Comptes-rendus*, January–March 1978, p. 166, pl. 14; for the seals, see Erich Kittel, *Siegel*, Bibliothek für Kunst und Antiquitätenfreunde 11 (Braunschweig, 1970), pp. 207–9, fig. 125; Wilhelm Ewald, *Siegekunde: Handbuch der mittelalterlichen und neueren Geschichte*, ed. G. von Below and F. Meinecke, pt. 4, Hilfswissenschaften und Altertümer (Munich, 1914), pp. 183–84, pl. 16; *Charlemagne: Oeuvre, rayonnement et Survivances*, pp. 183–84 and remarks in Friedrich Heer, *Charlemagne and His World* (New York, 1975), p. 34. The discovery a decade ago of a cache of more than 4000 Roman coins dating from the middle of the second century after Christ dramatically establishes the presence and availability of such material in Gaul. For a description of the underwater find in the hull of a boat shipwrecked in the summer of A.D. 161 and illustrations of the coins, see the report by Robert Etienne and Marguerite Rachet, "Les Monnaies romaines de Garonne," *Archéologia* 48 (1972): 20–27. Retreating German armies unearthed a terra cotta vase filled with more than 1000 Roman coins in 1944, at a site near Airvault. Details of that discovery have recently been clarified by Jean Hiernard, "Du Nouveau sur le trésor de monnaies romaines Soulièvre (Deux-Sèvres)," *Bulletin de la Société des antiquaires de l'Ouest*, 4th ser., 13 (1975): 255–79.

The *escrain*'s jewels have been discussed by John Beckwith, "Some Early Byzantine Rock Crystals," *Studies in Memory of David Talbot Rice*, ed. Giles Robertson and George Henderson (Edinburgh, 1975), pp. 1–5. Jean Adhémar suggested that ancient cameos may have served as sources of inspiration for a twelfth-century sculpture in "La Fontaine de Saint-Denis," *Revue Archéologique*, 6 ser., 7 (1936): 224–32.

42. On base and canopy tombs, see Toynbee, *Death and Burial*, pp. 125–29, and on tower tombs, pp. 164–65. Richard Brilliant's chapter on triumphal monuments and ostentatious display (*Roman Art* [New York, 1974]) offers useful remarks on the important category of monuments discussed here and below (trophies). He includes a brief mention of funeral pyres on p. 87. For La Turbie, see Jules Formigé, *Le Trophée des Alpes (La Turbie)*, Gallia, supplement 2 (1949) and, on the monument at Saint-Rémy, H. Rolland, *Le Mausolée de Glanum*, Gallia, supplement 21 (1969), esp. pp. 71–78. The circular *tropaeum* at Adamklissi, together with its adjacent circular mausoleum, provide another example of the association of death and victory in Roman military art. For these

structures, which lie just beyond Bucharest, see the study by I. A. Richmond, "Adamklissi," *Papers of the British School at Rome* 35, n.s. 22 (1967): 29–39.

43. André Grabar, *Martyrium: Recherches sur le culte des reliques et l'art chrétien antique*, 2 vols. ([Paris], 1946), pp. 416–18. See also the article by Richard Krautheimer on early Christian burial practices, "Mensa-Coemeterium-Martyrium," reprinted in his *Studies in Early Christian, Medieval and Renaissance Art*, pp. 35–58. A monolithic sculpture in Narbonne, possibly commemorating the Holy Sepulcher, is described by May Vieillard-Troiekouroff, *Les Monuments religieux de la Gaule d'après les oeuvres de Grégoire de Tours* (Paris, 1976), p. 187. An early article on related structures is by Philippe Lauzun, "Inventaire général des piles gallo-romaines du sud-ouest de la France," *Bulletin monumental* 63 (1898): 5–68.

44. For illustration of the Milan and Munich ivories, see Ernst Kitzinger, *Byzantine Art in the Making* (Cambridge, Mass., 1977), pls. 76 and 77; a Carolingian ivory from Liverpool with a related tomb representation is illustrated in pl. 78. A wooden bread mold in the Cleveland Museum of Art, dated before A.D. 1000 and thought to have been used in the preparation of bread offerings if not of Eucharistic wafers themselves, is decorated with a detailed architectural rendering of the structures of the Holy Sepulcher in Jerusalem. See George Galavaris, *Bread and the Liturgy: The Symbolism of Early Christian and Byzantine Bread Stamps* (Madison, 1970), pp. 153–61 and fig. 82.

45. Ivories of this type were studied by Stanley Ferber, who emphasized the particularly triumphant nature of the representations ("Crucifixion Iconography in a Group of Carolingian Ivory Plaques," *Art Bulletin* 48 [1966]: 323–33). Ferber commented that the type of sepulcher depicted was related to early medieval tower reliquaries and suggested a visual exegetical tradition for the reappearance of this form. Such a multistoried tomb is used in the Drogo Sacramentary to represent Christ's sepulcher in the scene of the three Marys' visit on Easter morning. Illustrated in Mütherich and Gaehde, *Carolingian Painting*, pl. 29. See also a similar shrine on a rock crystal discussed by Beckwith in "Some Early Byzantine Rock Crystals," *Studies in Memory of David Talbot Rice*, p. 3 and fig. 2a.

46. Philippe Verdier, "Deux plaques d'ivoire de la résurrection avec la représentation d'un Westwork," *Zeitschrift für schweizerische Archäologie und Kunstgeschichte* 22 (1962): 3–9, and Carol Heitz, *Recherches sur les rapports entre architecture et liturgie à l'époque carolingienne* (Paris, 1963), pp. 124–25. Hubert had earlier noted that the *escrain* recalled ciboria in the shape of a tower that were used to shelter tombs and relics ("L'Escrain," pp. 74–75). See remarks on the development of canopies in the early church from an essentially funerary context to associations with the altar; Molly Teasdale Smith, "The 'Ciborium' in Christian Architecture at Rome, 300–600 A.D.," *Marsyas* 14 (1968–69): 84, and the venerable study by Yrjo Hirn, *The Sacred Shrine* (Boston, 1957), pp. 13–30. Alfred Frazer has recently remarked on the similarity between temporary pyre structures (associated in my discussion with the Carolingian *escrain*) and permanent tower mausolea; he questioned whether the one might have influenced the design of the other ("The Pyre of Faustina Senior," *Studies in Classical Art and Archaeology: A Tribute to Peter Heinrich von Blanckenhagen*, ed. G. Kopcke and M. B. Moore [Locust Valley, N.Y., 1979], pp. 271–74). The suggestion was made earlier as well by Rolland, *Le Mausolée de Glanum*, p. 78.

47. The reliquary is discussed in Lasko, *Ars Sacra*, pp. 56–57, where it is called a miniature of a Roman funerary monument, and by M. Gauthier in Georges Gaillard, et al., *Rouergue roman* (La-Pierre-qui-Vire, 1963), pp. 141–42.

It is dated to the eleventh century in the exhibition catalog *Les Trésors des églises de France*, Musée des arts decoratifs, 2d ed. (Paris, 1965), pp. 301–4, no. 540, and pl. 40. There are relevant remarks on such objects by André Grabar in "Quelques reliquaires de St. Demetrios et le martyrium du Saint à Salonique," *Dumbarton Oaks Papers* 5 (1950): 22, and, more recently, on a group of ritual boxes of architectural form that were used as lanterns, in "Observations sur l'arc de triomphe de la Croix," pp. 76–83. See also the remarks on such objects in the article by Peter Cornelius Classen, "Das Reliquiar von Moutier-en-Der," *Pantheon* 36 (1978): 308–19, esp. p. 317.

48. The basic, though not the earliest, studies of these structures are by René Crozet, "Les Lanternes des morts," *Bulletin de la Société des antiquaires de l'Ouest*, 3d ser., 13 (1943): 115–44, and L. Fayolle, "Origine et destination des lanternes des morts," ibid., pp. 144–155. Earlier literature is cited there.

49. René Crozet, "De l'art romain à l'art roman," in *Actes du XVII^me Congrès international d'histoire de l'art*, Amsterdam, 1952 (The Hague, 1955), pp. 107–12, esp. pp. 110–12, and George H. Forsyth, Jr., "St. Martin's at Angers and the Evolution of Early Medieval Church Towers," *Art Bulletin* 32 (1950): 308–18; the quote is from p. 318. Several of the monuments Forsyth cites, such as the monument of the Julii at Saint-Rémy and ivories of the fifth and ninth centuries, have been used in my argument as well; see his figs. 4, 5, and 7. The suggestion that ancient funerary monuments may have influenced the design of medieval lanterns is not infrequently found in the literature; see, for example, R. F. Jessup, "Barrows and Walled Cemeteries in Roman Britain," *Journal of the British Archaeological Association* 22 (1959): 1–32, esp. p. 16. Krautheimer mentioned that copies of the Holy Sepulcher were sometimes located in cemeteries. He also emphasized that precise imitation of the model was *not* a primary concern; rather the "copy" was intended as a "memento of a venerated site" and a "symbol of promised salvation." Until the thirteenth century, Krautheimer noted, transmission of the content and significance of the imitated building mattered more than a precise rendering of its visible aspects ("Introduction to an 'Iconography of Medieval Architecture,'" esp. pp. 17 and 20).

50. "Obtinet autem medium coemeterii locum, structure quaedam lapidea, habens in summitate sui quantitatem unius lampadis capacem, quae ob reverentiam fidelium ibi quiescentium totis noctibus fulgore suo locum illum sacratum illustrat" (*De miraculis*, Bk. 2, ch. 27; *Patrologiae cursus completus*, Series Latina, 189:942). The passage has frequently been cited although this interpretation, to my knowledge, has not been made. Daras referred to the text in *Angoumois roman*, p. 55; earlier it was quoted by E. Bequet, "La Lanterne des morts et la cella de Cellefrouin," *Bulletin et mémoires de la Société archéologique et historique de la Charente* 22 (1932): 88, n. 1, and by Crozet, "Les Lanternes," pp. 119–20, where he comments on the collective rather than personal aspect of the monument.

51. Crozet, "Les Lanternes," p. 129; similar forms occur in the region as supports for a cross and are easily confused with the lanterns. See the list and discussion in Crozet, *L'Art roman en Poitou*, pp. 266–67, and *L'Art roman en Saintonge*, p. 115. Crozet observed that eleven of the buildings that had lanterns were Benedictine while nine related to Augustinian structures. It would appear that no particular association with a single order can be made.

52. See the study by H. Schaeffer, "The Origin of the Two-Tower Façade in Romanesque Architecture," *Art Bulletin* 27 (1945): 85–108, esp. pp. 97–98, where a relationship between Civray and Echillais in western France (which lack tower elements) and ancient city gates is considered, and the similarity of funerary lanterns to the façade turrets at Poitiers and at Saint-Jouin is noted. The article

by Hamann McLean, "Les Origines du portails," *Cahiers de civilisation médiévale* 2 (1959): 157–75, also explored the development of the tower façade.

53. From the vast literature on westworks, see Etienne Fels and Hans Reinhardt, "Etude sur les églises-porches carolingiennes et leur survivances dans l'art roman," *Bulletin monumental* 92 (1933): 331–65, and 96 (1937): 425–69; Wolfgang Lotz, "Zum Problem das karolingische Westwerks," *Kunstchronik* 5 (1952): 65–71, a review of the study by Alois Fuchs; and Heitz (*Recherches*), who deals at length with this type of structure. Crozet's observations are in *L'Art roman en Poitou*, pp. 40, 47, 59, and there are earlier comments on western "accretions" to churches in A. Grabar, *Martyrium*, 2:533, 580. Hans Reinhardt returned to the subject in "L'Eglise carolingienne de Saint-Riquier," *Mélanges offerts à René Crozet*, 1:90, and Daras studied it in "Les Eglises au onzième siècle," pp. 184–85. On Lesterps, see the early study by Valentin de Courcel, "L'Eglise de Lesterps," *Congrès archéologique* 79, no. 2 (1912): 231–69.

54. The introductory "complementary" studies on imperial and liturgical symbolism might be Baldwin Smith's *Architectural Symbolism*, chap. 3, and Heitz, *Recherches*, esp. pp. 160ff. The latter must be used with caution as pointed out most recently by David Parsons, "The Pre-Romanesque Church of St.-Riquier: The Documentary Evidence," *Journal of the British Archaeological Association* 30 (1977): 21–51. Krautheimer's remarks are found in his paper on the Carolingian revival in *Studies in Early Christian, Medieval and Renaissance Art*, pp. 228–29, and Pierre Francastel's in "A Propos des églises-porches: Du carolingien au roman," *Mélanges d'histoire du moyen-âge: Dédiés à la mémoire de Louis Halphen* (Paris, 1951), pp. 247–57, esp. 255–56.

Fritz Saxl, in his study of the Lincoln façade, discussed both its descent from Carolingian westworks and its relation to Roman triumphal arches. But he rejected the latter possibility in particular arguing that it was "unlikely" that familiarity with a far-off arch could lead to the invention of the Lincoln façade with its monumental, recessed arches ("Lincoln Cathedral: The Eleventh Century Design for the West Front," *Archaeological Journal* 103 [1946]: 105–17, esp. 109–11).

55. Crusader chronicles, in discussing the disposal of Saracen corpses, note that "funeral pyres were formed of them like pyramids," and these are described as being as large as houses (James A. Brundage, *The Crusades: A Documentary Survey* [Milwaukee, 1962], p. 65).

56. For a discussion of the availability of portable riches in medieval society, see n. 33, above, and chap. 3, n. 80, below, particularly the studies by Lesne, Riché and Martindale.

57. Panofsky, *Renaissance and Renascences*, p. 57.

58. Krautheimer, once again, rightly cautioned that the twelfth-century revival might depend less on early Christian prototypes than on the Carolingian imitation of early Christian architecture ("The Carolingian Revival," p. 227). From the historian's point of view, the Carolingian revival has been characterized as a reform rather than a renaissance, in other words, an attempt to revive the vigor and promise of Christian Rome and not the spirit of antiquity. See the remarks of Karl F. Morrison, "The Church, Reform and Renaissance in the Early Middle Ages," *Life and Thought in the Early Middle Ages*, ed. Robert S. Hoyt (Minneapolis, 1967), pp. 143–69, esp. p. 158. Likewise, Walter Ullmann remarked that Charlemagne was primarily concerned with the religious regeneration of the Franks and that the classical renascence was a by-product of this (*The Carolingian Renaissance and the Idea of Kingship* [London, 1969], p. 5). Warren Sanderson made relevant observations on the fusion of the imperial and the ecclesiastic in the Aachen *aula regia* ("The Sources and Significance of the

Ottonian Church of St. Pantaleon at Cologne," *Journal of the Society of Architectural Historians* 29 [1970]: 83–96, esp. p. 95). A Carolingian "revival" may explain the reutilization of Carolingian sculptures in southern France (G. Buis, "Recherches sur les sculptures carolingiennes à entrelacs dans le sud-est de la France," *Ecole antique de Nîmes*, n.s., 8–9 [1973–74]: 11–26).

59. Otto Pächt made interesting remarks about the origins of the phrase, "out-Herod Herod," which inspired me here (*The Rise of Pictorial Narrative in Twelfth-Century England* [Oxford, 1962], p. 53). In regard to the cultural significance of the late eleventh-century revival of antiquity, see the articles by Ernst Kitzinger, "The Gregorian Reform and the Visual Arts: A Problem of Method," *Transactions of the Royal Historical Society*, 5th ser., 22 (1972): 87–102, and "The First Mosaic Decoration of Salerno Cathedral," *Jahrbuch der österreichischen Byzantinistik* 21 (1972): 149–62; I am obviously indebted to Professor Kitzinger's critical remarks concerning the shortsighted concepts of a "sovereign artist and mindless patron," as expressed particularly in these two papers.

The concept of the transfer of power from one civilization to another and from past to present has been explored in literature. See, in particular, Ernst Robert Curtius, *European Literature and the Latin Middle Ages*, trans. Willard R. Trask (New York, 1953), esp. pp. 28–29, for his discussion of such a *topos*. More recently, the idea has been explored by Douglas Kelley, "*Translatio Studii*: Translation, Adaptation and Allegory in Medieval French Literature," *Philological Quarterly* 57 (1978): 287–91.

The Aquitainian Romanesque use of monumental architectural decoration comes very close to the antique concept of the function of triumphant sculpture, as summarized in Jonathan B. Riess, "The Civic View of Sculpture in Alberti's *De re aedificatoria*," *Renaissance Quarterly* 32 (1979): 1–17. Trophies could be understood both "offensively" and "defensively" in Roman times—as a manifestation of the prowess of the victor and also as a sign of the humiliation of the vanquished. For a study of the transformation of the concept of triumph from a purification ritual to an honorific ceremony, see Larissa Bonfante Warren, "Roman Triumphs and Etruscan Kings: The Changing Face of the Triumph," *Journal of Roman Studies* 60 (1970): 49–66. The concept of the trophy in Romanesque art is discussed further in the next chapter.

### Chapter Three

1. The seminal formulation of these ideas concerning ritual appears in Mircea Eliade, *The Sacred and the Profane* (New York, 1959). Related concepts are employed by T. B. Stroup, "Ritual and Ceremony in Drama," *Comparative Drama* 11 (1977): 139–46, with older, relevant literature. There are interesting remarks on liturgy as communication rather than as law in Janet Nelson, "Ritual and Reality in the Early Medieval Ordines," in *The Materials, Sources and Methods of Ecclesiastical History*, ed. Derek Baker, Studies in Church History 11 (Cambridge, 1974), pp. 41–51. Repetition as an essential structural order in literary work is discussed by Stephen G. Nichols, Jr., "The Rhetoric of Recapitulation in the Chanson de Guillaume," *Studies in Honor of Tatiana Fotitch*, ed. J. M. Sola-Solé, A. S. Crisafulli, and S. A. Schulz (Washington, D. C. [1975]), pp. 79–92.

2. For Mendell's discussion, see *Romanesque Sculpture in Saintonge*, pp. 61–62, 68, 85, and 87; Crozet's treatment of the material appears especially in *L'Art roman en Poitou*, pp. 191, 197 and *L'Art roman en Saintonge*, pp. 139, 144ff., and 171. Mâle's interpretation of the theme is in *Religious Art in France, the Twelfth Century*, pp. 406, 413 and 442. All seem to go back to Charles Dangibeaud, "L'Ecole de sculpture romane saintongeaise," *Bulletin archéologique du Comité des travaux historiques et scientifiques*, 1910, pp. 22–62, with his very helpful

*répertoire* of themes (pp. 50ff.), which the reader seeking detailed enumerations is advised to consult.

3. Mendell, *Romanesque Sculpture in Saintonge,* pp. 83–84; Crozet, *L'Art roman en Poitou,* p. 211 and *L'Art roman en Saintonge,* pp. 167–68; Chan. Tonnellier, "L'Art roman en Saintonge," *Bulletin du Centre international d'études romanes,* 1964, pp. 18–37.

4. Dubourg-Noves, for example, remarked in the case of the screen façade of Petit-Palais that the "decorative gains only what the spiritual loses" (*Guyenne romane,* p. 298). See, as well, his review of Françoise Leriche-Andrieu, *Itinéraires romans en Saintonge* (La-Pierre-qui-Vire, 1976), in which he applauded the author's impatience with "pseudo-esoteric exaggerations" that try to explain everything, that is, to find a meaning for all forms (*Cahiers de civilisation médiévale* 21 [1978]: 300–303).

5. Fletcher Collins, Jr., *The Production of Medieval Church Music-Drama* (Charlottesville, Va., 1972), pp. 57–84 on the *visitatio sepulchri;* more recently, Blandine-Dominique Berger, *Le Drame liturgique de Pâques: Liturgie et Théâtre* (Paris, 1976). Also, A. Grabar, *Christian Iconography,* pp. 123–25. The Chadenac capital is briefly discussed by François-Georges Pariset, "Les Eglises de Chadenac et de Pérignac," *CA* 114 (1956): 248.

6. Mendell, *Romanesque Sculpture in Saintonge,* pp. 69, 79–81, and Crozet, *L'Art roman en Saintonge,* p. 140 and pl. 61, *B* and *C* for illustrations of the capitals at Saintes and Saujon.

7. On Michael and the cult of the dead, see Heitz, *Recherches,* and the extensive remarks by J. J. G. Alexander, *Norman Illustration at Mont St. Michel, 966–1100* (Oxford, 1970), pp. 85–100, especially the suggestion that the theme of Michael and the dragon does not go back beyond the Carolingian period. There is a vast literature on martyrs based on Hippolyte Delehaye, *Sanctus,* Subsidia Hagiographica 17 (Brussels, 1928) and *Les Origines du culte des martyres,* Subsidia Hagiographica 20 (Brussels, 1933). For more local material, see E. Delaruelle, "Les Saints militaires de la région de Toulouse," *Cahiers de Fanjeux* 4 (1969): 173–83. The Chadenac façade carvings are identified and discussed in *CA* 114 (1956): 246–56. For additional churches on which Saint Michael and Saint George appear, see Crozet, *L'Art roman en Saintonge,* p. 152, and *L'Art roman en Poitou,* p. 204; Mendell, *Romanesque Sculpture in Saintonge,* pp. 73 and 82.

8. This is Schapiro's characterization of the Daniel story in "The Sculptures of Souillac," *Romanesque Art,* p. 121. For representations of Daniel on capitals at Saint-Eutrope at Saintes, Saujon, Rouffignac, and Marestay, among other churches, see Crozet, *L'Art roman en Saintonge,* pp. 134–35.

9. For the appearance of the angels in Aquitaine, see Mendell, *Romanesque Sculpture in Saintonge,* pp. 70–71 and 74; Crozet, *L'Art roman en Saintonge,* pp. 144 and 171, and *L'Art roman en Poitou,* p. 197. On the relation of the Christian angel to the Roman Victory, see the categorizations of K. Fel, "Die Niken und die Engel in der altchristlichen Kunst," *Römische Quartalschrift für christliche Altertumskunde und für Kirchengeschichte* 26 (1912): 3–25, and the studies by Alfons C. M. Beck, *Genien und Niken als Engel in der altchristlichen Kunst* (Düsseldorf, 1936); Alfred R. Bellinger and Marjorie Alkins Berlincourt, *Victory as a Coin Type,* Numismatic Notes and Monographs 149 (New York, 1962), pp. 44–64; Gunnar Berefelt, *A Study of the Winged Angel: The Origin of the Motif* (Stockholm, 1968); and Robert Grigg, "Symphōnian Aeidō tēs Basileias: An Image of Imperial Harmony on the Base of the Column of Arcadius," *AB* 59 (1977): 469–82 with additional references. On the Barberini panel most recently, see Ernst Kitzinger, *Byzantine Art in the Making* (Cambridge, Mass., 1977), p. 96,

and, on an issue not immediately relevant, Jean Vezin, "Une Nouvelle lecture de la liste de noms copiés au dos de l'ivoire Barberini," *BA*, n.s., 7 (1971): 19–53. In the preparation of this study I was unable to consult the relatively recent work by A. Stapert, *L'Ange roman dans la pensée et dans l'art* (Paris, 1975).

10. Deschamps, "Etude sur la naissance." The study by Friedrich Gerke is *Der Tischaltar des Bernard Gilduin in St-Sernin in Toulouse*, Akademie der Wissenschaften und der Literatur in Mainz (Wiesbaden, 1958).

11. Most recently see Charles Daras's entry on Angoulême in *Dictionnaire des Eglises de France* 3 (Tours, 1967): C 10.

12. See the plates in Bernhart, *Handbuch*, vol. 2, pl. 12, no. 9 and 84, no. 12 and the illustration and brief discussion of the type in Bellinger and Berlincourt, *Victory as a Coin Type*, pl. 12, no. 2 and p. 60. See also Gisela M. A. Richter, *Catalogue of Engraved Gems: Greek, Etruscan, Roman* (Rome, 1956), pl. 46, nos. 357, 358; pl. 64, nos. 559, 560.

13. André Grabar, *Ampoules de Terre Sainte* (Paris, 1958), pp. 55–58, esp. pl. 33. The objects were singled out by Yves Christe as supporting evidence for an early date for the cross and bust motif in the apse of Saint John in Lateran in Rome ("A Propos du décor absidial de Saint-Jean du Latran à Rome," *Cahiers archéologiques* 20 (1970): 197–206). Kurt Weitzmann referred to several of the ampullae in his paper "*Loca Sancta* and the Representational Arts in Palestine," *Dumbarton Oaks Papers* 28 (1974): 31–55, and Peter Lasko related them to a jewelled reliquary of Carolingian workmanship in Reims (*Ars Sacra*, p. 22 and pl. 21).

14. Storch, "Trophy and Cross," pp. 111–18.

15. The Roman cuirass is illustrated in Christe's article, "A Propos du décor absidial," p. 203, fig. 4. For the Monza ampulla (no. 3), with sprouts growing from the roof of the tomb, see Grabar, *Ampoules*, pl. 9 and pp. 20–21. An important relevant study is A. Frolow, *Les Reliquaires de la Vraie Croix* (Paris, 1965).

16. On the living tree, see most recently the comments of Gerhart B. Ladner, "Medieval and Modern Understanding of Symbolism: A Comparison," *Speculum* 54 (1979): 223–56, esp. pp. 236–38, and the important article by Penelope C. Mayo, "The Crusaders under the Palm: Allegorical Plants and Cosmic Kingship in the *Liber Floridus*," *Dumbarton Oaks Papers* 27 (1973): 29–67. On contemporary decoration in Italy and the motivation behind its Roman revival, see the paper by Hélène Toubert, "Aspects du renouveau paléochrétien à Rome au début du XII<sup>e</sup> siècle," *Cahiers archèologiques* 20 (1970): 99–154.

17. *L'Art roman en Saintonge*, p. 171.

18. Tampering with the Civray portal in the nineteenth century does not seem to have interfered with a basic reading of subject matter. See the remarks in R. Oursel, *Haut-Poitou roman*, pp. 332–33. On the concept and image of death in the *Song of Roland*, see Gérard Brault, "Le thème de la Mort dans la Chanson de Roland," *Studia Romanica* 14 (1969): 220–36, and A.-J. Dickman, *Le Rôle du surnaturel dans les Chansons de Geste* (Paris, 1926; reprinted Geneva, 1974), who stresses the recurrent appearance of angels or saints as messengers of God. "Iconographic documentation" of the Roland legend, that is to say the illustration of specific events, has been selectively collected by Rita Lejeune and Jacques Stiennon, *La Légende de Roland dans l'art du moyen âge* (Brussels, 1966).

19. R. Levine, "Ingeld and Christ: A Medieval Problem," *Viator* 2 (1971): 105–28, esp. p. 110.

20. Penn R. Szittya, "The Angels and the Theme of *Fortitudo* in the *Chanson de Roland*," *Neuphilologische Mitteilungen* 72 (1971): 193–223, esp. pp. 198–99.

21. On the program at Saint-Jouin, see the study by E. Maillard, "La Façade de l'église romane de Saint-Jouin-de-Marnes en Poitou," *Gazette des beaux-arts*, 5th ser., 9, pt. 1 (1924): 137–50.

22. See Mendell, *Romanesque Sculpture in Saintonge*, pp. 62, 78, 80–81.

23. Cf. Chenu's remarks on the presentness of past history in *Nature, Man, and Society*, pp. 160–61. Rhythmic repetition is an effective device in contemporary literature. For the European examples, see the discussion in Erich Auerbach, *Mimesis*, pp. 103–5, and S. Gilman, "The Poetry of the 'Poema' and the Music of the 'Cantar,'" *Philological Quarterly* 51 (1972): 1–11. For parallel examples in Arabic literature, see James T. Monroe, "The Historical Arjūza of the Ibn 'Abd Rabbihi, a Tenth-century Hispano-Arabic Epic Poem," *Journal of the American Oriental Society* 91 (1971): 78. Themes related to those considered here—repetition, angels, martyrs—are considered by Mario Pei, *French Precursors of the Chanson de Roland* (New York, 1948), pp. 36, 44, 103–4.

24. For Crozet's observations see *L'Art roman en Saintonge*, pp. 139, 143–44, and 157; also Mendell, *Romanesque Sculpture in Saintonge*, pp. 63, 65, 67. The archivolt with the Last Supper at Saintes is enclosed by a molding on which nude figures are seen "climbing" a grape vine that follows, in its design, the contour of the arch. The extension of the Eucharistic idea is obvious here; the implication of the different arrangement is discussed below.

25. *Romanesque Sculpture in Saintonge*, p. 63.

26. *L'Art roman en Poitou*, p. 140, and *Congrès archéologique* 114 (1956): 115–16.

27. Some of the recent literature on martyrologies includes Sirarpie Der Nersessian, "The Illustrations of the Metaphrastian Menologium," *Late Classical and Medieval Studies in Honor of A. M. Friend, Jr.*, ed. K. Weitzmann (Princeton, 1955), pp. 222–31, and Ihor Ševčenko, "The Illuminators of the Menologium of Basil II," *Dumbarton Oaks Papers* 16 (1962): 243–76, as well as the important early paper by Hippolyte Delehaye, "Le Témoignage des martyrologes," *Analecta Bollandiana* 26 (1907): 78–99. The icons are discussed and illustrated by K. Weitzmann in "Byzantine Miniature and Icon Painting in the Eleventh Century," *Studies in Classical and Byzantine Manuscript Illumination* (Princeton, 1971), pp. 271–313, esp. fig. 301, the Sinai icon, with comments on the relation of icon to monumental work (p. 309), and in his earlier paper, "Icon Painting in the Crusader Kingdom," *Dumbarton Oaks Papers* 20 (1966): 49–84. For the discussion of door decoration, see the study by Margaret English Frazer, "Church Doors and the Gates of Paradise: Byzantine Bronze Doors in Italy," ibid. 27 (1973): 145–62. She likens the probably original arrangement of panels on the south portal door of San Marco, dated around 1080, to a litany of saints (p. 152 and fig. 10).

For the representation of the Massacre of the Innocents on the Chartres frieze, see the article by Adelheid Heimann, "The Capital Frieze and Pilasters of the Portail Royal, Chartres," *Journal of the Warburg and Courtauld Institutes* 31 (1968), pl. 33, fig. 20, and pp. 80 and 82. Heimann proposes that the extensive treatment given the scene here depends upon Byzantine prototypes.

28. D. H. Green, *The Millstätter Exodus; A Crusading Epic* (Cambridge, 1966), on this matter especially, pp. 307–25. A Sacramentary from Mont Saint Michel, now in the Morgan Library MS. 641, and dated in the second half of the eleventh century, presents, in the place of the customary illustration of the massacre, an illumination that emphasizes more broadly, according to Alexander, "the idea of martyrdom and its rewards" (*Norman Illumination*, pp. 135–36).

29. The original manuscript in Ghent has been studied in detail (*Liber Floridus*

*Colloquium,* ed. Albert Derolez [Ghent, 1973]). The manuscript in Wolfenbüttel, from which the illustration under discussion comes, is dated to the third quarter of the twelfth century by Swarzenski (ibid., p. 28, Bibl. ducale, cod. Gud. Lat. I.2°, f.10ʳ). The content of the manuscript has been considered by Mayo, "The Crusaders under the Palm." On the Romanesque façades and the spirituality of the Crusades, see chap. 4, below.

30. Mendell, *Romanesque Sculpture in Saintonge,* p. 63. James W. Earl, in his study "Typology and Iconographic Style in Early Medieval Hagiography," *Studies in the Literary Imagination* 7 (1975): 15–46, compared martyrologies to a town monument in which "an idealized figure represents an ethical ideal," a useful association between literary and visual manifestation.

In contrast to the representation of the *process* of martyrdom on the central door of the Abbaye-aux-Dames, elsewhere already martyred saints—the deed *done* rather than in the doing—form a heavenly choir and are depicted as inhabiting an elevated realm where they stand ready to welcome newcomers. In this context, their forms follow the contour of the arch, for example, around a window on the second story of the façade at Corme-Royal, in a type of arrangement that is discussed at length in the following pages.

31. Crozet, *L'Art roman en Saintonge,* p. 115.

32. The large, ornamented central door was evidently added at a later date. Discussion of this monument is regrettably brief. See ibid., p. 112.

33. See chap. 1, notes 25–28. The south transept portal of Saint-Sernin in Toulouse was discussed in terms of its retrospective triumphant and funerary imagery by Thomas W. Lyman, "The Sculpture Programme of the Porte des Comtes Master at Saint-Sernin in Toulouse," *Journal of the Warburg and Courtauld Institutes* 34 (1971): 12–39.

34. On this point see Barbara Rosenwein, "Feudal War."

35. The point was suggested by Sauer in an early study (*Symbolik der Kirchengebäudes und seiner Ausstattung in der Auffassung des Mittelalters*) and has been revived and explored by Yves Christe in "Les Représentations médiévales d'Apoc. IV–V en visions de second parousie: Origines, textes et contexte," *Cahiers archéologiques* 23 (1974): 61–72. There are some relevant remarks on the differences discussed here in *Congrès archéologique* 114 (1956): 253.

36. Crozet added that the theme may have been visible once at Saint-Jean in Parthenay (*L'Art roman en Saintonge,* pp. 156–77).

37. Dickinson, *Austin Canons,* p. 47. The prominence of the canons regular is noted in a letter of Hilaire d'Orléans, cited in Jean Leclercq, "Un formulaire écrit dans l'Ouest de la France au XIIᵉ siècle," *Mélanges offerts à René Crozet,* 2:765–76. See also the literature on the regular canons cited in chap. 1, n. 28.

In characterizing the nature of the Chadenac façade, François-Georges Pariset suggested a distinction similar to the one I have drawn here: "Bonne nouvelle de la Résurrection . . . et du triomphe chrétien, leçons morales, de sagesse et de vigilance, rien de commun avec les thèmes des abbayes savantes, les terribles visions des jugements apocalyptiques, mais une religion optimiste qui convient à un peuple villageois" ("Les Eglises de Chadenac et de Pérignac," *Congrès archéologique* 114 [1956]: 253).

38. On Tertullian, the convert to Christianity and his treatise on discipline, *De spectaculis,* written ca. 200, see *New Catholic Encyclopedia* 13 (1967): 1021. Heroic virtue and its relation to martyrdom in the thought of Origen and Cyprien is remarked upon in ibid. 14 (1967): 709.

39. Paul Deschamps, "Le Combat des vertus et des vices sur les portails romans de la Saintonge et de Poitou," *Congrès archéologique* 79, no. 2 (1912): 309–24. There is a brief discussion in Emile Mâle, *Religious Art in France in the*

*Thirteenth Century,* trans. D. Nussey (London, 1913), pp. 98–102, and *Religious Art in France, the Twelfth Century,* pp. 25–26 and 440–43. Mâle's remarks have become basic to subsequent literature. J. Sauer touched on the theme in *Symbolik des Kirchengebäudes,* pp. 234–35, as did Werner Weisbach, *Reforma Religiosa y Arte Medieval,* trans. H. Schlunk and L. Vazquez de Parga (Madrid, 1949), pp. 103–5. R. J. Adams, "The Virtues and Vices at Aulnay Re-examined," in Bernard Levy and Sandro Sticca, eds., *The Twelfth Century* (Binghamton, N.Y., 1975), pp. 53–73, revises some of the identifications. He follows Deschamps, who related certain representations to depictions of Saint Michael casting out Lucifer. In these cases, Adams identifies the subject as the War in Heaven.

40. See Mâle, *Religious Art in France in the Thirteenth Century,* p. 102. On the ritual aspects of battle form in the written *Psychomachia,* see Angus J. S. Fletcher, *Allegory: The Theory of a Symbolic Mode* (Ithaca, N.Y., 1964), pp. 157–61.

41. Oursel provides an extensive discussion of voussoirs in which he differentiates the earlier ornamental type from the more progressive type that points toward Gothic (*Haut-Poitou roman,* pp. 396–99); Aulnay, where the voussoirs around the south transept portal are arranged radially while the ones above, around the window, are carved circumferentially, is singled out as an example. Contrast this, however, with the west façade at Echillais where the archivolts on the second story are radially designed while those around the main door bear figures that follow the curve of the arch.

Radial and tangential voussoirs were also distinguished by Rupprecht, who emphasized the way in which the latter merge with the arch (*Romanische Skulptur,* p. 13). Wilhelm Messerer spoke of "figural architecture" in connection with the western door at Aulnay (*Romanische Plastik in Frankreich* [Cologne, 1964], pp. 83–88). Archivolts were said to be an "iconologically unprescribed space" in the recent book by Frans Carlsson, *The Iconology of Tectonics in Romanesque Art* (Hässleholm, 1976), pp. 65–67. He observed, however, the two different types of composition and the depiction not just of Christians but of abstract ideas as well. I am grateful to Leah Rutchick for bringing this book to my attention. Focillon's comments on the subject, always sensitive, are in *Art of the West: Romanesque,* pp. 107–8.

42. Adolf Katzenellenbogen, *The Allegory of the Virtues and the Vices in Medieval Art* (New York, 1964). A portion of what follows is based on this basic text. There are discussions of this theme also in Mendell, *Sculpture in Saintonge,* p. 87; Crozet, *L'Art roman en Poitou,* p. 198, and *L'Art roman en Saintonge,* pp. 146–47.

43. Prudentius's text is appealingly discussed in Helen Waddell's *The Wandering Scholars,* 3d ed. (Boston, 1927), pp. 17–22. I have used the Loeb Library edition of the poem in my work (*Prudentius,* ed. and trans. H. J. Thomson, 2 vols. [London, 1962]) and have been helped substantially by Macklin Smith's recent analysis, *Prudentius' 'Psychomachia': A Reexamination* (Princeton, 1976). The illustrated copies of the poem were examined by Richard Stettiner in a scarce study, *Die illustrierten Prudentiushandschriften* (Berlin, 1905), and then by Helen Woodruff, "The Illustrated Manuscripts of Prudentius," *Art Studies* 7 (1929): 33–79, and were touched on most recently by Danielle Gaborit-Chopin, "Les Dessins d'Adémar de Chabannes," *Bulletin archéologique,* n.s., 3 (1967): 163–225, esp. 168–78. For additional Carolingian background to this textual material, see R. Pierce, "The 'Frankish' Penitentials," in *The Materials, Sources and Methods of Ecclesiastical History,* ed. Derek Baker, Studies in Church History 11 (Cambridge, 1974), pp. 31–39.

44. The piece is discussed by Peter Lasko, *Ars Sacra*, pp. 29–30, pl. 27, and in considerable detail by Joseph Déer, "Ein Doppelbildnis Karls des Grosse," *Wandlungen Christlicher Kunst im Mittelalter*, Forschungen zur Kunstgeschichte und christlichen Archäologie 2 (Baden-Baden, 1953), pp. 103–37.

45. For a discussion of the Roman type, especially the Arcadius example, see, among others, Laura Breglia, *Roman Imperial Coins: Their Art and Their Technique*, trans. Peter Green (London, 1968), p. 230 and no. 99.

See the representations of Faith in Bern, Stadtbibliothek, MS. 264, Scene 10, and Munich, Stadtbibliothek, clm 29031b in Woodruff, "The Illustrated Manuscripts of Prudentius," figs. 27, 120. The theme was majestically dealt with by André Grabar in *L'Empéreur dans l'art byzantin*, esp. p. 195, and was commented upon briefly in relation to Prudentius by Philippe Verdier in *New Catholic Encyclopedia* 14 (1967): 710–11.

46. There are important remarks on this theme in Ernst H. Kantorowicz, "Gods in Uniform," *Selected Studies*, ed. Michael Cherniavsky and Ralph E. Giesey (Locust Valley, N.Y., 1965), pp. 7–24, esp. pp. 18–19. He noted that the infrequent medieval representations of Christ as a warrior serve mostly as illustrations of Psalm 90:13, where the trampling of the demons is described.

47. Déer's interpretation, "Ein Doppelbildnis."

48. André Grabar discussed the association with church portals of representations of archangels trampling on demonic figures in "Deux portails sculptés paléochrétiens d'Egypte et d'Asie Mineure, et les portails romans," *Cahiers archéologiques* 20 (1970): 15–28, esp. pp. 25–26. See also his remarks "A Propos des mosaiques de la coupole de St-George à Salonique," ibid. 17 (1967): 80, in which he explicitly linked western French portal schemes to earlier traditions.

49. McKitterick, *Frankish Reforms*, pp. 155–83. For further information on the *florilegia* or medieval anthologies, see the papers by B. L. Ullman, "Tibullus in the Mediaeval *Florilegia*," *Classical Philology* 23 (1928): 128–74, and "Classical Authors in Certain Mediaeval *Florilegia*," ibid., 27 (1932): 1–42.

50. For the antependium, see Tilmann Buddensieg, "Die Basler Altartafel Heinrichs II," *Wallraf-Richartz Jahrbuch* 19 (1957): 133–92. Lyman's observations on the decline in metalwork production during the second half of the eleventh century and the possible absorption of techniques and even metalworkers into the stonemasons' craft complement the iconographic ideas developed here ("Les arts sumptuaires").

51. The martyr's crown was a pervasive literary metaphor for salvation or the just life; see the quotation from Bernard of Clairvaux in John Sommerfeldt, "The Social Theory of Bernard of Clairvaux," in *Studies in Medieval Cistercian History*, Cistercian Studies 13 (Kalamazoo, Mich., 1971), p. 40: "Turn your eyes toward any state of life you please and you shall everywhere discover a multitude of heroes hastening with fortitude towards the martyr's crown." On the Aquitainian sculptures, see Mendell, *Romanesque Sculpture in Saintonge*, pp. 70–74, and Crozet, *L'Art roman en Poitou*, pp. 198–99; also Deschamps, "Le Combat."

52. Weisbach noted that the story of the wise and foolish virgins was, like that of the virtues and vices, an allusion to celestial recompense (*Reforma Religiosa*, p. 104). On the *sponsus* play, see Collins, *Medieval Church Music-Drama*, pp. 189–95; he cites Hugo of Saint Victor's emphasis that the play was a parable of mankind waiting for the last judgment (ibid., p. 190). An important, detailed study is that of Lucien-Paul Thomas, *Le "Sponsus": Mystère des Vierges sages et des Vierges folles* (Paris, 1951).

An ironic and erotic analogue of the story occurs in Andreas Capellanus' treatise on Love where the women who refuse love are associated with the north side of an edifice and a closed door (like the foolish Virgins) while those who discriminate, choosing lovers wisely, are placed at the south standing in the doorway. See the discussion by Betty Bowden, "The Art of Courtly Copulation," *Medievalia et Humanistica,* n.s., 9 (1979): 67–85.

53. Chenu, *Nature, Man, and Society,* pp. 99–145, esp. p. 136; Henri de Lubac, *Exégèse médiévale* (Paris, 1959–), 1, pt. 2, 645–58 for the four levels of scriptural exegesis and Erich Auerbach, "Figura," in *Scenes from the Drama of European Literature* (New York, 1959), pp. 11–76. The use of chiasmus, a rhetorical figure, as a metaphor in literature of the time is discussed by George S. Tate, "Chiasmus as Metaphor," *Neuphilologische Mitteilungen* 79 (1978): 114–25.

54. The doors in the representation of the wise and foolish virgins at Fenioux were referred to by Isa Ragusa, who considered them within the Last Judgment context proposed by Mâle. She pointed out the explicit depiction of a lion's head on the pull on the closed door in her study *"Terror demonum* and *terror inimicorum:* The Two Lions of the Throne of Solomon and the Open Door of Paradise," *Zeitschrift für Kunstgeschichte* 40 (1977): 108–9. For the interpretation of miniature architectural elements in sculpture as representations of the Holy City, see, for example, the discussion by Elbern of a mid-eleventh-century Eucharistic chalice at Silos, which is decorated with arcades. It can be compared in its treatment with the Lebuinus Chalice and to the composition of the Romanesque façades ("Der eucharistische Kelch," p. 45 and ill. p. 53). Marie-Madeleine Gauthier identified the arcaded architectural canopy on the mid-twelfth-century enameled funerary plaque in Le Mans as a "tomb on tomb" image of celestial abode ("Art, savoir-faire médiéval et le laboratoire moderne, à propos de l'effigie funéraire de Geoffroy Plantagenêt," *Académie des Inscriptions et Belles-Lettres,* January–March 1979, p. 122).

55. Woodruff, "The Illustrated Manuscripts of Prudentius," fig. 47, from Leyden, Universitatsbibliothek, Cod. Burm Q3, scene 89. Bernard McGinn refers to such metaphors of Jerusalem in *"Iter Sancti Sepulchri:* The Piety of the First Crusaders," *Essays on Medieval Civilization,* Walter Prescott Webb Memorial Lectures, ed. Bede Lackner and K. Philp (Austin, Texas, 1978), pp. 40–42. For Carolingian representations of the heavenly city, see M. T. Gousset, "La représentation de la Jérusalem céleste à l'époque carolingienne," *Cahiers archéologiques* 23 (1974): 47–60.

56. Chenu, *Nature, Man, and Society,* p. 113. For other metaphors of the temple, see I. Glier, in *Claustrum Animae: Untersuchungen zur Geschichte der Metaphor vom Herzen als Kloster* 1 (Munich, 1973): 126–28. Walter Cahn has made important observations on the representation of architecture in the twelfth century in "Architectural Draftsmanship in Twelfth Century Paris," *Gesta* 15 (1976): 247–54. In the Paris Prudentius manuscript, BN lat. 15158, the virtues are shown arriving on horseback at a city that is depicted as a crenelated wall with a central arch, the doors of which are flung open and framed by two conically roofed turrets. The resemblance of this gateway to those presented by the Aquitainian façades is obvious. See Woodruff, "The Illustrated Manuscripts of Prudentius," fig. 123. An analogous association between specific and ideal structures has been suggested in the preceding pages in regard to the Holy Sepulcher, represented explicitly as Christ's tomb at Chadenac, and the prevailing Romanesque regional façade design. For a discussion of the popularity of the edifice metaphor in the writings of Saint Bernard of Clairvaux, see the paper by Ford Lewis Battles, "Bernard of Clairvaux and the Moral Allegorical Tradition," *Innovation in Medieval Literature: Essays to the Memory of Alan Markham,* ed. D. Radcliff-Umstead (Pittsburgh, 1971), pp. 1–19.

57. Lubac, *Exégèse,* I, ii:645.

58. E. O. Blake, "The Formation of the 'Crusade' Idea," *Journal of Ecclesiastical*

*History* 21 (1970): 25; *Histoire littéraire de la France*, nouv. ed., 11 (Paris, 1869): 102–13, esp. 104–6.

59. *Gesta Francorum et Aliorum Hierosolymitanorum*, ed. Rosalind M. Hill (London, 1962), pp. 98–101. See the article by Philippe Verdier, "La Colonne de Colonia Aelia Capitolina et l'*imago clipeata* du Christ-Helios," *Cahiers archéologiques* 23 (1974): 17–40 for references to other similar accounts of the "middle of the world."

60. On liturgical and natural time, see Eliade, *Sacred and Profane*, pp. 68–69, and Jean Leclercq, "Experience and Interpretation of Time in the Early Middle Ages," *Studies in Medieval Culture* 5 (1975): 9–19. Willibald Sauerländer related the carved calendars to the cycle of church feasts, though he was by no means the first to do so (*Gothic Sculpture in France*, trans. Janet Sondheimer [London, 1972], p. 41). Phila Calder Nye compared the continuous band of the zodiac to the "heavens bearing witness to the solemnization of a rite" ("Romanesque Signs of the Zodiac," *Art Bulletin* 5 [1922]: 55–57). See also the brief comment on the relation of the seasons to medieval man's "ritual . . . management of the earth," in Derek Pearsall and Elizabeth Salter, *Landscapes and Seasons of the Medieval World* (Toronto and London, 1973), p. 128. For a depiction of the signs of the zodiac in a ring around an enthroned Zeus, see the large bronze medallion of Severus Alexander in *Romans and Barbarians* (Boston, 1976), C60.

61. Discussions about Jerusalem as the center of the universe are treated in A. J. Bredero, "Jérusalem dans l'Occident médiéval," *Mélanges offerts à René Crozet*, 1:259–71, esp. p. 264; R. Konrad, "Das himmelische und das irdische Jerusalem im mittelalterlichen Denken," *Speculum Historiale*, ed. C. Bauer, L. Boehm, and M. Muller (Munich, 1965), pp. 531–33.

A recent study of some Romanesque zodiacal reliefs in Spain emphasizes a moralizing content for them based on a homily by the late fourth-century bishop of Verona, Zeno (see Serafín Moralejo Alvarez, "Pour l'interprétation iconographique du portail de l'agneau à Saint-Isidore de Léon: Les Signes du zodiaque," *Les Cahiers de Saint-Michel de Cuxa* 8 [1977]: 137–73). The basic study of the labors of the months, James Carson Webster's *The Labors of the Months in Antique and Medieval Art to the End of the Twelfth Century* (Princeton, 1938), is by now in need of revision. The important position given to cycles of the labors both inside the church, in the vicinity of the altar, and at the doorway deserves emphasis. See the discussion of the now fragmentary cycle that originally formed a U-shaped frame in the pavement in front of the altar in the chapel of Saint Firmin at Saint-Denis by Jean-Pierre Darmon and Henri Lavagne, *Recueil Général des Mosaïques de la Gaule*, Gallia Supplement 10, pt. ii, 3 (1977): 177–83.

Arabic astrological texts that were translated into Latin in the mid twelfth century stress many of the same elements seen in the Christian material: the "unerring and fixed course" of the heavenly bodies, their division into twelve parts and the centrality of the earth. See the article by C. S. F. Burnett, "A Group of Arabic-Latin Translators Working in Northern Spain in the Mid-Twelfth Century," *Journal of the Royal Asiatic Society of Great Britain and Ireland*, 1977, pp. 64–108.

62. M.-T. Gousset, "La Représentation de la Jérusalem Céleste," MSS at Valenciennes and Cambrai, and the article by Carl-Otto Nordström, "Text and Myth in Some Beatus Miniatures, Pt. ii," *Cahiers archéologiques* 26 (1977): 120–23 and fig. 4, Vat. gr. 1291, f. 9r. The article by Karl Lehmann, "The Dome of Heaven," *Art Bulletin* 27 (1945): 1–27, relates the theme to architectural traditions. Charlemagne is known to have had a set of round silver tables one of which appears, from descriptions, to have been decorated with relief figures of

celestial bodies in imitation of the circular maps (F. N. Estey, "Charlemagne's Silver Celestial Table," *Speculum* 18 [1943]: 112–17).

63. There is a discussion of the symbolism of Romanesque doors based on their "circular" axes in Gérard de Champeaux and Sébastian Sterckx, *Introduction au Monde des symboles* (La-Pierre-qui-Vire, 1966), pp. 390–407, esp. p. 393. Schapiro associated in an expressive way the secular theme of music-making with the radial placement of figures on voussoirs ("Silos," *Romanesque Art*, p. 42, n. 77, and p. 43).

The calendars are not subject to a rigid system of presentation. At Aulnay, for example, while the zodiacal signs maintain a regular radial disposition, the labors revert to a circumferential presentation along the lower sides. And at Fenioux and Cognac, an alternation between modes is observed in the juxtaposition of labor and sign, differentiating thereby the fixed and the figural.

64. Mâle, and more explicitly Tonnellier, perceived a unity in the Aquitainian archivolts as well. For their interpretations see *Religious Art in France; the Twelfth Century*, p. 442 and "L'Art roman" (both papers). Oursel also suggested that there was an intentional relationship between the gradual descent from the labor scenes at the outside to the mystic lamb on the keystone of the deepest voussoir (*Haut-Poitou roman*, pp. 329–30). A very brief paper by Pierre Bouffard alluded to a sense of larger issues such as the struggle between good and evil, depicted as an earthly vision of the church's teachings ("La Psychomachie sur les portails romans de la Saintonge," *Zeitschrift für schweizerische Archäologie und Kunstgeschichte* 22 [1962]: 19–21). These ideas have been perpetuated in a general way, for example, in Robert Calkins, *Monuments of Medieval Art* (New York, 1979), p. 93.

The interpretation suggested here coincidentally illustrates one of the modern historical "models" used to describe the relation of salvation history, church history, and secular history as a series of concentric circles with *Heilsgeschichte* at the center. See the paper by Lewis W. Spitz, "History: Sacred and Secular," *Church History* 47 (1978): 17, with its reference to the work of Peter Meinhold. Interesting comments on allegory as a sequence of metaphors on distinct though interpenetrating levels is found in Fletcher, *Allegory*, esp. p. 70.

65. Northrop Frye's distinctions of mythical and fabulous, which he sees as overlapping the sacred and secular, have been helpful to me in differentiating between types of content in the sculpture (*The Secular Scripture* [Cambridge, Mass., 1976], chap. 1, esp. pp. 6–16).

One group of carvings to which I have paid little apparent attention in these pages is the corpus of corbels that punctuate the arches and moldings on the exterior of the churches. These are occasionally decorated with motifs that appear in more prominent zones, but frequently they are distinguished solely by the presentation of individualized heads. Zarnecki tentatively proposed a relationship between the isolated heads on archivolts in western France and the severed heads that were employed as trophies in Roman Gaul. He suggested no meaningful connection between the elements, however, and hypothesized a transmission of the motif through Byzantium (Françoise Henry and George Zarnecki, "Romanesque Arches Decorated with Human and Animal Heads," *Journal of the British Archaeological Association* 20–21 [1957–58]: 1–34, esp. pp. 29–30). A recent study discusses at some length the conservation, display, and representation of severed heads by the Celts in pre-Roman Gaul. The association of the heads with carvings of warriors and horsemen, themes discussed here in the following pages, is particularly striking. See the articles by François Salviat, "La Sculpture pré-romane en Provence," and Patrice Arcelin,

"Croyances et vie religieuse," *Dossiers de l'archéologie* 35 (June 1979): 31–51 and 99–107. Human masks, as both Christian and apotropaic protectors in Merovingian art, are discussed by Edouard Salin, *La Civilisation mérovingienne* (Paris, 1959), 4:278–81; he comments as well upon the ritual mutilation or decapitation that was widespread in Merovingian Gaul.

An earlier study suggested a possible relation between such elements and the cult of decapitated saints, such as Saint Denis, whose legend flourished in medieval France. A remark of John Chrysostom that martyrs can present themselves before God carrying their head in their hand as proof of their suffering for the faith is cited in support of this idea (Pierre Lambrechts, *L'Exaltation de la tête dans la pensée et dans l'art des celtes* [Bruges, 1954], p. 109, where the initial article by Adolphe Reinach is cited, "Les Têtes coupées et les trophées en Gaule," *Revue celtique*, 1913, pp. 38–60 and 253–86). Saint Adalbert of Prague's head is displayed on a stick near his corpse, after his martyrdom by heathens, on the twelfth-century bronze doors at Gniezno Cathedral. See the illustration in Beryl Smalley, *Historians in the Middle Ages* (London, 1974), p. 125, fig. 62, and Adolph Goldschmidt, *Die Bronzetüren von Nowgorod und Gnesen* (Marburg, 1932), pp. 27–38 and pl. 97. Immediately adjacent to this scene (pl. 97) is one of the saint before a turreted chapel said to represent the graves of martyrs (ibid., pl. 77 and p. 29). Evidence of the ritualistic beheading of enemies during the period in which the façades were being built exists. The anonymous *Gesta Francorum* reports that Syrians and Armenians beheaded a Turkish lord during the capture of Antioch and "brought his head to Bohemund so that they might thereby obtain their liberty" (Brundage, *The Crusades*, p. 56). A Hebrew poem recounting the Turkoman defeat in Egypt in 1079 describes how the heads of the defeated were cut off and carried in baskets upon the shoulders of the victorious chiefs; see Julius H. Greenstone, "The Turkoman Defeat at Cairo," *American Journal of Semitic Languages and Literatures* 22 (1905–6): 144–75. Greenstone relates this passage to biblical texts of both submission and victory. The theme of bodies in baskets is discussed in greater detail in connection with images of women; see pp. 62–64. An association between the motif of detached heads and the themes of trophies and martyrs, key subjects on the Aquitainian façades, is plausible and worthy of further consideration.

66. Erich Auerbach, *Mimesis*, and, more briefly, W. T. H. Jackson, *Medieval Literature* (New York, 1966), p. 76. Auerbach's remarks were recapitulated in Eugene Vance, "Notes on the Development of Formulaic Language in Romanesque Poetry," *Mélanges offerts à René Crozet* 1:427–34, esp. p. 429. E. J. Mickel, Jr. ("Parallels in Prudentius' *Psychomachia* and *La Chanson de Roland*," *Studies in Philology* 67 [1970]: 439–52, and "Christian Duty and the Structure of the Roland," *Romance Notes* 9 [1967]: 126–33) develops the comparison extensively. Lejeune and Stiennon identified the *Psychomachia* as one of three thematic forms for the Roland story ("Le Héro Roland, 'Neveu de Charlemagne,' dans l'iconographie médiévale," *Karl der Grosse* 4:215–28). See also the abstract of Gérard Brault's talk on character portrayal in the *Song of Roland* in which he tries to identify the virtue or vice that lies at the heart of each figure (*Olifant* 2 [1974]: 65). Brault has recently summarized many of these ideas in "The French Chansons de Geste," *Heroic Epic and Saga*, ed. Felix J. Oinas (Bloomington, Ind., 1978), pp. 193–215. Muslim epics use the same motifs for similar ends. The caliph's forces are depicted as being loyal and courageous while the rebels are drawn as disloyal, cowardly, and passive (Monroe, "The Historical Arjuza," p. 74). See a related interpretation of another piece of literature by J. P. Herman, "The Theme of Spiritual Warfare in the OE Judith," *Philological Quarterly* 55 (1976): 1–9.

67. On the chronicle, see H. M. Smyser, ed., *The Pseudo-Turpin*, Mediaeval Academy of America Publication, no. 30 (Cambridge, Mass., 1937); the earlier publication of the text, *De vita Caroli Magni et Rolandi* (Florence, 1882); more recently Christopher Hohler, "A Note on *Jacobus*," *Journal of the Warburg and Courtauld Institutes* 35 (1972): 31–80; and the introduction in Ronald N. Walpole, *The Old French Johannes-Translation of the Pseudo-Turpin Chronicle* (Berkeley and Los Angeles, 1976), pp. xi–xxii.

68. Smyser, *Pseudo-Turpin*, pp. 24, 63–64. A frequently cited commentary in the Saint Albans Psalter, in which fighting soldiers are likened to spiritual warriors, was related to the virtue and vice theme by Folke Nordström, *Virtues and Vices on the Fourteenth Century Corbels in the Choir of Uppsala Cathedral*, 7 (Stockholm, 1956): pp. 107–8.

69. Smith, *Prudentius' "Psychomachia*," p. 289; Lester Little, "Pride Goes before Avarice: Social Change and the Vices in Latin Christendom," *American Historical Review* 76 (1971): 16–49.

70. Schapiro, "Silos," *Romanesque Art*, p. 37.

71. David Herlihy, "Land, Family and Women in Continental Europe, 701–1200," *Women in Medieval Society*, ed. Susan Mosher Stuard (Philadelphia, 1976), pp. 13–45, esp. 34.

72. A useful source here is H. von Roques de Maumont, *Antike Reiterstandbilder* (Berlin, 1958). For other bibliography, see Seidel, "Holy Warriors," notes 1–6, and the remarks of Walter Cahn, *The Romanesque Wooden Doors of Auvergne* (New York, 1974), esp. pp. 98, 102. The ancient coins with riders in different poses appear in Harold Mattingly, *Roman Coins from the Earliest Times to the Fall of the Western Empire* (London, 1928), pls. 2:2, 7:20, 36:14, 17. The early Christian adaptation was traced by André Grabar, *L'Empéreur*, pp. 45ff.

73. Ernst Gunther Grimme, "Novus Constantinus," *Aachener Kunstblätter* 22 (1961): 7–20, esp. pp. 12–14, and Lasko, *Ars Sacra*, p. 18.

74. For the Roman coins, see the sestertius of Claudius in Anne S. Robertson, *Roman Imperial Coins in the Hunter Coin Cabinet, University of Glasgow* 1 (London, 1962): 97, pl. 18, no. 79. There are splendid illustrations in John P. C. Kent, Bernhard Overbeck, and Armin U. Stylow, *Die römische Münze* (Munich, 1973), e.g., pl. 47, no. 179. A helpful series of illustrations accompanies the article of Ferdinand Noack, "Triumph und Triumphbogen," *Vorträge der Bibliothek Warburg* [vol. 5], 1925–26, pp. 147–201, pl. 38. For the coin of Septimius Severus, see Robertson, *Roman Imperial Coins* 3 (London, 1977): 21 and pl. 7, no. 78.

75. Much has been written about Einhard's arch in the last few years while I have been considering, independently, its impact on subsequent centuries. Some of my remarks are closely related to conclusions of Kurt Weitzmann, "Der Aufbau und die unteren Felder der Einhard-Reliquiars," in Hauck, ed., *Das Einhardkreuz*, pp. 45–46, and to remarks of Donald Bullough, who suggested that here, "for the first time in Carolingian art, the mystical triumph of the Christian Cross is linked with the earthly triumphs of secular rulers engaging in 'just wars' against the forces of evil" ("'Imagines Regum,'" p. 250). Belting's recent interpretation offers yet another, more political perspective on the possible program of the arch, in "Der Einhardsbogen." One of the issues would seem to be whether the riders on the arch represent specific figures, and whether these are emperors, or whether they stand for a class of individuals to which emperors might belong. In light of the testimony from coins, along with the handling of other antique themes on Carolingian objects and the subsequent treatment of the theme, my interpretation supports the latter position. See the additional remarks above, chap. 2, note 32.

Kantorowicz's paper "Gods in Uniform," makes important remarks on the "imperialization of deities" in art and comments on the substitution of the victorious cross for the pagan trophy (*Selected Studies*, ed. Michael Cherniavsky and Ralph E. Giesey [New York, 1965], pp. 7–24, esp. pp. 18, 21). The recent article by Hubert Le Roux on the equestrian figure emphasizes the availability in western France of certain images on Roman coins and medals as well as on ruins although the conclusions he draws from the evidence are quite different from my own; see Le Roux, "Les Enigmatiques cavaliers romans, St. Jacques ou Constantin?" *L'Archéologie* 20 (1977): 75–78.

Baldwin Smith mentioned a mid-third-century Thracian coin minted for Philippus Senior which showed, as part of a bird's-eye view of a city, a city gate decorated to the left of the entry with a horseman. He suggested that its rather elaborate sculptural treatment might indicate a particularly commemorative function for the gateway; in other words, it would approach in purpose the triumphal arch (*Architectural Symbolism*, pp. 39–40 and fig. 28).

The importance of late Roman monuments for the formation of medieval iconography has often been suggested. See, for example Yves Christe, "La Colonne d'Arcadius, Sainte-Prudentienne, l'arc d'Eginhard et le Portail de Ripoll," *Cahiers archéologiques* 21 (1971): 31–42, esp. pp. 35–36, and "Le Portail de Beaulieu: Etude iconographique et stylistique," *Bulletin archéologique*, n.s. 6 (1970): 57–76, where he likens the instruments of Christ's Passion to trophies of victory.

Observations on the relation of Romanesque to the antique have also been made by Dorothy Glass, "Romanesque Sculpture in Campania and Sicily: A Problem of Method," *Art Bulletin* 56 (1974): 315–24, esp. p. 319. Margaret English Frazer commented on the triumphal imperial source for the image of the personification of Hell impaled ("Hades Stabbed by the Cross of Christ," *Metropolitan Museum Journal* 9 [1974]: 153–61) and O. K. Werckmeister associated Roman triumphal columns with Romanesque narrative ("Political Ideology of the Bayeux Tapestry," *Studi Medievalii* 3d ser., 17, no. 2 [1976]: 535–89, esp. pp. 535–36).

76. The essential reference is in the article by Montesquiou-Fézensac, "L'Arc d'Eginhard," p. 170.

77. For this useful concept, see the early article by Georgiana Goddard King, "The Rider on the White Horse," *Art Bulletin* 5 (1922): 3–9. The emergence of vernacular historical writing in France at about this time in place of the more ecclesiastical Latin has been related to the need for information among contemporary people (Diana B. Tyson, "Patronage of French Vernacular History Writers in the Twelfth and Thirteenth Centuries," *Romania* 100 [1979]: 180–222).

78. See Lynn White's interpretation of the importance of the horse in the Middle Ages in *Medieval Technology and Social Change* (Oxford, 1962). His argument concerning the importance of the early mounted fighters has been criticized recently by Bernard S. Bachrach ("Charles Martel, Mounted Shock Combat, the Stirrup and Feudalism," *Studies in Medieval and Renaissance History* 7 [1970]: 47–75), who, however, commented positively on the importance of horses to the Franks in "Procopius, Agathias and the Frankish Military," *Speculum* 45 (1970): 435–41. Georges Duby made significant remarks on the contribution of the horse to the transformation of society in his paper "The Origins of Knighthood," *Chivalrous Society*, p. 163.

On the seals of Parthenay, see François Eygun, "Un Thème iconographique commun aux églises romanes de Parthenay et aux sceaux de ses seigneurs," *Bulletin archéologique*, 1927, pp. 387–90, and idem, *Sigillographie du Poitou* (Poitiers, 1938), pl. 1, no. l; pl. 8, no. 207; pl. 18, nos. 533–34. George Henderson has recently considered images on seals in relation to contemporary personages

("Romance and Politics on Some Medieval English Seals," *Art History* 1 [1978]: 26–42).

79. On the identification of imperial rider figures in the Middle Ages, see my brief remarks, "Constantine and Charlemagne," *Gesta* 15 (1976): 237–39; on Charlemagne as the new Constantine, see Hauck, *Das Einhardkreuz*, p. 202. The main commentaries on Constantine were in Byzantium; see the article by A. Linder, "The Myth of Constantine the Great in the West: Sources and Hagiographic Commemoration," *Studi Medievalii*, 3d ser. 16, no. 1 (1975): 43–95. On the transferral to the chivalric class of rituals previously reserved for the king, see the important article by J. Flori, "Chevalerie et liturgie," *Le Moyen âge* 84 (1978): 247–78 and 409–42.

The image of the hunt, a royal occupation, was used rhetorically by Saint Bernard to evoke and condemn the negative aspects of cunning and contrived behavior. See the brief discussion by Elizabeth T. Kennan, "Rhetoric and Style in the *De Consideratione*," *Studies in Medieval Cistercian History*, no. 2, ed. John R. Sommerfeldt, Cistercian Studies 24 (Kalamazoo, Mich., 1976), pp. 40–41.

80. For the material cited here, see Schapiro, "Silos," *Romanesque Art*, p. 51, and W. S. Heckscher, "Relics of Pagan Antiquity in Mediaeval Settings," *Journal of the Warburg Institute* 1 (1937–38): 209–10 and 215. On the collection and use of antique carved gems in the Middle Ages, see Emile Lesne, *Histoire de la propriété ecclésiastique en France*, 6 vols. (Lille and Paris, 1910–43), vol. 3, *L'Inventaire de la propriété; églises et trésors des églises du commencement du VIII^e à la fin du XI^e siècle* (1936), chaps. 13 and 15, pp. 173–79, 191–99, and esp. p. 239; G. Demay, *Des Pierres gravées employées dans les sceaux du moyen âge* (Paris, 1877), nos. 1–309; Ernest Babelon, *Histoire de la gravure sur gemmes en France* (Paris, 1902), pp. 19–20; Jean Adhémar, *Influences Antiques*, pp. 106–9 and 249. For discussions of the wealth of medieval aristocracy, see Pierre Riché, "Trésors et Collections d'aristocrates laïques carolingiens," *Cahiers archéologiques* 22 (1972): 44, and his brief communication in *Bulletin de la Société Nationale des Antiquaires*, 1971, pp. 132–34; also Martindale, "French Aristocracy," p. 26.

81. H. Wentzel, "Portraits 'à l'antique' on French medieval gems and seals, " *Journal of the Warburg and Courtauld Institutes* 16 (1953): 342.

82. Pertinent to these remarks are the studies by G. A. S. Snijder, "Antique and Medieval Gems on Bookcovers at Utrecht," *Art Bulletin* 14 (1932): 14–18; Heckscher, "Relics of Pagan Antiquity," pp. 219–20; Jean Maury, M.-M. Gauthier, and Jean Porcher, *Limousin roman*, 2d ed. (La-Pierre-qui-Vire, 1974), pp. 290–91, on the Grandmont treasure. See as well Jean Taralon's recent study of the celebrated seated statue at Conques with its many cameos and inset intaglios, "La Majesté d'or de Sainte-Foy du trésor de Conques," *Revue de l'art* 40–41 (1978): 17 and figs. 30–33.

83. See the discussions of crowns and of crown-bearing saints in the monumental fresco painting of the region by André Grabar, "L'Etude des fresques romanes," *Cahiers archéologiques* 2 (1947): 170–71, where the theme is associated with early Christian apse decoration, and by William M. Hinkle, "The Iconography of the Apsidial Fresco at Montmorillon," *Münchener Jahrbuch der bildenden Kunst* 23 (1972): 37–62. Marie-Madeleine Gauthier commented on the association of crowns with athletic triumph, sovereign power, and homage rendered to God in "L'Or et l'église au moyen âge," *Revue de l'art* 26 (1974): 70. Courtiers are associated with the "glorious crown of martyrdom" in the writing of Peter of Blois, one of many possible examples (Peter Dronke, "Peter of Blois and Poetry at the Court of Henry II," *Mediaeval Studies* 38 [1976]: 193). The classic study of crowns as symbols of political power but also as military decoration and as funeral embellishment is that of Percy E. Schramm,

*Herrschaftszeichen und Staatssymbolik,* 3 vols. (Stuttgart, 1954–56), esp. vols. 2 and 3. More recently, crowns have been studied primarily as rewards for "spiritual success" (Edwin Hall and Horst Uhr, "*Aureola* and *Fructus*: Distinctions of Beatitude in Scholastic Thought and the Meaning of Some Crowns in Early Flemish Painting," *Art Bulletin* 60 [1978]: 249–70). In Rev. 6:2, after the Lamb opens one of the seven seals, a rider on a white horse appears and is given a crown before he goes out conquering. On the English rider relief see George Zarnecki, *Later English Romanesque Sculpture* (London, 1953), pp. 9–13; also Selma Jónsdóttir, "The Portal of Kilpeck Church: Its Place in English Romanesque Sculpture," *Art Bulletin* 32 (1950): 171–80, fig. 2. There are extensive comments on warriors and riders in W. Cahn, *Wooden Doors,* pp. 98–99.

84. Peter Dronke commented on the shared values and conventions linking poet and patron out of which the courtly genre emerges; he observed them already in eleventh-century work ("The Rise of the Medieval Fabliau: Latin and Vernacular Evidence," *Romanische Forschungen* 85 [1973]: 275–97, esp. p. 284). See also A. R. Harden, "The Depreciatory Comparison: A Literary Device of the Medieval French Epic," *Medieval Studies in Honor of U. T. Holmes, Jr.,* University of North Carolina Studies in the Romance Languages and Literatures 56 (Chapel Hill, N.C., 1965), pp. 63–78, esp. p. 78.

85. S. G. Nichols, Jr., "Canso-Conso: Structures of Parodic Humor in Three Songs of Guilhelm IX," *L'Esprit Créateur* 14, no. 1 (1976): 16–29, and his remarks on language in "Rhetorical Metamorphoses in the Troubadour Lyric," *Mélanges de langue,* pp. 569–85. On the confusing or ambiguous meanings of some of William's poems, see G. A. Bond, "Philological Comments on a New Edition of the First Troubadour," *Romance Philology* 30 (1976): 343–61. Bond's reinterpretation of William's boasting poem emphasizes the multiple layers of meaning in the poet's work ("The Structure of the *Gap* of the Count of Poitiers," *Neuphilologische Mitteilungen* 79 [1978]: 162–72).

86. W. J. W. Field, ed., *Raimon Vidal, Poetry and Prose,* University of North Carolina Studies in Romance Languages and Literatures 110 (Chapel Hill, N.C., 1971), esp. pp. 15 and 61–65. A. Stainton called attention to the vivid evocations as a manifestation of the heightened sensitivity to time in "The Time Motif in the Poetry of Bernart de Ventadorn," *Neuphilologische Mitteilungen* 78 (1977): 202–14, esp. 202. See also James Wilhelm, *The Cruelest Month* (New Haven, Conn., 1965), pp. xiii–xiv. Moshé Lazar suggested that the themes of seasons and love helped evoke an erotic dream ("Classification des thèmes amoureux et des images poetiques dans l'oeuvre de Bernard de Ventadour," *Filologia Romanza* 6 (1959): 371–400, esp. pp. 371–72. More recently, on related topics, see Peter Dronke, "The Interpretation of the Ripoll Love Songs," *Romance Philology* 33 (1979): 35–41.

87. D. Nelson, "Animal Imagery in Marcabru's Poetry," *Studies in Medieval Culture* 11 (1977): 51–55, esp. p. 54; Bond, "Philological Comments," pp. 343–61; Moshé Lazar, *Amour courtois et fin'amors dans la littérature du XIIᵉ siècle* (Paris, 1964), p. 128, and Peter Dronke, "Guillaume IX et Courtoisie," *Romanische Forschungen* 73 (1961): 327–38, esp. pp. 329–30.

88. Lazar, *Amour courtois,* p. 129, and idem, *Bernard de Ventadour, Troubadour du XIIᵉ siècle* (Paris, 1966), pp. 20–21, 25–26. Gérard Brault suggested that the idea of military conquest expressed in representations of the rider may also express, on the metaphoric plane, the concept of spiritual conquest ("'Truvet Li unt le num de Juliane,' Sur le role de Bramimonde dans la Chanson de Roland," *Mélanges de langue,* pp. 134–49). Such imagery even invaded religious writing. Peter the Venerable used military terminology in an "attempt to speak language best calculated to make sense and produce desired results" (James Kritzeck, *Peter the Venerable and Islam* [Princeton, 1964], pp. 44–45).

89. Illustrations of Luxuria appear in Woodruff, "The Illustrated Manuscripts of Prudentius"; for remarks on the role of women in twelfth-century poetry see René Nelli, *L'Erotique des Troubadours*, Bibliothèque méridionale, 2d ser., 38 (Toulouse, 1963), pp. 24–25.

90. Schapiro enumerated other examples of the theme, at Morlaas, Varaize, Bordeaux, Aulnay, Foussais, and Oloron—all in western France—in his article on "Silos," note 77. Luxuria is seen dancing in the *Psychomachia* manuscript in the British Library, Add. 24199, f. 18$^r$, illustrated in Louis Grodecki et al., *Le Siècle de l'an mil*, L'univers des formes (Paris, 1973), fig. 249. A scene of music-making and dancing appears on a capital to the left of the center door at Blasimon (Francis Salet, "Blasimon," *Congrès archéologique* 102 [1939]: 212).

91. The Chartres carving is illustrated and discussed by Adelheid Heimann, "The Capital Frieze and Pilasters of the Portail Royal, Chartres," *Journal of the Warburg and Courtauld Institutes* 31 (1968): pl. 30, fig. 5, and p. 76. For the date of the Leyden manuscript, see Woodruff, "The Illustrated Manuscripts of Prudentius." Zarnecki singled out the Parthenay figures as a "slightly odd version" of the head motif on Aquitainian archivolts (Henry and Zarnecki, "Romanesque Arches," p. 8).

92. Grace D. Guest and Richard Ettinghausen, "The Iconography of a Kashan Lustre Plate," *Ars Orientalis* 4 (1961): 25–64, esp. pp. 43–45. See the comments on the representation of women by Oleg Grabar, *Sasanian Silver* (Ann Arbor, 1967), pp. 60–63, and the summation of western attitudes in C. Meredith Jones, "The Conventional Saracen of the Songs of Geste," *Speculum* 17 (1942): 201–25. The Freer plate is illustrated and discussed in Esin Atil, *Ceramics from the World of Islam* (Washington, D.C., 1973), no. 50, pp. 112–15.

93. For these texts, see Álvaro Galmés de Fuentes, "Le 'Charroi de Nîmes' et la tradition arabe," *Cahiers de civilisation médiévale* 22 (1979): 129–30; Monroe, "The Historical Arjūza," p. 84, for the image of a woman in a litter; and Brian Stock, "Antiqui and Moderni as 'Giants' and 'Dwarfs': A Reflection of Popular Culture?" *Modern Philology* 76 (1979): 371, for the quote from Ordericus, *Ecclesiastical History*, bk. 8, chap. 17. A passage in the Koran quotes Muhammad as saying that a bad omen is found in a woman, a house, or a horse (see T. P. Hughes, *A Dictionary of Islam* [Lahore, 1964], pp. 677–80, from the hadith on women). Schapiro called attention to the theme of the adulterous woman in Arabic accounts of the afterlife ("Silos," *Romanesque Art*, p. 38 and n 33)

94. A series of nude women in baskets, arranged in a ring on a Renaissance map, are reminiscent of the French Romanesque carvings. The figures are identified as representations of stars by Robert S. Brumbaugh, "The Voynich 'Roger Bacon' Cipher Manuscript: Deciphered Maps of Stars," *Journal of the Warburg and Courtauld Institutes* 39 (1976): 139–50. He suggests that the figures depend on a twelfth- or thirteenth-century model and, because of the identity of certain figures on the maps, he notes the possibility of Arabic ancestry for them. See also the paper by Dalu Jones, "Notes on a Tattooed Musician: A Drawing of the Fatimid Period," *Art and Archaeology Research Papers* 7 (1975): 1–14, in which a drawing of a nude musician is closely associated with illustrations of the constellations in the eleventh-century Book on the Fixed Stars in Oxford.

95. Smyser, *Pseudo-Turpin*, pp. 80–83; Walter E. Kaegi, "Initial Byzantine Reactions to the Arab Conquest," *Church History* 38 (1969): 139, 143. Robert S. Lopez described a "Byzantine Roland," riding along frontiers, killing animals and infidels, seducing countless women, and repenting ("Marquis et Mono-stratèges," *Mélanges offerts à René Crozet*, 1:77.

96. Raymond d'Aguilers, the canon of le Puy who also wrote an account of the First Crusade, likewise attributed military reverses to prostitutes (see J. H. Hill and L. L. Hill, *Raymond d'Aguilers, Historia Francorum* [Philadelphia, 1968], p. 8).

97. Hughes, *Dictionary of Islam*, p. 244. Official attitudes toward plunder, both the legitimate retention of spoils and the unjustly taken booty that required penance, are discussed in Frederick H. Russell, *The Just War in the Middle Ages* (Cambridge, 1975), pp. 244–45.

98. J. Waltz, "Carolingian Attitudes Regarding Muslims," *Studies in Medieval Culture* 5 (1975): 35.

99. Bachrach, "Charles Martel," p. 68.

100. Hill and Hill, *Raymond d'Aguilers*, p. 43. See the translation of a passage from the Annals of Genoa describing the taking of Saracen booty by Genoese crusaders and their return from the Holy Land in 1101 "... in triumph and covered with glory" (Lopez and Raymond, *Medieval Trade*, pp. 88–89).

101. Ernst Kantorowicz, "The 'King's Advent' and the Enigmatic Panels on the Doors of Santa Sabina," *Selected Studies* (Locust Valley, N.Y., 1965), pp. 37–38.

102. The two other privileges promised the martyr were safety from the grave and hell and a role as intercessor for relatives (Alfred Guillaume, *The Traditions of Islam* [Oxford, 1924], p. 112). Elsewhere in the hadith, pride is put forth as the worst attribute of man, another analogue to the position of the Christian warrior (*Al-Hadis: An English Translation and Commentary of Mishkat-al-Masabih*, trans. Fazlul Karim; 2 vols; 2d ed. [Calcutta, 1960], 2:352–55; the six privileges are enumerated in 2:358). Most scholars associate these texts with the first centuries after Muhammad; they were probably complete by A.D. 1000. See, for example, Fazlur Rahman, *Islam*, 2d ed. (Chicago, 1979), chap. 3.

103. Kritzeck, *Peter the Venerable*, p. 135. The translation was supervised by Peter the Venerable's secretary, Peter of Poitiers, a monk originally from the monastery of Saint-Jean d'Angély in Poitou (Giles Constable, *The Letters of Peter the Venerable*, Harvard Historical Studies 78, 2 vols. [Cambridge, Mass., 1967], 2:342). The concept of the Muslim paradise as a place of sensual delight was introduced into the West as early as ca. 1106, according to Dorothee Metlitzki, *The Matter of Araby in Medieval England* (New Haven and London, 1977), p. 210.

104. Relevant discussion appears in Dronke, "Guillaume IX," pp. 327–38; William Calin, *The Old French Epic of Revolt* (Geneva, 1962); Frederick Goldin, *The Mirror of Narcissus in the Courtly Love Lyric* (Ithaca, N.Y., 1967), p. 2; and E. Kohler, "Sens et Fonction du terme 'jeunesse' dans la poésie des troubadours," *Mélanges offerts à René Crozet*, 1:569–83, on the social groups for whom some of the poetry was intended.

105. Compare the suggestion by Jacques Thirion that the women and riders on a capital in the Musée de Sisteron recall "quelques héros des chansons de geste ou des romans courtois" ("Sculptures romanes de haute-Provence," *Bulletin monumental* 130 [1972]: 29). The theme informed real life as well. William of Malmesbury wrote that the troubadour William of Aquitaine established a "monastery" at Niort and peopled it with prostitutes in imitation of what happened in real religious houses (cited in A. Richard, *Histoire des Comtes*, pp. 496–97).

106. Susan Olson, "Immutable Love: Two Good Women in Marcabru," *Neophilologus* 60 (1976): 190–99. She emphasizes in the article that virtue (or vice?) is not an abstraction for the poet but is often localized in noble men and women.

107. On the theme see Jacqueline Leclerq-Kadaner, "De la Terre-Mère à la Luxure," *Cahiers de civilisation médiévale* 18 (1975): 37–43.

108. The moral goal of this poem was emphasized by Alan R. Press, who likened the work to exempla ("Quelques observations sur la chanson V de Guillaume IX: *Farai un vers pos mi sonelh*," *Etudes de civilisation médiévale*, pp. 603–9).

109. The representation of asses on the archivolt at Aulnay may be another allusion to the lasciviousness of sensual people as described in Hrabanus Maurus; see Peter Dronke, "The Rise of Medieval Fabliaux," pp. 285–86. The animals may be intended to invoke, simultaneously, the Arabs, descendants of Ishmael, who was described in Gen. 16:12 as a "wild ass of a man"; see the article by J. Waltz, "Carolingian Attitudes Regarding Muslims," pp. 33–40 for the earlier literature. In the poetry of Marcabru, the cuckolded noble is likened to a "jackass with the sense of a goat"; see Nelson, "Animal Imagery."

110. On the rider asleep, see Lynne Lawner, "Notes toward an Interpretation of the *vers de dreyt nien*," *Cultura Neolatina* 28 (1968): 160–61. The rider asleep on a horse is a familiar motif in psalters, where it is used as an image of the stouthearted men of war stripped of their spoils who sink into sleep (Psalm 75 (76): 5–7). See the brief remarks and illustration in Anthony Cutler, "The Marginal Psalter in the Walters Art Gallery," *Journal of the Walters Art Gallery* 35 (1977): 49 and fig. 17. The use of different styles of writing is addressed by Press, "Quelques observations." The quotation from Auerbach is found in *Mimesis*, pp. 11–13.

111. Joan M. Ferrante, *Woman as Image in Medieval Literature from the Twelfth Century to Dante* (New York, 1975), p. 1.

112. J. George and A. Guérin-Boutard, *Les Eglises romanes de l'ancien diocèse d'Angouleme* (Paris, 1928), pp. 266–67, fig. 235 A–K. See also the metopes at La Jarne with Luxuria, a warrior and a centaur. These are discussed by René Crozet, "Le Chasseur et le combattant dans la sculpture romane en Saintonge," *Mélanges offerts à Rita Lejeune-Dehousse*, 1:672–73. A recent survey of related material in Spain appears in Maria I. Ruiz Montejo, "La Temática obscena en la iconografía del románico rural," *Goya* 147 (1978): 136–46, but, for the most part, licentious themes on or in a church are not viewed as significant material for investigation. See, for example, Françoise Brisset, "Etude comparée des modillons des galeries de circulation de l'église Ste-Radegonde et de la cathédrale St-Pierre de Poitiers," *Bulletin de la Société des antiquaires de l'Ouest*, 4th ser., 14 (1978): 483–510.

113. Charles Daras, "Les Cavaliers de La Rochette," *Mémoires de la Société archéologique et historique de la Charente*, 1957, pp. 1–5.

114. D. C. Munro, "The Western Attitude toward Islam during the Crusades," *Speculum* 6 (1931): 332; Jones, "Conventional Saracen," ibid., 17 (1942): 201–5; R. W. Southern, *Western Views of Islam in the Middle Ages* (Cambridge, Mass., 1962), pp. 29–30. These attitudes are discussed in relation to some Romanesque sculpture by John Williams, "*Generationes Abrahae*: Reconquest Iconography in León," *Gesta* 16, no. 2 (1977): 8–9.

115. Mattingly, *Roman Coins* (1928), pl. xv: 6 and p. 67.

116. Lejeune and Stiennon, "Le Héro Roland," pp. 215–28.

117. Comments on biblical guidance for Carolingian kings is found in J. M. Wallace-Hadrill, "The Via Regia of the Carolingian Age," *Early Medieval History* (New York, 1976), pp. 181–200, esp. pp. 184–89. On David as the lion-killer, see the recent comments of Henderson, "Romance and Politics," pp. 27–28. For comparisons of rulers with both David and Samson and a discussion of the rider theme, see Margarita Ruiz Maldonado, "La Contraposición 'Superbia-Humilitas': El sepulcro de Doña Sancha y otras obras," *Goya* 146 (1978): 75–81, and "El 'caballero victorioso' en la escultura románica española: Algunas consideraciones y nuevos ejemplos," *Boletín del Seminario de Estudios de Arte y Arqueología*, Universidad de Valladolid 45 (1979): 271–86.

118. In the middle of the twelfth-century, Saint Bernard characterized the opposition between Goliath and David as pride vanquished by humble faith; cited by Jean Leclercq, "Le Thème de la jonglerie chez S. Bernard et ses con-

temporains," *Revue d'histoire de la spiritualité* 48 (1972): 385–99, esp. 387, 396.

119. See the comments of Howard Helsinger, "Images on the *Beatus* Page of Some Medieval Psalters," *Art Bulletin* 53 (1971): 174–75. The lantern of Bégon, discussed in the preceding chapter, had added to it in the twelfth century plaques showing Christ treading on the beasts and a lion fight; see the comments by Verdier, "Deux plaques d'ivoire," p. 7, n. 23. The association of Samson with Adam and Eve can be seen as well in sculpture near Figeac; see Jacques Bousquet, "Trois Tympans sculptés des environs de Figeac: Saint-Félix et Saint-Jean de Mirabel, Saint-Pierre-Toirac," *Figeac et le Quercy* (Cahors, 1969), pp. 254–57.

120. In connection with the milieu for which this piece was carved, see H. Mayer, "Studies in the History of Queen Melisende of Jerusalem," *Dumbarton Oaks Papers* 26 (1972): 93–182. The basic article is by T. S. R. Boase, "The Arts in the Latin Kingdom of Jerusalem," *Journal of the Warburg and Courtauld Institutes* 2 (1938–39): 2–21. A crozier in Florence with David imagery has recently been associated with the Melisende ivory by M. L. Campbell, " 'Scribe faber lima': A Crozier in Florence Reconsidered," *Burlington Magazine* 121 (1979): 364–69. The death of Goliath is seen here as a visual echo of that of Superbia. For the symbolism of David imagery on another twelfth-century liturgical object, see Piotr Skubiszewski, "The Iconography of a Romanesque Chalice from Trzemeszno," *Journal of the Warburg and Courtauld Institutes* 34 (1971): 40–64, as well as the article by Adelheid Heimann for remarks on David as psalmist *and* dancer, "A Twelfth-Century Manuscript from Winchecombe and Its Illustrations," *Journal of the Warburg and Courtauld Institutes* 28 (1965): 86–109, esp. pp. 94–103.

121. See Yvonne Labande-Mailfert's interpretation of the lion-fighter as *sacerdotium*, which fails to take account of some of these subordinate themes ("L'iconographie des laïcs dans la société aux XI^e siècles," *I Laici nella 'Societas Christiana' dei secoli XI e XII*, Miscellanea del centro di Studi Medioevali 5 [Milan, 1968], pp. 515–18). Schapiro pointed out that Theophilus counseled craftsmen in his handbook to represent Samson or David tearing the jaws of the lion ("The Bowman and the Bird on the Ruthwell Cross and Other Works," *Art Bulletin* 45 [1963]: 351–55).

122. There is controversy over the authenticity of this scene in the Roland. It is doubted by D. D. R. Owen ("Charlemagne's Dreams, Baligant and Turoldus," *Zeitschrift für romanische Philologie* 87 [1971]: 197–208). J. J. Duggan (*The Song of Roland: Formulaic Style and Poetic Craft* [Berkeley and Los Angeles, 1973], pp. 63–104) accepts it as part of the same tradition of oral composition as the rest of the poem. W. G. van Emden supports the suggestion that the dream refers to Baligant and is intended to portray him as one of the precursors of the Antichrist in "Another Look at Charlemagne's Dreams in the *Chanson de Roland*," *French Studies* 28 (1974): 257–71, esp. p. 267. Sylvia Huntley Horowitz, in a recent paper tries to explain the significance of multiple allusions to some of these figures in "Beowulf, Samson, David and Christ," *Studies in Medieval Culture* 12 (1978): 17–23.

123. Helsinger, "Images on the *Beatus* Page," p. 165.

124. Ian Short, "Roland's Final Combat," *Cultura Neolatina* 30 (1970): 135–55.

125. The influence of Prudentius on medieval imagery is cited with increasing frequency. See, for example, M.-L. Thérel, "*Caritas et Paupertas* dans l'iconographie médiévale inspirée de la Psychomachie," *Etudes sur l'histoire de la pauvreté: Moyen âge–XVI^e siècle* (Paris, 1974), pp. 295–317, and Ilene H. Forsyth, "The Theme of Cockfighting in Burgundian Romanesque Sculpture," *Speculum* 53 (1978): 252–82.

126. Interesting comments were made by Eugène Vance on the function of the

commemorative in pre-Scholastic Christian culture ("Roland et la poétique de la mémoire," *Cahiers d'études médiévales* 1 [1974]: 103–15) and by S. G. Nichols, Jr., on the evocation and reinterpretation of the past in the present ("The Interaction of Life and Literature in the *Peregrinationes ad Loca Sancta* and the Chansons de Geste," *Speculum* 44 [1969]: 51–77). See also Peter Dronke's description of the Angevin and Plantagenet fancy with retelling the splendors of the past and then linking them with an equally glorious present ("Peter of Blois," p. 185). The medieval "inability" to distinguish past and present was important to Otto von Simson's interpretation in *The Gothic Cathedral* (New York, 1956; 2d ed., 1962). Even looting has been characterized as a way of bringing the past into the present (A. Guilhou, "Demography and Culture in the Exarchate of Ravenna," *Studi Medievalii*, 3d ser., 10 [1969]: 201–19).

127. J. D. Niles, "The Ideal Depiction of Charlemagne in 'La Chanson de Roland,'" *Viator* 7 (1976): 123–39, esp. p. 138.

128. "Silos," *Romanesque Art*, p. 46.

129. More reading than I could hope to acknowledge contributed to my thinking in this area. Lévi-Strauss's remarks on the importance of focussing on Totality rather than sequence in the understanding of myth and music are especially relevant in this context (*Myth and Meaning*, pp. 44–45). Several of the themes I intertwine have been explored in isolation in recent years by numerous scholars. A fraction of that literature is cited in the following paragraph.

George Fenwick Jones related the values of the *Song of Roland* to that of its intended audience, concluding that the poem depicted the "moral physiognomy of the age in which it was composed." His conclusions and the method he employed are in ways similar to mine, but his emphasis on the heroic to the exclusion of the Christian is, I believe, shortsighted (*The Ethos of the Song of Roland* [Baltimore, 1963], p. 191; cf., for example, Constance Hieatt, "Roland's Christian Heroism," *Traditio* 24 [1968]: 420–29). Studies of the relationships between art and literature in this period include, in addition to the work of Auerbach, that of H. Hatzfeld, *Literature through Art: A New Approach to French Literature*, University of North Carolina Studies in the Romance Languages and Literatures 86 (Chapel Hill, N.C., 1969), pp. 3–8, and "Les Etudes de style et la littérature médiévale," *Mélanges offerts à Rita Lejeune-Dehousse*, 2:1601–11. Fern Farnham applied principles of composition in poetry to an analysis of the Moissac tympanum in "Romanesque Design in the Song of Roland," *Romance Philology* 18, no. 2 (1964): 143–84. A specifically structuralist attempt has been made by B. Schuchard, "Architecture, littérature et art figuratif dans la France du XII^e siècle," *Les Cahiers de St-Michel de Cuxa* 4 (1973): 48–67, esp. p. 66. The close relationship between historical and cultural concerns has been explored by Karl D. Uitti, *Story, Myth, and Celebration in Old French Narrative Poetry* (Princeton, N.J., 1973), and S. G. Nichols, Jr., "The Spirit of Truth: Epic Modes in Medieval Literature," *New Literary History* 1 (1970): 365–86. Literature and geography have been brought together by E. R. Labande, "Le Poitou dans les chansons de geste," *Bulletin de la Société des antiquaires de l'Ouest*, 4th ser., 13 (1976): 329–52; literature and history have been correlated by D. D. R. Owen, "The Secular Inspiration of the Song of Roland," *Speculum* 37 (1962): 390–400, J. Frappier, "Réflexions sur les rapports des chansons de geste et de l'histoire," *Zeitschrift für romanische Philologie* 73 (1957): 1–19, and René Louis, "L'Epopée français est carolingienne," *Coloquios de Roncesvalles* (Zaragoza, 1956), pp. 327–460.

Several of the themes treated in this chapter—martyred soldier-saints, horsemen, musicians, the Holy Sepulcher, and even lion struggles—were equally popular inside these same churches. They are often found in the vicinity of the choir or main apse. Léon Pressouyre has recently discussed some capitals from a small "princely" church in southwestern France. His association of two capitals with the triumphal arch that framed the entry to the apse suggests how explicit and deliberate the choice and arrangement of subjects was. A depiction of the Marys, fashionably attired, faced out toward the nave on one side, while a scene of soldiers, shields readied and swords raised, faced the worshipers on the other side of the arch. Together, they formed a "contemporary" crusading representation that directed the worshiper's eye toward the scenes of the angel at the tomb and the betrayal on the main faces. On the eastern or altar sides of the carvings, detached and more symbolic images of force were displayed. The first capital showed a man astride and overcoming a lion while the second one presented two men dramatically armed with hatchet-like weapons, familiar from scenes of martyrdom (Pressouyre, "Les Chapiteaux romans de Ste-Croix-du-Mont au château de Castelnau-Bretenoux," *Bulletin monumental* 136 [1978]: 1–33).

Finally, Emile Mâle made a comparison similar to the one I have arrived at here in the closing paragraph of his essay, "L'Espagne arabe et l'art roman." Although he provides none of the evidence I have tried to marshal, I am confident that his remarks contributed, as a *souvenir*, to the formulation of my own conclusion: "Cette grande epopée du pèlerinage de Saint-Jacques et de la lutte contre les Maures n'est pas seulement dans la Chanson de Roland: elle est écrite au front des vieilles églises de la route d'Espagne" (*Art et artistes du moyen âge* [Paris, 1927], p. 88).

*Chapter Four*

1. The literature on the Crusades, specifically as an *imitatio Christi*, in which the knight is guaranteed martyrdom should he die in the service of Christ, is too vast to be cited in any measure of detail here. Among the recent articles from which the discussion here has profited considerably are H. E. J. Cowdrey, "Pope Urban II's Preaching of the First Crusade," *History* 55 (1970): 177–88 and "The Genesis of the Crusades," in *The Holy War*, ed. T. R. Murphy (Columbus, Ohio, 1976), pp. 9–32; E. O. Blake, "The Formation of the 'Crusade' Idea," *Journal of Ecclesiastical History* 21 (1970): 11–31; J. S. Preus, "Theological Legitimation for Innovation in the Middle Ages," *Viator* 3 (1972): 1–26, esp. pp. 14–16; I. S. Robinson, "Gregory VII and the Soldiers of Christ," *History* 58 (1973): 169–92; and Bernard McGinn, "*Iter Sancti Sepulchri*: The Piety of the First Crusaders," *Essays on Medieval Civilization*, ed. Bede Lackner and K. R. Philp (Austin, 1978), pp. 33–72. See also the introduction to *The First Crusade: The Chronicle of Fulcher of Chartres and Other Source Materials*, ed. E. Peters (Philadelphia, 1971), pp. xxi–xxii. The basic and majestic study, newly available in translation with updated notes and commentary, is by Carl Erdmann, *The Origin of the Idea of Crusade*, with a foreword by Marshall W. Baldwin, trans. Marshall W. Baldwin and Walter Goffart (Princeton, N.J., 1977), originally published in 1935. *The First Hundred Years*, ed. Marshall W. Baldwin, in *A History of the Crusades*, ed. Kenneth M. Setton, 2d ed. (Madison, Wis., 1969), presents an informative series of essays on significant aspects of the Crusades. A useful handbook, summarizing much recent scholarship, is by Jonathan Riley-Smith, *What Were the Crusades?* (Totowa, N.J., 1977). The important study of vernacular crusading literature, with many observations pertinent to my own conclusions, recently came to my attention: D. H. Green, *The Millstätter Exodus: A Crusading Epic* (Cambridge, 1966).

2. The quotation is from B. Rosenwein (Lester Little and Barbara Rosenwein, "Social Meaning in the Monastic and Mendicant Spiritualities," *Past and Present* 63 [1974]: 13). Rosenwein's emphasis on the nature of the activity of the Cluniacs has been essential to my appreciation of Cluniac art.

3. For the situation in the west of France, in particular, see the article by Daniel F. Callahan, "Adémar de Chabannes et la Paix de Dieu," *Annales du Midi* 89 (1977): 21–43. The situation is summarized and discussed in its much broader context in Russell, *The Just War*, pp. 34–39, and also Duby, "Laity," pp. 131–33.

4. Robinson, "Gregory VII," p. 185; the quotation is from John of Mantua's commentary on the *Song of Songs* written in the late eleventh century for Matilda of Tuscany.

5. Cited in Blake, "'Crusade' Idea," p. 25, and again in Colin Morris, "*Equestris ordo*: Chivalry as a Vocation in the Twelfth Century," in *Religious motivation: Biographical and Sociological Problems for the Church Historian*, Studies in Church History 15 (Cambridge, 1978), p. 87. There are useful recent publications on Guibert. His so-called autobiography has been revised and published as *Self and Society in Medieval France*, ed. John F. Benton (New York, 1970); his writing has been analyzed by Jacques Chaurand, "La Conception de l'histoire de Guibert de Nogent," *Cahiers de civilisation médiévale* 8 (1965): 381–95, and his scriptorium has been studied by Monique-Cécile Garand, "Le Scriptorium de Guibert de Nogent," *Scriptorium* 31 (1977): 3–29.

6. J. J. Duggan, "The Generation of the Episode of Baligant, Charlemagne's Dream and the Normans at Manzikert," *Romance Philology* 30 (1976): 59–82, esp. p. 70. It was, of course, in the vicinity of Poitiers that Charles Martel's famous battle against the Saracens took place. See the comments by J.-H. Roy and J. Deviosse in *La Bataille de Poitiers* (Paris, 1966), and the article by J. Waltz, "Carolingian Attitudes," pp. 33–40.

7. J. Verdon, "Une Source de la reconquête chrétienne en Espagne: la Chronique de Saint-Maixent," *Mélanges offerts à René Crozet* 1:273–82 and S. de Vajay, "Ramire II le Moine, roi d'Aragon, et Agnes de Poitou dans l'histoire et dans la légende," ibid. 2:727–50. The subject was treated earlier by P. Boissonade, "Les Relations des ducs d'Aquitaine, comtes de Poitiers, avec les états Chrétiens d'Aragon et de Navarre," *Bulletin de la Société des antiquaires de l'Ouest*, 3d ser., 10 (1934): 264–316.

8. A. C. Krey, "A Neglected Passage in the *Gesta* and Its Bearing on the Literature of the First Crusade," in *The Crusades and Other Essays Presented to Dana C. Munro by His Former Students*, ed. Louis J. Paetow (New York, 1928), pp. 57–78.

9. See the revisionist edition by J. H. Hill and L. L. Hill, *Peter Tudebode* (Philadelphia, 1974). For a summary of the other "eyewitness" accounts, see the Hills' introduction to *Raymond d'Aguilers: Historia Francorum Qui Ceperunt Iherusalem* (Philadelphia, 1968).

10. On the centrality of Jerusalem and the moral posture of the crusader, see Blake, "'Crusade' Idea," pp. 18, 24, 27. For the Crusade *excitatoria* see Palmer Throop, *Criticism of the Crusade: a Study of Public Opinion and Crusade Propaganda* (Amsterdam, 1940). On Saint Bernard and the Second Crusade, see Giles Constable, "The Second Crusade as Seen by Contemporaries," *Traditio* 9 (1953): 213–79, and "A Report on a Lost Sermon by St. Bernard on the Failure of the Second Crusade," in *Studies in Medieval Cistercian History*, no. 1, Cistercian Studies 13 (Kalamazoo, Mich., 1971), pp. 49–54. Varied aspects of Crusade propaganda were also emphasized by Jean Leclercq in "Pour l'histoire de l'encyclique de St. Bernard sur la croisade," *Etudes de civilisation médiévale*, pp. 479–90, and "St. Bernard's Attitude toward War," in *Studies in Medieval Cistercian History*, no. 2, ed. John Sommerfeldt, Cistercian Studies 24 (Kalamazoo, Mich., 1976), pp. 1–25.

11. Blake, "'Crusade' Idea," pp. 14–15. Duby observed that the diffusion of the ideology of peace made it possible for "the intellectuals of the church . . . to find spiritual justification for the violence implicit in the knight's calling"

("The History and Sociology of the Medieval West," *The Chivalrous Society*, p. 86).

12. E.g., Paul Deschamps, "Combats de cavalerie et episodes des Croisades dans les peintures murales du XII$^e$ et XIII$^e$ siècles," *Orientalia Christiana Periodica* 13 (1947): 454–74; Charles Daras, "L'Orientalisme dans l'art roman en Angoumois," *Bulletin et mémoires de la Société archéologique et historique de la Charente*, 1936, pp. 5–135; and, most recently, the dissertation by Carra Ferguson O'Meara, *The Iconography of the Façade of Saint-Gilles-du-Gard* (New York, 1977).

13. This observation parallels Norman F. Cantor's comments that the monastic orders lost "social utility" while a "new penetrating secularist spirit" emerged in European political life ("The Crisis of Western Monasticism, 1050–1130," *American Historical Review* 66 [1960]: 47–67). The citation reads in full: "And so, while the monastic order became spiritually embalmed behind the walls of its comfortable establishments, a new, grasping, penetrating, secularist spirit came to dominate European political life" (p. 67).

14. For the quotation and discussion of these matters see Erdmann, *Origin*, pp. 115 and 293–94. The possible "forgery" was considered by A. Gieysztor, "The Genesis of the Crusades: The Encyclical of Sergius IV (1009–1012)," tr. S. Harrison Thompson, *Medievalia et Humanistica* 5 (1948): 3–23 and 6 (1950): 3–34; the original text appears on pp. 33–34. More recently the document has been discussed by Jean Dufour, who would date it about a decade earlier than Gieysztor (*La Bibliothèque et le scriptorium de Moissac*, Centre de recherches d'histoire et de philologie 5, Hautes études médiévales et modernes 15 [Paris, 1972], pp. 101–2).

15. René Crozet, "Le Voyage d'Urbain II et ses négociations avec le clergé de France," *Revue historique* 179 (1937): 271–310. For a correction of the pervasive idea that Cluny was instrumental in the formulation of Crusade ideology, see the article by Etienne Delaruelle, "The Crusading Idea in Cluniac Literature of the Eleventh Century," in *Cluniac Monasticism in the Central Middle Ages*, ed. Noreen Hunt (Hamden, Conn., 1971), pp. 191–216. Aquitaine and its duke were openly at odds with Cluny, and with the papacy, during the early 1130s. See the remarks concerning Peter of Poitiers, secretary to Peter the Venerable in Giles Constable, *The Letters of Peter the Venerable*, 2 vols., Harvard Historical Studies 78 (Cambridge, Mass., 1967), 2:331–43.

16. Gieysztor, "The Genesis of the Crusades," p. 20. Additional material on the resistance to Cluny is in H. Claude, "Le Légat Gérard d'Angoulême et la résistance de l'abbaye de Baigne à la centralisation clunisienne," *Bulletin philologique et historique du Comité des travaux historiques et scientifiques* 2 (1971). In a recent paper, Giles Constable referred to Cluny at that time as "moving spiritually into the rearguard of monasticism" ("Cluniac Administration and Administrators in the Twelfth Century," in *Order and Innovation in the Middle Ages: Essays in Honor of Joseph R. Strayer*, ed. W. C. Jordan, B. McNab, T. F. Ruiz [Princeton, N.J., 1976], pp. 17–30; the quote is from the last page).

17. *Fulcher of Chartres, A History of the Expedition to Jerusalem*, trans. F. R. Ryan and ed. H. S. Fink (Knoxville, 1969), esp. the introduction. On the biblical propaganda for the crusades, see Aryeh Grabois, "The Hebraica Veritas and Jewish-Christian Intellectual Relations in the XIIth Century," *Speculum* 50 (1975): 613–34, esp. 613. Valuable also is Harold S. Fink, "Fulcher of Chartres, Historian of the Latin Kingdom of Jerusalem," *Studies in Medieval Culture* 5 (1975): 53–60.

18. The incumbent religious duty for the Muslim to fight against infidels is established in the Koran, sura 3. In addition, the hadith, companion volume to

NOTES TO PAGES 74–75

the Koran, identifies God as the sponsor of the soldier who, if he is not killed, returns with booty and, if he is, is taken to paradise (T. P. Hughes, *A Dictionary of Islam*, p. 244). Compare the remarks of James Brundage, "Holy War and the Medieval Lawyers," in Murphy, *The Holy War*, p. 103, and J. J. Saunders, "The Crusade as a Holy War," *Aspects of the Crusades*, University of Canterbury Publications 3 (Christchurch, N.Z., 1962), pp. 56–58. Saunders contrasts the Muslim goal of expansion in the *jihad* with the Christian one of recovery.

19. H. Adolf, "Christendom and Islam in the Middle Ages," *Speculum* 32 (1957): 103–55, esp. pp. 108–9.

20. Islam argues that Ishmael was prepared for sacrifice although neither son is actually named (Koran, sura 37). Meyer Schapiro discussed the unusual motif of the ram presented by an angel in scenes of the sacrifice in western France and associated them with the popularity of angelic representations in the art of that area in general. Schapiro also cited the comment by a ninth-century Arab chronicler that God had Gabriel descend holding a ram by the ear ("The Angel with the Ram in Abraham's Sacrifice: A Parallel in Western and Islamic Art," *Ars Islamica* 19 [1943]: 134–47). Abraham's sacrifice of Isaac is one of the first Old Testament events recounted in the preface to the *Psychomachia* and the event is illustrated in the Carolingian editions; see Woodruff, "Illustrated Prudentius," figs. 41, 49.

21. Southern, *Western Views of Islam*, pp. 11, 27, 38.

22. D. C. Munro, "The Western Attitude toward Islam during the Crusades," *Speculum* 6 (1931): 329–43.

23. James Kritzeck, "Moslem-Christian Understanding in Mediaeval Times," *Comparative Studies in Society and History* 4 (1962): 392–93.

24. The bibliography on the question is available in several places, most recently in Walter Cahn, *The Romanesque Wooden Doors of Auvergne* (New York, 1974), notes 46 and 68. See especially the early work by Emile Mâle, "Les Influences arabes sur l'art roman," *Revue des deux mondes* (1913) and "L'Espagne arabe et l'art roman," ibid. (1923). The latter article was reprinted in *Art et artistes du moyen âge* (Paris, 1927), pp. 39–88. Other works more directly relevant in this context are those by Elisa Maillard, "La Façade de l'église romane de Saint-Jouin-de-Marnes en Poitou," *Gazette des beaux-arts*, 5th ser., 9, pt. 1 (1924): 146–50, and A. Fikry, *L'Art roman du Puy et les influences islamiques* (Paris, 1934), with extensive bibliography, pp. 7–13. Fikry attributes similarities in decoration between Poitou, Catalonia, and Islam to the relations between these areas (p. 163). See also Daras, "L'Orientalisme," and J.-R. Colle, "Essais sur les influences mozarabes dans l'art roman du sud-ouest," *Revue de Saintonge et d'Aunis*, n.s., 2 (1956): 236–45; also Marcel Durliat, "L'Art dans le Velay," *Congrès archéologique* 133 (1975): 9–54, a critique of the "mirage oriental."

25. Daras linked this particular design element to the lack of a tympanum in Islamic architecture and in Aquitaine ("L'Orientalisme," pp. 104–5). The motif, of which there are more than a hundred examples, was considered previously by Pierre Héliot, "Les Portails polylobés de l'Aquitaine et des régions limitropes," *Bulletin monumental* 104 (1946): 63–89, and Daras returned to it in "Réflexions sur les influences arabes dans la décoration roman des églises charentaises," *Mélanges offerts a René Crozet* 2:751–53. More recently the form has been discussed in greater detail by E. Vergnolle, "Les Arcs polylobés dans le centre-ouest de la France," *L'Information d'histoire de l'art* 5 (1969): 217–23; she considers the south door at Cahors, completed in 1119, to be the first example of the use of the motif and emphasizes the Romanesque transformation of the polylobed arch elsewhere. Katherine Watson emphasizes the importance of this motif as evidence of Islamic influence on French Romanesque architecture,

123

citing in particular the lobed doorway at the church in Le Wast, founded in 1100 by the mother of the crusader Godfroy of Bouillon. Watson stresses the importance of the Andalusian impact on France during these critical years but stops short of suggesting specific motivation for the French appropriation of Islamic architectural elements ("French Romanesque and Islam: Influences from Al-Andalus on Architectural Decoration," *Art and Archaeology Research Papers* 2 (1972): 1–27.

26. For reference to objects brought back or sent to Europe from Byzantium in the earlier Middle Ages, see the remarks of Steven Runciman, "Byzantine Art and Western Medieval Taste," in *Byzantine Art: An European Art* (Athens, 1966), pp. 3–20. A series of documents provides an account of commerce, particularly in fabrics, between East and West at this early date; see Robert S. Lopez and Irving W. Raymond, *Medieval Trade in the Mediterranean World* (New York, 1955), pp. 19–48. For the survival of such objects see the representation of hunters on silk sleeve panels in the Victoria and Albert Museum in W. R. Lethaby, "Byzantine Silks in London Museums," *Burlington Magazine* 24 (1913–14): 138–46, no. 559, opposite p. 143; also, the study of some textile fragments that were probably inserted between the folios of a late eighth-century Carolingian manuscript at the time it was made; R. Pfister, "Les Tissus orientaux de la Bible de Theodulf," *Coptic Studies in Honor of Walter Ewing Crum, Bulletin of the Byzantine Institute* 2 (1950): 501–30.

27. Meyer Schapiro, "The South Transept Portal of St-Sernin at Toulouse," *Parnassus* 1 (1929): 22–23, and "The Sculpture of Souillac," *Romanesque Art,* p. 124.

28. Mendell, *Romanesque Sculpture of Saintonge,* p. 173.

29. Krautheimer, *Early Christian and Byzantine Architecture,* pp. 407–8.

30. Oleg Grabar, "Islamic Art and Byzantium," *Dumbarton Oaks Papers* 18 (1964): 67–88, and Richard Ettinghausen, *From Byzantium to Sassanian Iran and the Islamic World: Three Modes of Artistic Influence* (Leyden, 1972) for perspectives on this relationship. See also the discussion of the influence of Byzantium on Islam by Speros Vryonis Jr., "Byzantium and Islam, Seventh to Seventeenth Century," in *Byzantium: Its Internal History and Relation with the Muslim World* (London, 1971), pp. 205–40.

31. See the somewhat popular but very useful articles on some of these questions by John Beckwith, "The Influence of Islamic Art on Western Medieval Art," *Middle East Forum,* 1960, pp. 21–27, and *Apollo* 170 (1976): 270–81; also Dalu Jones, "Romanesque, East and West?" *Connoisseur* 191 (1976): 280–85, and the limited but pioneering article by A. J. Christie, "Islamic Minor Arts and Their Influence upon European Work," *The Legacy of Islam,* ed. Sir Thomas Arnold and Alfred Guillaume (Oxford, 1931), pp. 108–51. An important article, though one not particularly on art, is that by H. A. R. Gibb, "The Influence of Islamic Culture on Medieval Europe," *Bulletin of the John Rylands Library* 38 (1955): 82–98.

32. For the relationship between Muslims and European Christians, see especially Norman Daniel, *The Arabs and Medieval Europe* (London, 1975), pp. 167–91, and his more recent article "Learned and Popular Attitudes to the Arabs in the Middle Ages," *Journal of the Royal Asiatic Society of Great Britain and Ireland,* 1977, pp. 41–52; in addition, see the study by Rosalind Hill, "The Christian View of the Muslims at the Time of the First Crusade," in *The Eastern Mediterranean Lands in the Period of the Crusades,* ed. P. M. Holt (Warminster, 1977), pp. 1–8. Byzantine intellectual prejudice against the west in the twelfth century was described by Anthony Bryer, who characterized the societies as basically "incurious of each other" ("Cultural Relations between East and West

in the Twelfth Century," in *Relations between East and West in the Middle Ages,* Studies in Church History 10 (Cambridge, 1973), pp. 77–94, esp. pp. 87–88. On the differences between Christian East and West in the twelfth century, see Deno John Geanakoplos, *Interaction of the "Sibling" Byzantine and Western Cultures in the Middle Ages and Italian Renaissance* (New Haven and London, 1976), esp. chap. 3. Claude Cahen's summary of the background to the First Crusade draws attention to the differences between Byzantine Christians and western ones in the eleventh century ("An Introduction to the First Crusade," *Past and Present* 6 [1954]: 6–30).

33. In addition to the many papers of Oleg Grabar, now reformulated in *The Formation of Islamic Art* (New Haven, 1973), I have found invaluable the volumes by Marshall Hodgson, *The Venture of Islam* (Chicago, 1974), esp. 1:359–409 and 2:62–151. Montgomery Watts pointed out that certain Islamic mystics explained the *jihad* as a fight against the self; in other words, it was analogous to the moral struggle with which the Christian crusade was intimately allied ("Islamic Conceptions of the Holy War," in Murphy, *The Holy War,* p. 155). This theme is found in the hadith as well: "The greatest *jihad* is the fight against the evil passions of oneself," (*Al-Hadis,* 2:341). Muslim attitudes toward the Franks are described in Francesco Gabrieli, *Arab Historians of the Crusades* (Berkeley and Los Angeles, 1969; reprinted, 1978), pp. 73–84. Subtle class consciousness on the part of the Muslims is apparent in some of the remarks attributed to the commander of the Persian army by the French chronicler Peter Tudebode (*Historia,* p. 85). For the remarks on the characterization of Christians and Muslims in the *Song of Roland* see Auerbach, *Mimesis,* p. 102.

34. These are, of course, related to remnants of Roman monuments that survive in these regions; see above, chap. 2, note 42. Oleg Grabar studied the documentary evidence for such structures in a long article, "Earliest Islamic Commemorative Structures," *Ars Orientalis* 6 (1966): 7–46. See also the initial study by H. Thiersch, *Pharos in Antike, Islam und Occident* (Leipzig and Berlin, 1909), and the remarks by E. Diez on minarets in the *Encyclopedia of Islam* 3 (Leyden and London, 1936): 227–31.

A recent discussion of related material appears in G. A. Pugachenkova, "Little Known Monuments of the Balkh Area," *Art and Archaeology Research Papers* 13 (1978): 31–40.

35. The quote is from Monroe, "The Historical Arjuza," p. 69, where it is used exclusively in regard to the epic. See also his "Hispano-Arabic Poetry during the Almoravid Period: Theory and Practice," *Viator* 4 (1973): 65–98. On the controversy concerning direct contacts between Romance and Arabic poetry and on the southern orientation of Aquitainian language in general, see T. J. Gorton, "Arabic Words and Refrains in Provençal and Portuguese Poetry," *Medium Aevum* 45 (1976): 257–64, and M. Pfister, "La Langue de Guilhelm IX, Comte de Poitiers," *Cahiers de civilisation médiévale* 19 (1976): 91–113; also the earlier paper by Richard Lemay, "A Propos de l'origine arabe de l'art des troubadours," *Annales, économies-sociétés-civilisations* 21 (1966): 990–1011. The close relation between the French epic and the Hispano-Arab tradition has recently been emphasized by Álvaro Galmés de Fuentes, "Le 'Charroi de Nîmes' et la tradition arabe," pp. 125–37. The influence of Muslim customs and tactics on Christians was noted by Elena Lourie in "A Society Organized for War: Medieval Spain," *Past and Present* 35 (1966): 54–76.

36. Georges Duthuit and F. Volbach, *Art Byzantin* (Paris, n.d.), pl. 38C and pp. 50–51, and Oleg Grabar, *Sasanian Silver* (Ann Arbor, Mich., 1967) no. 18. On the relation between Arab and Byzantine society, see the paper by H. A. R. Gibb, "Arab-Byzantine Relations under the Umayyad Caliphate," *Dumbarton*

*Oaks Papers* 12 (1958): 21–33, and those by Oleg Grabar, "Islamic Art and Byzantium," Gustave E. von Grunebaum, "Parallelism, Convergence, and Influence in the Relations of Arab and Byzantine Philosophy, Literature, and Piety," and John Meyendorff, "Byzantine Views of Islam," all in *Dumbarton Oaks Papers* 18 (1964): 67–88, 89–112, and 113–32.

37. See the ivory plaque from Egypt now in the Louvre that is illustrated in M. Bernus, "Arts de l'Islam: Arts figuratifs," *Archeologia* 41 (1971): 26. There are illustrations also in John Beckwith, *Caskets from Cordoba* (London, 1960), and E. Kühnel, *Die islamischen Elfenbeinskulpturen VIII–XIII Jhr.* (Berlin, 1971), esp. no. 88, four narrow plaques, and idem, *The Minor Arts of Islam*, trans. Katherine Watson (Ithaca, N.Y., 1971), pp. 222–33. A casket now in Madrid was formerly in the Cathedral of Palencia in Spain; see the Arts Council of Great Britain, *The Arts of Islam* (London, 1976), no. 150, p. 153. On commerce in flat ivory boxes, see R. H. Pinder-Wilson and C. N. L. Brooke, "The Reliquary of St. Petroc and the Ivories of Norman Sicily," *Archaeologia* 104 (1973): 293. On trade in the Mediterranean in general, see the paper of N. A. Stillman, "The Eleventh Century Merchant House of Ibn 'Awkal," *Journal of the Economic and Social History of the Orient* 16 (1973): 15–88, and, on gold and fabrics particularly, Pierre Bonnassie, "La Monnaie et les échanges en Auvergne et Rouergue aux X$^e$ et XI$^e$ siècles d'après les sources hagiographiques," *Annales du Midi* 90 (1978): 275–88. Antonio Ubieto Arteta has written on the system of payments of both gold and precious objects by which Muslims living in Spain bought peace from the impoverished Christians on their borders ("L'Art roman en Aragon au XI$^e$ siècle," *L'Information d'histoire de l'art* 9, no. 4 [1964]: 158–60 and 230).

Related observations on exchanges between East and West through ceramics are made by Rudolf Schnyder, "Islamic Ceramics: A Source of Inspiration for Medieval European Art," *Islam and the Medieval West*, ed. Stanley Ferber (Binghamton, N.Y., 1975), pp. 27–38.

38. Grabar, *Formation*, chap. 6; idem, "The Visual Arts," in *The Cambridge History of Iran*, ed. J. A. Boyle (Cambridge, 1968), 5:626–58; idem, "Les Arts mineurs de l'Orient musulman à partir du milieu du XII$^e$ siècle," *Cahiers de civilisation médiévale* 11 (1968): 181–90; and idem, "Imperial and Urban Art in Islam: The Subject Matter of Fātimid Art," in *Colloque internationale sur l'histoire du Caire* (Cairo, 1969), pp. 173–89. Also important are the paper by Richard Ettinghausen, "The Flowering of Seljuk Art," *Metropolitan Museum Journal* 3 (1970): 113–31, and his seminal work, "The Bobrinski 'Kettle': Patron and Style of an Islamic Bronze," *Gazette des beaux-arts*, 6th ser., 24 (1943): 193–208.

39. H. A. R. Gibb, "The Influence of Islamic Culture," p. 98.

40. Thrupp, "Comparison of Cultures in the Middle Ages: Western Standards as Applied to Muslim Civilization in the Twelfth and Thirteenth Centuries," *Society and History*, ed. Raymond Grew and Nicholas H. Steneck (Ann Arbor, Mich., 1977), pp. 67–88.

41. Mendell, *Romanesque Sculpture in Saintonge*, p. 173.

42. Schapiro pointed out the use of Islamic ceramics in his early article "The South Transept Portal," pp. 22–23. They have been cited again more recently in the paper by Katherine Watson, "French Romanesque and Islam," pp. 4–5. On the Saint-Antonin and related carvings, see Linda Seidel, "Romanesque Capitals from the Vicinity of Narbonne," *Gesta* 11, no. 1 (1972): 34–45. Eva Baer has studied the harpy theme in detail, *Sphinxes and Harpies in Medieval Islamic Art*, Oriental Notes and Studies, no. 9 (Jerusalem, 1965).

43. M. S. Dimand, *A Handbook of Muhammedan Art*, 3d ed. (New York, 1958), p. 97, fig. 57. A similar carving of a horseman, called Saint George and said to have come from a now lost Romanesque house in Arles, appeared in a recent

publication as an example of twelfth-century French civilian art. (A. F., "Art roman en Provence," *Archéologia* 109 [1977]: 11 top).

44. Hugo Buchthal, "A Note on Islamic Enameled Metalwork and Its Influences in the Latin West," *Ars Islamica* 11–12 (1946): 195–98, and Ernest Rupin, *L'Oeuvre de Limoges* (Paris, 1890), pp. 543–50. J. Michael Rogers has noted that the Innsbruck dish discussed by Buchthal is, in fact, an *einzigartige Arbeit*, hardly typical for Islamic work and therefore an unlikely model for the Limoges examples (see Janine Sourdel-Thomine and Bertold Spuler, *Die Kunst des Islam*, Propyläen Kunstgeschichte 4 [Berlin, 1973], pp. 303–4 and pl. XLII; Robert Nelson kindly called this discussion to my attention). A still more recent paper on the Innsbruck enameled dish and other related objects localizes them in a workshop in northern Syria. See the article by G. Fehérvári, "Working in Metal: Mutual Influences between the Islamic World and the Medieval West," *Journal of the Royal Asiatic Society of Great Britain and Ireland*, 1977, pp. 3–16.

45. Compare Stanley Ferber's remarks on the contextual approach to the question of copies and influence in "Islamic Art and the Medieval West: The State of the Question," *Islam and the Medieval West* (Binghamton, N.Y., 1975), pp. 70–73.

46. The self-description comes from the twelfth-century pilgrim's guide (Jeanne Vielliard, *Le Guide du pèlerin de Saint-Jacques de Compostelle* [Mâcon, 1960], p. 18). The Muslim Usama's description of the orientalized Franks can be found in Gabrieli, *Arab Historians*, chap. 9, pp. 73–84. There are further remarks in Aharon Ben-Ami, *Social Change in a Hostile Environment* (Princeton, N.J., 1969), pp. 121–23. References to the manners and appearance of southern French nobles, in particular, abound in literature and contemporary western French documents refer to the presence of exotic foreigners for whom the word Saracen is employed. See J. Duquet, "Les Possessions de l'abbaye de Nouaillé en Aunis et Saintonge des environs de 940 à la fin du XIIᵉ siècle," *Bulletin de la Société des antiquaires de l'Ouest*, 4th ser., 9 (1967): 313–18, for the latter, and H. Platelle, "Le Problème du scandale: Les Nouvelles modes masculines aux XIᵉ et XIIᵉ siècles," *Revue belge de philologie et d'histoire* 53 (1975): 1071–96 for the former.

47. Mâle stressed throughout his paper, "L'Espagne arabe et l'art roman," the echo in Romanesque art of Islamic motifs. He attributed this phenomenon to pilgrimage traffic, in *Art et artistes du moyen âge* (Paris, 1927), p. 66, for example, and esp. the quote on p. 84.

48. Both the portability of small-scale objects as well as the availability of Saracenic work is suggested in Danielle Gaborit-Chopin, "Les Dessins d'Adémar de Chabannes," *Bulletin archéologique du comité des travaux historiques et scientifiques*, n.s., 3 (1967): 217, 214, 223. On varied levels of interpretation for the Islamic material, see Dorothy G. Shepherd, "Banquet and Hunt in Medieval Islamic Iconography," in *Gatherings in Honor of Dorothy E. Miner*, ed. U. E. McCracken, L. M. C. Randall, and R. H. Randall (Baltimore, 1974), pp. 79–92; the quote is from p. 84.

### Chapter Five

1. H. A. R. Gibb, "Arab-Byzantine Relations," pp. 221 and 232. The building was subsequently studied by Oleg Grabar, "The Umayyad Dome of the Rock," *Ars Orientalis* 3 (1959): 33–62.

2. I take exception here to older more traditional interpretations. In addition to those already cited, see the paper by Beatrice White, "Saracens and Crusaders: From Fact to Allegory," in *Medieval Literature and Civilization: Studies in Memory of G. N. Garmonsway*, ed. by D. A. Pearsall and R. A. Waldron (London,

1969), pp. 170–91. On the absence of Muslim hostility during and after the First and Second Crusade, see Emmanuel Sivan, *L'Islam et la croisade: Idéologie et propagande dans les réactions musulmanes aux croisades* (Paris, 1968).

3. R. W. Southern, *Western Views of Islam in the Middle Ages*, p. 38.

4. Richard Crocker has made illuminating remarks on the external foe as an extension of inner vices in "Early Crusade Songs," in Murphy, *The Holy War*, pp. 96–97. Richard Ettinghausen also characterized the "sporadic digestive process" by which eastern forms were absorbed by the West ("Muslim Decorative Arts and Painting: Their Nature and Impact on the Medieval West," in Ferber, *Islam and the Medieval West*, p. 21).

5. These three different aspects of the sculptured façades correspond to categories that have been suggested as stages in the development of religious culture: externalization, objectivization, and internalization (Peter L. Berger, *The Sacred Canopy: Elements of a Sociological Theory of Religion* [New York, 1967], p. 4).

# Bibliography

Adams, R. J. "The Virtues and Vices at Aulnay Re-examined." In *The Twelfth Century*. Edited by Bernard Levy and Sandro Sticca. Pp. 53–73. Binghamton, N.Y., 1975.

Adhémar, Jean. *Influences antiques dans l'art du moyen âge française*. Studies of the Warburg Institute 7. London, 1939.

Adolf, Helen. "Christendom and Islam in the Middle Ages." *Speculum* 32 (1957): 103–55.

Alexander, J. J. G. *Norman Illustration at Mont St. Michel, 966–1100*. Oxford, 1970.

*Al-Hadis: An English Translation and Commentary of Mishkat-al-Masabih*. Translated by Fazlul Karim. 2 vols. 2d ed. Calcutta, 1960.

Amy, R., et al. *L'Arc d'Orange*. 2 vols. *Gallia*, supplement 15. Paris, 1962.

Arcelin, Patrice. "Croyances et vie religieuse." *Dossiers de l'archéologie* 35 (1979): 99–107.

*Archives historiques du Poitou*. Poitiers, 1872–

Arnold, Sir Thomas, and Guillaume, Alfred, eds. *The Legacy of Islam*. Oxford, 1931.

Atil, Esin. *Ceramics from the World of Islam*. Freer Gallery of Art. Fiftieth Anniversary Exhibition, vol. 3. Washington, D.C., 1973.

Aubert, Marcel, ed. *L'Art roman en France*. Paris, 1961.

Auerbach, Erich. *Mimesis: The Representation of Reality in Western Literature*. Translated by Willard R. Trask. Princeton, N.J., 1953.

———. *Scenes from the Drama of European Literature*. New York, 1959.

Auzias, Léonce. *L'Aquitaine carolingienne*. Toulouse and Paris, 1937.

Babelon, Ernest. *Histoire de la gravure sur gemmes en France*. Paris, 1902.

Bachrach, Bernard S. "A Study in Feudal Politics: Relations between Fulk Nerra and William the Great, 995–1030." *Viator* 7 (1976): 111–22.

———. "Charles Martel, Mounted Shock Combat, the Stirrup and Feudalism." *Studies in Medieval and Renaissance History* 7 (1970): 47–75.

———. "Toward a Reappraisal of William the Great, Duke of Aquitaine (995–1030)." *Journal of Medieval History* 5 (1979): 11–21.

Baer, Eva. *Sphinxes and Harpies in Medieval Islamic Art*. Oriental Notes and Studies, no. 9. Jerusalem, 1965.

Bak, J. M. "Medieval Symbology of the State: Percy E. Schramm's Contribution." *Viator* 4 (1973): 33–63.

Barbier, Edmond. "Les Images, les reliques et la face supérieure de l'autel avant le XI$^e$ siècle." *Synthronon: Art et archéologie de la fin de l'antiquité et du moyen âge.* Pp. 199–207. Bibliothèque des cahiers archéologiques 2. Paris, 1968.

Battles, Ford Lewis. "Bernard of Clairvaux and the Moral Allegorical Tradition." In *Innovation in Medieval Literature: Essays to the Memory of Alan Markham.* Edited by D. Radcliff-Umstead. Pp. 1–19. Pittsburgh, 1971.

Bauer, Gerhard. *Claustrum Animae; Untersuchungen zur Geschichte der Metaphor vom Herzen als Kloster.* Munich, 1973–.

Beck, Alfons C. M. *Genien und Niken als Engel in der altchristlichen Kunst.* Düsseldorf, 1936.

Beckwith, John. *Caskets from Cordoba.* London, 1960.

———. *The Art of Constantinople.* London, 1961.

———. "The Influence of Islamic Art on Western Medieval Art." *Middle East Forum,* 1960, pp. 21–27 and *Apollo* 170 (1976): 270–81.

Becquet, Dom Jean. "La Paroisse en France aux XI$^e$ et XII$^e$ siècles." *Le Istituzioni ecclesiastiche della "Societas Christiana" dei secoli XI–XII: Diocesi, pieve e parrocchie,* pp. 199–229. Miscellanea del Centro di studi medioevali 8. Atti della sesta Settimana internazionale de studio, Mendola, 1974. Milan, 1977.

Beech, George T. *A Rural Society in Medieval France: The Gâtine of Poitou in the Eleventh and Twelfth Centuries.* Baltimore, 1964.

———. "A Feudal Document of Early Eleventh Century Poitou." *Mélanges offerts à René Crozet.* Edited by Pierre Gallais and Yves-J. Rioux. Vol. 1, pp. 203–13. Poitiers, 1966.

———. "Prosopography." In *Medieval Studies: An Introduction.* Edited by James M. Powell. Pp. 151–84. Syracuse, N.Y., 1976.

———. "The Origins of the Family of the Viscounts of Thouars." In *Etudes de civilisation médiévale, IX$^e$–XII$^e$ siècles: Mélanges offerts à Edmond-René Labande,* pp. 25–31. Poitiers, 1974.

Beeler, John. *Warfare in Feudal Europe.* Ithaca, N.Y., 1971.

Bellinger, Alfred R., and Berlincourt, Marjorie Alkins. *Victory as a Coin Type.* Numismatic Notes and Monographs 149. New York, 1962.

Belting, Hans. "Der Einhardsbogen." *Zeitschrift für Kunstgeschichte* 36 (1973): 93–121.

Ben-Ami, Aharon. *Social Change in a Hostile Environment.* Princeton, N.J., 1969.

Berefelt, Gunnar. *A Study of the Winged Angel: The Origin of the Motif.* Stockholm, 1968.

Berger, Blandine-Dominique. *Le Drame liturgique de Paques: Liturgie et théâtre.* Paris, 1976.

Berger, Peter L. *The Sacred Canopy: Elements of a Sociological Theory of Religion.* New York, 1967.

Bernhart, Max. *Handbuch zur Münzkunde der römischen Kaiserzeit.* 2 vols. Halle, 1926.

Blake, E. O. "The Formation of the 'Crusade' Idea." *Journal of Ecclesiastical History* 21 (1970): 11–31.

Bloomfield, Morton W. "Continuities and Discontinuities." *New Literary History* 10 (1979): 409–16.

Boase, T. S. R. "The Arts in the Latin Kingdom of Jerusalem." *Journal of the Warburg and Courtauld Institutes* 2 (1938–39): 1–21.

Boissonade, P. "Les Relations des ducs d'Aquitaine, comtes de Poitiers, avec les états Chrétiens d'Aragon et de Navarre." *Bulletin de la Société des antiquaires de l'Ouest*, 3d ser., 10 (1934): 264–316.

Bond, G. A. "Philological Comments on a New Edition of the First Troubadour." *Romance Philology* 30 (1976): 343–61.

———. "The Structure of the *Gap* of the Count of Poitiers." *Neuphilologische Mitteilungen* 79 (1978): 162–72.

Bonnassie, Pierre. "La Monnaie et les échanges en Auvergne et Rouergue aux X<sup>e</sup> et XI<sup>e</sup> siècles d'après les sources hagiographiques." *Annales du Midi* 90 (1978): 275–88.

Bonnaud-Delamare, Roger. "Les Institutions de paix en Aquitaine au XI<sup>e</sup> siècle." *Recueils de la Société Jean Bodin pour l'histoire comparative des institutions* 14 (1962): 415–87.

Bouffard, Pierre, "La psychomachie sur les portails romans de la Saintonge." *Zeitschrift für schweizerische Archäologie und Kunstgeschichte* 22 (1962): 19–21.

Bowden, Betty. "The Art of Courtly Copulation." *Medievalia et Humanistica*, n.s., 9 (1979): 67–85.

Brault, Gérard. "Le Thème de la Mort dans la Chanson de Roland," *Société Rencesvals, 4<sup>e</sup> Congrès international, Actes et mémoires*, pp. 220–36. Studia romanica 14. Heidelberg, 1969.

———. "The French Chansons de Geste." In *Heroic Epic and Saga*. Edited by Felix J. Oinas. Bloomington, Ind., 1978.

Braunfels, Wolfgang. *Monasteries of Western Europe: The Architecture of the Orders*. 3d ed. Princeton, N.J., 1972.

Braunfels, Wolfgang, ed. *Karl der Grosse: Lebenswerk und Nachleben*. 5 vols. Düsseldorf, 1965–68.

Breglia, Laura. *Roman Imperial Coins: Their Art and Their Technique*. Translated by Peter Green. London, 1968.

Brendel, Otto J. *Prolegomena to the Study of Roman Art*. New Haven, Conn., 1979.

Brilliant, Richard. *Roman Art*. New York, 1974.

Brisset, F. "Guillaume le Grand et l'église." *Bulletin de la Société des antiquaires de l'Ouest*, 4th ser., 11 (1972): 441–60.

———. "Etude comparée des modillons des galeries de circulation de l'église Ste-Radegonde et de la cathédrale St-Pierre de Poitiers." *Bulletin de la Société des antiquaires de l'Ouest*, 4th ser., 14 (1978): 483–510.

Brooke, Christopher. *The Twelfth Century Renaissance*. New York, 1970.

Bruhat, L. *Le Monachisme en Saintonge*. La Rochelle, 1907.

Brumbaugh, Robert S. "The Voynich 'Roger Bacon' Cipher Manuscript: Deciphered Maps of Stars." *Journal of the Warburg and Courtauld Institutes* 39 (1976): 139–50.

Brundage, James A. *The Crusades: A Documentary Survey*. Milwaukee, 1962.

Bryer, Anthony. "Cultural Relations between East and West in the Twelfth Century." In *Relations between East and West in the Middle Ages*. Edited by Derek Baker. Pp. 77–94. Studies in Church History 10. Cambridge, 1973.

Buchthal, Hugo. "A Note on Enameled Metalwork and Its Influences in the Latin West." *Ars Islamica* 11–12 (1946): 195–98.

Buddensieg, Tilmann. "Die Basler Altartafel Heinrichs II." *Wallraf-Richartz Jahrbuch* 19 (1957): 133–92.

Bullough, Donald. "'Imagines Regum' and Their Significance in the Early Medieval West." In *Studies in Memory of David Talbot Rice*. Edited by Giles Robertson and George Henderson. Pp. 223–76. Edinburgh, 1975.

———. "Roman Books and Carolingian *Renovatio*." In *Renaissance and Renewal in Christian History*. Edited by Derek Baker. Pp. 23–50. Studies in Church History 14. Cambridge, 1977.

Burnett, C. S. F. "A Group of Arabic-Latin Translators Working in Northern Spain in the Mid-Twelfth Century." *Journal of the Royal Asiatic Society of Great Britain and Ireland*, 1977, pp. 64–108.

Cahen, Claude. "An Introduction to the First Crusade." *Past and Present* 6 (1954): 6–30.

Cahn, Walter. "Architectural Draftsmanship in Twelfth Century Paris." *Gesta* 15 (1976): 247–54.

———. "The Artist as Outlaw and *Apparatchik*: Freedom and Constraint in the Interpretation of Medieval Art." In Stephen K. Scher, *The Renaissance of the Twelfth Century*, pp. 10–14. Providence, R.I., 1969.

———. *The Romanesque Wooden Doors of Auvergne*. New York, 1974.

Calin, William. *The Old French Epic of Revolt*. Geneva, 1962.

Calkins, Robert. *Monuments of Medieval Art*. New York, 1979.

Callahan, Daniel F. "Adémar de Chabannes et la Paix de Dieu." *Annales du Midi* 89 (1977): 21–43.

Campbell, M. L. "'Scribe faber lima': A Crozier in Florence Reconsidered." *Burlington Magazine* 121 (1979): 364–69.

Cantor, Norman F. "The Crisis of Western Monastacism, 1050–1130." *American Historical Review* 66 (1960): 47–67.

Carlsson, Frans. *The Iconography of Tectonics in Romanesque Art*. Hässleholm, 1976.

Cate, James Lea. "A Gay Crusader." *Byzantion* 16 (1942–43): 503–26.

Caumont, Arcisse de. "Essai sur l'architecture religieuse du moyen âge." *Mémoires de la Société des antiquaires de Normandie* 1 (1824): 535–677.

———. *Histoire sommaire de l'architecture religieuse, civile et militaire au moyen âge*. 2d ed. Caen, 1838.

Champeaux, Gérard de, and Sterckx, Sébastian. *Introduction au Monde des symboles*. La-Pierre-qui-Vire, 1966.

Chappuis, R. "Utilisation du trace ovale dans l'architecture des églises romanes." *Bulletin monumental* 134 (1976): 7–36.

*Charlemagne: Oeuvre, Rayonnement et Survivances*. Dixième Exposition sous les auspices du Conseil de l'Europe. Aix-la-Chapelle, 1965.

Charles-Picard, Gilbert. *Les Trophées romains: Contribution à l'histoire de la religion et de l'art triomphal de Rome*. Bibliothèque des écoles françaises d'Athènes et de Rome 187. Paris, 1957.

Chaurand, Jacques. "La Conception de l'histoire de Guibert de Nogent." *Cahiers de civilisation médiévale* 8 (1965): 381–95.

Chavanon, Jules. *Adémar de Chabannes: Chronique*. Paris, 1897.

Chenu, M.-D. *Nature, Man, and Society in the Twelfth Century*. Edited and translated by Jerome Taylor and Lester K. Little. Chicago, 1968.

Cheyette, F. L., ed. *Lordship and Community in Medieval France*. New York, 1968.

Christe, Yves. "A Propos du décor absidial de Saint-Jean du Latran à Rome." *Cahiers archéologiques* 20 (1970): 197–206.

———. "La Colonne d'Arcadius, Sainte-Pudentienne, l'arc d'Eginhard et le portail de Ripoll." *Cahiers archéologiques* 21 (1971): 31–42.

———. "Le Portail de Beaulieu: Etude iconographique et stylistique." *Bulletin archéologique*, n.s., 6 (1970): 57–76.

———. *Les Grands portails romans.* Geneva, 1969.

———. "Les Représentations médiévales d'Apoc. IV–V en visions de seconde parousie: Origines, textes et contexte." *Cahiers archéologiques* 23 (1974): 61–72.

Christie, A. J. "Islamic Minor Arts and Their Influence upon European Work." In *The Legacy of Islam.* Edited by Sir Thomas Arnold and Alfred Guillaume. Pp. 108–51. Oxford, 1931.

Cocke, Thomas H. "Pre-Nineteenth-Century Attitudes in England to Romanesque Architecture." *Journal of the British Archeological Society*, 3d ser., 36 (1973): 72–97.

Colle, J.-R. "Essais sur les influences mozarabes dans l'art roman du sud-ouest." *Revue de Saintonge et d'Aunis*, n.s., 2 (1956): 236–45.

Collins, Fletcher, Jr. *The Production of Medieval Church Music-Drama.* Charlottesville, Va., 1972.

Conant, Kenneth. *Cluny: Les Eglises et la maison du chef d'ordre.* Cambridge, Mass., 1968.

*Congrès archéologique de France: Poitiers* 70 (1903).

*Congrès archéologique de France: Angoulême* 79 (2 vols.; 1912).

*Congrès archéologique de France: Bordeaux, Bayonne* 102 (1939).

*Congrès archéologique de France: Poitiers* 109 (1951).

*Congrès archéologique de France: La Rochelle* 114 (1956).

Constable, Giles. "A Report on a Lost Sermon by St. Bernard on the Failure of the Second Crusade." In *Studies in Medieval Cistercian History*, no. 1, pp. 49–54. Cistercian Studies 13. Kalamazoo, Mich., 1971.

———. "Monastic Possession of Churches and 'Spiritualia' in the Age of Reform." In *Il Monachesimo e la Riforma Ecclesiastica, 1049–1122*, pp. 304–31. Atti della quarta Settimana internazionale di studio, Mendola, 1968. Milan, 1971.

———. *The Letters of Peter the Venerable.* 2 vols. Harvard Historical Studies 78. Cambridge, Mass., 1967.

———. "The Second Crusade as Seen by Contemporaries." *Traditio* 9 (1953): 213–79.

Corcia, Joseph di. "*Bourg, Bourgeois, Bourgeois de Paris* from the Eleventh to the Eighteenth Century." *Journal of Modern History* 50 (1978): 207–33.

Coulson, C. H. "Fortresses and Social Responsibility in Late Carolingian France." *Zeitschrift für Archäologie des Mittelalters* 4 (1976): 29–36.

Cowdrey, H. E. J. *The Cluniacs and the Gregorian Reform.* Oxford, 1970.

———. "Pope Urban II's Preaching of the First Crusade." *History* 55 (1970): 177–88.

Crozet, René. "Aspects sociaux de l'art du moyen-âge en Poitou." *Bulletin de la Société des antiquaires de l'Ouest*, 4th ser., 3 (1955): 7–19.

———. "De l'art romain à l'art roman, recherches sur quelques ordonnances architecturales." In *Actes du XVIIᵐᵉ Congrès international d'histoire de l'art, Amsterdam 1952*, pp. 107–12. The Hague, 1955.

————. *L'Art roman en Poitou.* Paris, 1948.

————. *L'Art roman en Saintonge.* Paris, 1971.

————. "Les Etablissements clunisiens en Saintonge." *Annales du Midi* 75 (1963): 575–81.

————. "Les Lanternes des morts." *Bulletin de la Société des antiquaires de l'Ouest,* 3d ser., 13 (1943): 115–44.

————. "Le Voyage d'Urbain II et ses négociations avec le clergé de France." *Revue historique* 179 (1937): 271–310.

————. "Recherches sur les sites de châteaux et de lieux fortifiés en Haut-Poitou au moyen-âge." *Bulletin de la Société archéologique de l'Ouest,* 4th ser., 11 (1971): 187–217.

————. "Survivances antiques dans le décor roman de Poitou, de l'Angoumois et la Saintonge." *Bulletin monumental* 114 (1956): 7–33.

Curtius, Ernst Robert. *European Literature and the Latin Middle Ages.* Translated by Willard R. Trask. New York, 1953.

Dangibeaud, Charles. "L'Ecole de sculpture romane saintongeaise." *Bulletin archéologique du Comité des travaux historiques et scientifiques,* 1910, pp. 22–62.

Daniel, Norman. *The Arabs and Medieval Europe.* London, 1975.

————. "Learned and Popular Attitudes to the Arabs in the Middle Ages." *Journal of the Royal Asiatic Society of Great Britain and Ireland,* 1977, pp. 41–52.

Daras, Charles. *Angoumois roman.* La-Pierre-qui-Vire, 1961.

————. *La Cathédrale d'Angoulême: Chef-d'oeuvre monumental de Girard II.* Angoulême, 1942.

————. "La Cathédrale d'Angoulême." *Bulletins et mémoires de la Société archéologique et historique de la Charente,* 1941, pp. 11–176.

————. "Les Cavaliers de La Rochette." *Mémoires de la Société archéologique et historique de la Charente,* 1957, pp. 1–5.

————. "Les Eglises au onzième siècle en Charente." *Bulletin de la Société archéologique de l'Ouest,* 4th ser., 5 (1959): 177–213.

————. "L'Evolution de l'architecture aux façades des églises romanes ornées d'arcatures en Charente: Leur origine, leur filiation." *Bulletin monumental* 119 (1961): 121–38.

————. "L'Orientalisme dans l'art roman en Angoumois." *Bulletins et mémoires de la Société archéologique et historique de la Charente,* 1936, pp. 5–135.

Dawson, Christopher. *Medieval Essays.* London, 1953.

Déer, Joseph. "Ein Doppelbildnis Karls des Grosse." In *Wandlungen christlicher Kunst im Mittelalter,* pp. 103–37. Forschungen zur Kunstgeschichte und christlichen Archäologie 2. Baden-Baden, 1953.

Delaruelle, Etienne. "Les Saints militaires de la région de Toulouse." *Cahiers de Fanjeux* 4 (1969): 173–83.

————. "The Crusading Idea in Cluniac Literature of the Eleventh Century." In *Cluniac Monasticism in the Central Middle Ages.* Edited by Noreen Hunt. Pp. 191–216. Hamden, Conn., 1971.

Delehaye, Hippolyte. *Les Origines du culte des martyres.* Subsidia hagiographica 20. Brussels, 1933.

————. "Le Témoignage des martyrologes." *Analecta Bollandiana* 26 (1907): 78–99.

————. *Sanctus.* Subsidia hagiographica 17. Brussels, 1928.

Demay, G. *Des Pierres gravées employées dans les sceaux du moyen âge*. Paris, 1877.

Demus, Otto. *The Church of San Marco in Venice: History, Architecture, Sculpture*. Washington, D.C., 1960.

Dereine, Charles. "Vie commune, règle de Saint Augustin et chanoines réguliers." *Revue d'histoire écclesiastique* 41 (1946): 365–406.

Deschamps, Paul. "Combats de cavalerie et episodes des Croisades dans les peintures murales du XII ͤ et XIIIͤ siècles." *Orientalia Christiana Periodica* 13 (1947): 454–74.

———. "Etude sur la naissance de la sculpture en France à l'époque romane." *Bulletin monumental* 84 (1925): 5–98.

———. "Le Combat des vertus et des vices sur les portails romans de la Saintonge et de Poitou." *Congrès archéologique* 79² (1912): 309–24.

Deshoulières, F. "La Théorie d'Eugène Lefèvre-Pontalis sur les écoles romanes: Ecole du sud-ouest." *Bulletin monumental* 85 (1926): 5–22.

*De vita Caroli Magni et Rolandi*. Florence, 1822.

Dickman, A.-J. *Le Rôle du surnaturel dans les Chansons de Geste*. 1926. Reprint, Geneva, 1974.

Dickinson, J. C. *The Origins of the Austin Canons and Their Introduction into England*. London, 1950.

*Dictionnaire des églises de France*. Vol. 3. Tours, 1967.

Dillange, Michel. *Vendée romane: Bas-Poitou roman*. La-Pierre-qui-Vire, 1976.

Dimand, M. S. *A Handbook of Muhammedan Art*. 3d ed. New York, 1958.

Dronke, Peter. "Guillaume IX and Courtoisie." *Romanische Forschungen* 73 (1961): 327–38.

———. "Learned Lyric and Popular Ballad in the early Middle Ages." *Studi Medievali*, 3d ser., 17 (1976): 1–40.

———. "Peter of Blois and Poetry at the Court of Henry II." *Medieval Studies* 38 (1976): 185–235.

———. "The Interpretation of the Ripoll Love-Songs." *Romance Philology* 33 (1979): 14–42.

———. "The Rise of the Medieval Fabliau: Latin and Vernacular Evidence." *Romanische Forschungen* 85 (1973): 275–97.

Dubourg-Noves, Pierre. *Guyenne romane*. La-Pierre-qui-Vire, 1969.

———. "Remarques sur les portails romans à fronton de l'ouest de la France." *Cahiers de civilisation médiévale* 17 (1974): 25–39.

Duby, George. *The Chivalrous Society*. Translated by Cynthia Postan. Berkeley and Los Angeles, 1977.

Dufour, Jean. *La Bibliothèque et le scriptorium de Moissac*. Centre de recherches d'histoire et de philologie 5. Hautes études médiévales et modernes 15. Paris, 1972.

Duggan, J. J. "The Generation of the Episode of Baligant, Charlemagne's Dream and the Normans at Manzikert." *Romance Philology* 30 (1976): 59–82.

———. *The Song of Roland: Formulaic Style and Poetic Craft*. Berkeley and Los Angeles, 1973.

Durand-Lefébvre, M. *Art gallo-romain et sculpture romane*. Paris, 1937.

Durliat, Marcel. "L'Art dans le Velay." *Congrès archéologique* 133 (1975): 9–54.

———. *Haut-Languedoc roman*. La-Pierre-qui-Vire, 1978.

Earl, James W. "Typology and Iconographic Style in Early Medieval Hagiography." *Studies in the Literary Imagination* 7 (1975): 15–46.

Elbern, Victor. "Der eucharistische Kelch im frühen Mittelalter." *Zeitschrift des deutschen Vereins für Kunstwissenschaft* 17 (1963): 1–76, 117–88.

Eliade, Mircea. *Myths, Rites, Symbols: A Mircea Eliade Reader*. Edited by Wendell E. Beane and William G. Doty. 2 vols. New York, 1976.

——. *The Sacred and the Profane*. New York, 1959.

Emden, W. G. van. "Another Look at Charlemagne's Dreams in the *Chanson de Roland*." *French Studies* 28 (1974): 257–71.

Erdmann, Carl. *The Origin of the Idea of Crusade*. Translated by Marshall W. Baldwin and Walter Goffart. Princeton, N.J., 1977.

Erlande-Brandenburg, Alain. "Iconographie de Cluny III." *Bulletin monumental* 126 (1968): 293–322.

Espérandieu, E. "L'Arc de Triomphe de Saintes." *Revue poitevine et santongeaise* 46 (1887): 289–307.

Estey, F. N. "Charlemagne's Silver Celestial Table." *Speculum* 18 (1943): 112–17.

Etienne, Robert, and Rachet, Marguerite. "Les monnaies romaines de Garonne." *Archéologia* 48 (1972): 20–27.

Ettinghausen, Richard. *From Byzantium to Sassanian Iran and the Islamic World: Three Modes of Artistic Influence*. Leyden, 1972.

——. "The Bobrinski 'Kettle': Patron and Style of an Islamic Bronze." *Gazette des beaux-arts*, 6th ser., 24 (1943): 193–208.

——. "The Flowering of Seljuk Art." *Metropolitan Museum Journal* 3 (1970): 113–31.

*Etudes de civilisation médiévale, IX<sup>e</sup>–XII<sup>e</sup> siècles: Mélanges offerts à Edmond-René Labande*. Poitiers, 1974.

Evans, Joan. *Cluniac Art of the Romanesque Period*. Cambridge, 1950.

Evergates, Theodore. "Historiography and Sociology in Early Feudal Society: The Case of Hariulf and the 'Milites' of St-Riquier." *Viator* 6 (1975): 35–49.

Ewald, Wilhelm. *Siegekunde: Handbuch der mittelalterlichen und neueren Geschichte*. Edited by G. von Below and F. Meinecke. Pt. 4: Hilfswissenschaften und Altertümer. Munich, 1914.

Eydoux, Henri-Paul. *La France antique*. Paris, 1962.

Eygun, François. *Art des pays d'Ouest*. Paris, 1965.

——. *Saintonge roman*. La-Pierre-qui-Vire, 1970.

——. *Sigillographie du Poitou*. Poitiers, 1938.

——. "Un thème iconographique commun aux églises romanes de Parthenay et aux sceaux de ses seigneurs." *Bulletin archéologique*, 1927, pp. 387–90.

Farnham, Fern. "Romanesque Design in the Song of Roland." *Romance Philology* 18, no. 2 (1964): 143–64.

Fayolle, L. "Origine et destination des lanternes des morts." *Bulletin de la Société des antiquaires de l'Ouest*, 3d ser., 13 (1943): 144–55.

Fehérvári, G. "Working in Metal: Mutal influences between the Islamic World and the Medieval West." *Journal of the Royal Asiatic Society of Great Britain and Ireland*, 1977, pp. 3–16.

Fel, K. "Die Niken und die Engel in der altchristichen Kunst." *Römische Quartalschrift für christliche Altertumskunde und für Kirchengeschichte* 26 (1912): 3–25.

Fels, Etienne, and Reinhardt, Hans. "Etude sur les églises-porches carolin-giennes et leur survivances dans l'art roman." *Bulletin monumental* 92 (1933): 331–65; 96 (1937): 425–69.

Ferber, Stanley. "Crucifixion Iconography in a Group of Carolingian Ivory Plaques." *Art Bulletin* 48 (1966): 323–33.

Ferber, Stanley, ed. *Islam and the Medieval West.* Binghamton, N.Y., 1975.

Ferrante, Joan M. *Woman as Image in Medieval Literature from the Twelfth Century to Dante.* New York, 1975.

Février, Paul-Albert. "The Origin and Growth of the Cities of Southern Gaul to the Third Century A.D." *Journal of Roman Studies* 63 (1973): 1–28.

Fikry, A. *L'Art roman du Puy et les influences islamiques.* Paris, 1934.

Fillitz, H. "Die Elfenbeinreliefs zur Zeit Kaiser Karls des Grossen." *Aachener Kunstblätter* 32 (1966): 14–45.

Fink, H. S. "Fulcher of Chartres: Historian of the Latin Kingdom of Jerusalem." *Studies in Medieval Culture* 5 (1975): 53–60.

Fletcher, Angus J. S. *Allegory: The Theory of a Symbolic Mode.* Ithaca, N.Y., 1964.

Flori, J. "Chevalerie et liturgie." *Le Moyen âge* 84 (1978): 247–78, 409–42.

Focillon, Henri. *The Art of the West in the Middle Ages.* Edited by Jean Bony and translated by Donald King. 2 vols. London, 1963.

Folz, Robert. *Le Souvenir et la légende de Charlemagne dans l'empire germanique médiévale.* Publications de l'Université de Dijon, n.s., 7. Paris, 1950.

Formigé, Jules. *Le Trophée des Alpes (La Turbie). Gallia,* supplement 2. Paris, 1949.

Forsyth, George H., Jr. "St. Martin's at Angers and the Evolution of Early Medieval Church Towers." *Art Bulletin* 32 (1950): 308–18.

Forsyth, Ilene H. "The Theme of Cockfighting in Burgundian Romanesque Sculpture." *Speculum* 53 (1978): 252–83.

Francastel, Pierre. "A Propos des églises-porches: Du carolingien au roman." *Mélanges d'histoire du moyen-âge: Dédiés à la mémoire de Louis Halphen,* pp. 247–57. Paris, 1951.

Frappier, J. "Réflexions sur les rapports des chansons de geste et de l'histoire." *Zeitschrift für romanische Philologie* 73 (1957): 1–19.

Frazer, Alfred. "The Pyre of Faustina Senior." *Studies in Classical Art and Archaeology: A Tribute to Peter Heinrich von Blanckenhagen.* Edited by Günter Kopcke and Mary B. Moore, pp. 271–74. Locust Valley, N.Y., 1979.

Frazer, Margaret English. "Church Doors and the Gates of Paradise: Byzantine Bronze Doors in Italy." *Dumbarton Oaks Papers* 27 (1973): 145–62.

————. "Hades Stabbed by the Cross of Christ." *Metropolitan Museum Journal* 9 (1974): 153–61.

Freeman, Ann. "Theodulf of Orleans and the *Libri Carolini.*" *Speculum* 32 (1957): 663–705.

Frolow, A. *Les Reliquaires de la Vraie Croix.* Paris, 1965.

Frye, Northrop. *The Secular Scripture.* Cambridge, Mass., 1976.

*Fulcher of Chartres: A History of the Expedition to Jerusalem.* Edited by H. S. Fink and translated by F. R. Ryan. Knoxville, 1969.

Gaborit-Chopin, Danielle. "Les Dessins d'Adémar de Chabannes." *Bulletin archéologique du comité des travaux historiques et scientifiques,* n.s., 3 (1967): 163–225.

————. "Les Arts précieux au IX<sup>e</sup> siècle." *Dossiers de l'archéologie* 30 (1978): 50–65.

Gabrieli, Francesco. *Arab Historians of the Crusades.* Berkeley and Los Angeles, 1978.

Gaillard, Georges, et al. *Rouergue roman.* La-Pierre-qui-Vire, 1963.

Galavaris, George. *Bread and the Liturgy: The Symbolism of Early Christian and Byzantine Bread Stamps.* Madison, 1970.

Galmés de Fuentes, Álvaro. "Le 'Charroi de Nîmes' et la tradition arabe." *Cahiers de civilisation médiévale* 22 (1979): 125–37.

Ganshof, François L. *The Carolingians and the Frankish Monarchy: Studies in Carolingian History.* Translated by Janet Sondheimer. Ithaca, N.Y., 1971.

Garaud, Marcel. "L'Aquitaine carolingienne et l'histoire du Poitou à propos d'un livre récent." *Revue historique* 186 (1939): 78–84.

————. *Les Châtelains de Poitou et l'avènement du régime féodale, XI<sup>e</sup> et XII<sup>e</sup> siècle.* Poitiers, 1967.

————. "Observations sur les vicissitudes de la propriété écclesiastique dans le diocèse de Poitiers du IX<sup>e</sup> au XIII<sup>e</sup> siècle." *Bulletin de la Société des antiquaires de l'Ouest,* 4th ser., 5 (1960): 357–77.

————. "Recherches sur les défrichements dans la Gâtine poitevine aux XI<sup>e</sup> et XII<sup>e</sup> siècles." *Bulletin de la Société des antiquaires de l'Ouest,* 4th ser., 9 (1967): 11–27.

————. "L'Organisation administrative du Comté de Poitou au X<sup>e</sup> siècle et l'avènement des Châtelains et des Châtellenies." *Bulletin de la Société des antiquaires de l'Ouest,* 4th ser., 2 (1953): 411–54.

Gardelles, Jacques. "Recherches sur les origines des façades à étages d'arcatures des églises médiévales." *Bulletin monumental* 136 (1978): 113–33.

Gauthier, Marie-Madeleine. "Art, savoir-faire médiéval et laboratoire moderne, à propos de l'effigie funéraire de Geoffroy Plantagenêt." *Académie des inscriptions et belles-lettres: Comptes rendus,* 1979, pp. 105–31.

————. "L'Or et l'église au moyen âge." *Revue de l'art* 26 (1974): 64–76.

Geanakoplos, Deno John. *Interaction of the "Sibling" Byzantine and Western Cultures in the Middle Ages and Italian Renaissance.* New Haven and London, 1976.

Genicot, Léopold. "The Nobility in Medieval *Francia*: Continuity, Break or Evolution?" In *Lordship and Community in Medieval Europe.* Edited by F. L. Cheyette. Pp. 128–36. New York, 1968.

George, J., and Guérin-Boutard, A. *Les Eglises romanes de l'ancien diocèse d'Angoulême.* Paris, 1928.

Gerke, Friedrich. *Der Tischaltar des Bernard Gilduin in Saint-Sernin in Toulouse.* Akademie der Wissenschaften und der Literatur in Mainz, Abhandlungen der geistes- und sozialwissenschaftlichen Klasse, 8. Wiesbaden, 1958.

Gibb, H. A. R. "Arab-Byzantine Relations under the Umayyad Caliphate." *Dumbarton Oaks Papers* 12 (1958): 218–33.

————. "The Influence of Islamic Culture on Medieval Europe." *Bulletin of the John Rylands Library* 38 (1955): 82–98.

Gieysztor, A. "The Genesis of the Crusades: The Encyclical of Sergius IV (1009–1012)." Translated by S. Harrison Thompson. *Medievalia et Humanistica* 5 (1948): 3–23; 6 (1950): 3–34.

Gilman, S. "The Poetry of the 'Poema' and the Music of the 'Cantar.'" *Philological Quarterly* 51 (1972): 1–11.

Goldin, Frederick. *The Mirror of Narcissus in the Courtly Love Lyric*. Ithaca, N.Y., 1967.

Goldschmidt, Adolph. *Die Bronzetüren von Nowgorod und Gnesen*. Marburg, 1932.

Gorton, T. J. "Arabic Words and Refrains in Provençal and Portuguese Poetry." *Medium Aevum* 45 (1976): 257–64.

Gousset, M. T. "La Représentation de la Jérusalem céleste à l'époque carolingienne." *Cahiers archéologiques* 23 (1974): 47–60.

Grabar, André. *Ampoulles de terre sainte*. Paris, 1958.

———. *Christian Iconography: A Study of Its Origins*. Bollingen Series 35. A. W. Mellon Lectures in the Fine Arts 10. Princeton, N.J., 1968.

———. *L'Empéreur dans l'art byzantin: Recherches sur l'art officiel de l'empire d'Orient*. Publications de la Faculté des lettres de l'Université de Strasbourg, fasc. 75. Paris, 1936.

———. "L'Etude des fresques romanes." *Cahiers archéologiques* 2 (1947): 163–77.

———. *Martyrium: Recherches sur le culte des reliques et l'art chrétien antique*. 2 vols. [Paris], 1946.

———. "Observations sur l'arc de triomphe de la Croix dit Arc d'Eginhard, et sur d'autres bases de la Croix." *Cahiers archéologiques* 27 (1978): 61–83.

Grabar, Oleg. "Earliest Islamic Commemorative Structures." *Ars Orientalis* 6 (1966): 7–46.

———. "Islamic Art and Byzantium." *Dumbarton Oaks Papers* 18 (1964): 67–88.

———. *The Formation of Islamic Art*. New Haven, Conn., 1973.

———. "Les Arts mineurs de l'Orient musulman à partir du milieu du XIIe siècle." *Cahiers de civilisation médiévale* 11 (1968): 181–90.

———. "The Visual Arts." In *The Cambridge History of Iran*, 5:626–58. Edited by J. A. Boyle. Cambridge, 1968.

———. "Imperial and Urban Art in Islam: The Subject Matter of Fatimid Art." In *Colloque internationale sur l'histoire du Caire*, pp. 173–89. Cairo, 1969.

———. *Sasanian Silver*. Ann Arbor, 1967.

———. "The Umayyad Dome of the Rock." *Ars Orientalis* 3 (1959): 33–62.

Grabois, Aryeh. "The Hebraica Veritas and Jewish-Christian Intellectual Relations in the XIIth Century." *Speculum* 50 (1975): 613–34.

Green, D. H. *The Millstätter Exodus: A Crusading Epic*. Cambridge, 1966.

Greenstone, Julius H. "The Turkoman Defeat at Cairo." *American Journal of Semitic Languages and Literatures* 22 (1905–6): 144–75.

Grimme, Ernst Gunther. "Novus Constantinus." *Aachener Kunstblätter* 22 (1961): 7–20.

Grunebaum, Gustave E. von. "Parallelism, Convergence, and Influence in the Relations of Arab and Byzantine Philosophy, Literature, and Piety." *Dumbarton Oaks Papers* 18 (1964): 89–112.

Guest, Grace D., and Ettinghausen, Richard. "The Iconography of a Kāshān Lustre Plate." *Ars Orientalis* 4 (1961): 25–64.

Guillaume, Alfred. *The Traditions of Islam*. Oxford, 1924.

Guillot, Oliver. *Le Comte d'Anjou et son entourage au XIe siècle*. 2 vols. Paris, 1972.

Hajdu, Robert. "Castles, Castellans and the Structure of Politics in Poitou, 1152–1271." *Journal of Medieval History* 4 (1978): 27–53.

———. "Family and Feudal Ties in Poitou, 1100–1300." *Journal of Interdisciplinary Studies* 8 (1977): 117–39.

Hall, Edwin, and Uhr, Horst. "*Aureola* and *Fructus*: Distinctions of Beatitude in Scholastic Thought and the Meaning of Some Crowns in Early Flemish Painting." *Art Bulletin* 60 (1978): 249–70.

Hamann McLean, Richard. "Les Origines des portails et façades sculptés gothiques." *Cahiers de civilisation médiévale* 2 (1959): 157–75.

Harden, A. R. "The Depreciatory Comparison: A Literary Device of the Medieval French Epic." In *Medieval Studies in Honor of U. T. Holmes, Jr.*, pp. 63–78. University of North Carolina Studies in the Romance Languages and Literatures 56. Chapel Hill, N.C., 1965.

Hartigan, F. X. "Reform of the Collegiate Clergy in the Eleventh Century: The Case of St-Nicholas at Poitiers." *Studies in Medieval Culture* 11 (1977): 55–62.

Haskins, Charles Homer. *The Renaissance of the Twelfth Century.* Cambridge, Mass., 1927.

Hatzfeld, H. *Literature through Art: A New Approach to French Literature.* University of North Carolina Studies in the Romance Languages and Literatures 86. Chapel Hill, N.C., 1969.

Hauck, Karl, ed. *Das Einhardkreuz.* Abhandlungen der Akademie der Wissenschaften in Gottingen, philologisch-historische Klasse, 3d ser., 87. Gottingen, 1974.

Heer, Friedrich. *Charlemagne and His World.* New York, 1975.

Heckscher, W. S. "Relics of Pagan Antiquity in Mediaeval Settings." *Journal of the Warburg Institute* 1 (1937–38): 204–20.

Heimann, Adelheid. "The Capital Frieze and Pilasters of the Portail Royal, Chartres." *Journal of the Warburg and Courtauld Institutes* 31 (1968): 73–102.

Heitz, Carol. *Recherches sur les rapports entre architecture et liturgie à l'époque carolingienne.* Paris, 1963.

Héliot, Pierre. "Les Portails polylobés de l'Aquitaine et des régions limitropes." *Bulletin monumental* 104 (1946): 63–89.

———. "Observations sur les façades décorées d'arcades aveugles dans les églises romanes." *Bulletin de la Société archéologique de l'Ouest,* 4th ser., 4 (1958): 367–99, 419–58.

———. "Sur la façade des églises romanes d'Aquitaine à propos d'une étude récente." *Bulletin de la Société archéologique de l'Ouest,* 4th ser., 2 (1952): 243–71.

Helsinger, Howard. "Images on the *Beatus* Page of Some Medieval Psalters." *Art Bulletin* 53 (1971): 161–76.

Henderson, George. *Early Medieval.* Style and Civilization. Harmondsworth, 1972.

———. "Romance and Politics on Some Medieval English Seals." *Art History* 1 (1978): 26–42.

Henning, Edward B. "Patronage and Style in the Arts: A Suggestion concerning Their Relations." In *The Sociology of Art and Literature.* Edited by Milton C. Albrecht, James A. Barnett, and Mason Griff. Pp. 353–62. New York, 1970.

Henry, Françoise, and Zarnecki, George. "Romanesque Arches Decorated with

Human and Animal Heads." *Journal of the British Archaeological Association* 20–21 (1957–58): 1–34.

Herlihy, David. "Land, Family and Women in Continental Europe, 701–1200." *Women in Medieval Society*. Edited by Susan Mosher Stuard. Pp. 13–45. Philadelphia, 1976.

Herman, J. P. "The Theme of Spiritual Warfare in the OE Judith." *Philological Quarterly* 55 (1976): 1–9.

Hieatt, Constance. "Roland's Christian Heroism." *Traditio* 24 (1968): 420–29.

Hiernard, Jean. "Du nouveau sur le trésor de monnaies romaines Soulièvre (Deux-Sèvres)." *Bulletin de la Société des antiquaires de l'Ouest*, 4th ser., 13 (1975): 255–79.

Higounet, Charles. "Le Groupe aristocratique en Aquitaine et en Gascogne, fin X^e–début XII^e siècle." In *Les Structures sociales de l'Aquitaine, du Languedoc et de l'Espagne au premier âge féodal*, pp. 221–37. Colloques internationales du Centre nationale de la recherche scientifique. Paris, 1969.

Higounet, Charles, et al. *Histoire de l'Aquitaine: Documents*. Toulouse, 1973.

Hill, John H., and Hill, Laurita L., trans. *Peter Tudebode: Historia de Hierosolymitano itinere*. Philadelphia, 1974.

———, trans. *Raymond d'Aguilers: Historia Francorum qui ceperunt Iherusalem*. Philadelphia, 1968.

Hill, Rosalind. "The Christian View of the Muslims at the Time of the First Crusade." In *Eastern Mediterranean Lands in the Period of the Crusades*. Edited by P. M. Holt. Pp. 1–8. Warminster, 1977.

Hill, Rosalind, ed. *Gesta Francorum et Aliorum Hierosolymitanorum*. London, 1962.

Hinkle, William M. "The Iconography of the Apsidial Fresco at Montmorillon." *Münchener Jahrbuch der bildenden Kunst* 23 (1972): 37–62.

Hirn, Yrjo. *The Sacred Shrine*. Boston, 1957.

*Histoire littéraire de la France*. 12 vols. Paris, 1865–69.

Hodgson, Marshall. *The Venture of Islam*. 3 vols. Chicago, 1974.

Hohler, Christopher. "A Note on Jacobus." *Journal of the Warburg and Courtauld Institutes* 35 (1972): 31–80.

Hoyt, Robert S., ed. *Life and Thought in the Early Middle Ages*. Minneapolis, 1967.

Hubert, Jean. "Introïbo ad Altare." *Revue de l'art* 24 (1974): 9–21.

———. "L'Escrain dit de Charlemagne." *Cahiers archéologiques* 4 (1949): 71–77.

Hughes, T. P. *A Dictionary of Islam*. Lahore, 1964.

Hunt, Noreen, ed. *Cluniac Monasticism in the Central Middle Ages*. Hamden, Conn., 1971.

*I Laici nella "Societas Christiana" dei secoli XI e XII*. Miscellanea del centro di studi medioevali 5. Atti della terza Settimana internazionale de studio, Mendola, 1965. Milan, 1968.

Imbert, Hugues. *Histoire de Thouars*. Niort, 1870; Marseilles, 1976.

Jackson, W. T. H. *The Literature of the Middle Ages*, New York, 1960.

———. *Medieval Literature*. New York, 1966.

Jarousseau, Gérard. "Essai de localisation de la Porte-le-Comte et de la Porte Mainard dans l'enceinte du bas empire à Poitiers." *Bulletin de la Société des antiquaires de l'Ouest*, 4th ser., 13 (1975): 143–53.

Jeanroy, Alfred, ed. *Les Chansons de Guillaume IX, duc d'Aquitaine.* Paris, 1913.

Jones, Dalu. "Romanesque, East and West?" *Connoisseur* 191 (1976): 280–85.

————. "Notes on a Tattooed Musician: A Drawing of the Fatimid Period." *Art and Archaeology Research Papers* 7 (1975): 1–14.

Jones, George Fenwick. *The Ethos of the Song of Roland.* Baltimore, 1963.

Jones, C. Meredith. "The Conventional Saracen of the Songs of Geste." *Speculum* 17 (1942): 201–25.

Jordan, W. C.; McNab, B.; and Ruiz, T. F.; eds. *Order and Innovation in the Middle Ages: Essays in Honor of Joseph R. Strayer.* Princeton, N.J., 1976.

Kaegi, Walter E. "Initial Byzantine Reactions to the Arab Conquest." *Church History* 38 (1969): 139–149.

Kahler, M. "Triumphbogen." *Realencyclopädie der classischen Altertumswissenschaft,* vol. 13, pp. 371–491. Edited by A. F. von Pauly. Stuttgart, 1894–1959.

Kantorowicz, Ernst H. *Selected Studies.* Edited by Michael Cherniavsky and Ralph E. Giesey. Locust Valley, N.Y., 1965.

Katzenellenbogen, Adolf. *Allegories of the Virtues and Vices in Medieval Art from Early Christian Times to the Thirteenth Century.* Translated by Alan J. P. Crick. Studies of the Warburg Institute 10. London, 1939; New York, 1964.

Kelley, Douglas. "*Translatio Studii:* Translation, Adaptation and Allegory in Medieval French Literature." *Philological Quarterly* 57 (1978): 287–310.

Kent, John P. C.; Overbeck, Bernhard; and Stylow, Armin U. *Die römische Münze.* Munich, 1973.

King, Georgiana Goddard. "The Rider on the White Horse." *Art Bulletin* 5 (1922): 3–9.

Kittel, Erich. *Siegel.* Bibliothek für Kunst und Antiquitätenfreunde 11. Braunschweig, 1970.

Kitzinger, Ernst. *Byzantine Art in the Making.* Cambridge, Mass., 1977.

————. "The First Mosaic Decoration of Salerno Cathedral." *Jahrbuch der österreichischen Byzantinistik* 21 (1972): 149–62.

————. "The Gregorian Reform and the Visual Arts: A Problem of Method." *Transactions of the Royal Historical Society,* 5th ser., 22 (1972): 87–102.

Konrad, R. "Das himmelische und das irdische Jerusalem im Mittelalterlichen Denken." *Speculum Historiale.* Edited by C. Bauer, L. Boehm, and M. Muller. Munich, 1965.

Krautheimer, Richard. *Early Christian and Byzantine Architecture.* Baltimore, 1967.

————. "Introduction to an 'Iconography of Medieval Architecture.'" *Journal of the Warburg and Courtauld Institutes* 5 (1942): 1–33.

————. *Studies in Early Christian, Medieval and Renaissance Art.* Edited by Elizabeth MacDougall. New York, 1969.

Krey, A. C. "A Neglected Passage in the *Gesta* and Its Bearing on the Literature of the First Crusade." In *The Crusades and Other Essays Presented to Dana C. Munro by His Former Students.* Edited by Louis J. Paetow. Pp. 57–78. New York, 1928.

Krinsky, Carol H. "Romanesque Architecture and Some Eighteenth-Century Critics." *Gesta* 1, no. 2 (1964): n.p.

Kritzeck, James. "Moslem-Christian Understanding in Mediaeval Times." *Comparative Studies in Society and History* 4 (1962): 388–401.

———. *Peter the Venerable and Islam.* Princeton, N.J., 1964.

Kubach, H. Erich, and Bloch, Peter. *Kunst der Welt: Früh und Hochromanik.* Baden-Baden, 1964.

Kubach, H. Erich. *Romanesque Architecture.* New York, 1975.

Kühnel, E. *Die islamischen Elfenbeinskulpturen VIII–XIII Jhr.* Berlin, 1971.

———. *The Minor Arts of Islam.* Translated by Katherine Watson. Ithaca, N.Y., 1971.

Labande, E. R. "Le Poitou dans les chansons de geste." *Bulletin de la Société des antiquaires de l'Ouest,* 4th ser., 13 (1976): 329–52.

———. "L'Historiographie de la France de l'Ouest au Xe et XIe siècles." In *La storiografia Altomedievale,* vol. 2, pp. 751–91. Settimane di Studio del Centro Italiano di Studi sull'alto Medioevo 17. Spoleto, 1970.

Labande-Mailfert, Yvonne. *Poitou roman.* La-Pierre-qui-Vire, 1957.

Laborde, Alexandre de, ed. *La Chanson de Roland: Reproduction phototypique du manuscrit Digby 23.* Paris, 1933.

Lafaurie, Jean. "Les Monnaies impériales de Charlemagne." *Académie des inscriptions et belles-lettres. Comptes rendues,* 1970, pp. 154–76.

Lasko, Peter. *Ars Sacra, 800–1200.* Harmondsworth, 1972.

———. "The *Escrain* de Charlemagne." In *Beiträge zur Kunst des Mittelalters: Festschrift für Hans Wentzel zum 60. Geburtstag,* pp. 127–34. Berlin, 1975.

Lauzun, Philippe. "Inventaire général des piles gallo-romaines du sud-ouest de la France." *Bulletin monumental* 63 (1898): 5–68.

*La Vita commune del clero nei secoli XI e XII.* 2 vols. Miscellanea del centro di studi medioevali 3. Atti della prima Settimana internazionale de studio, Mendola, 1959. Milan, 1962.

Lawner, Lynne. "Notes Toward an Interpretation of the *vers de dreyt nien.*" *Cultura Neolatina* 28 (1968): 147–64.

Lazar, Moshé. *Amour Courtois et fin amors dans la littérature du XIIe siècle.* Paris, 1964.

———. *Bernard de Ventadour: Troubadour du XIIe siècle.* Paris, 1966.

———. "Classification des thèmes amoureux et des images poetiques dans l'oeuvre de Bernard de Ventadour." *Filologia Romanza* 6 (1959): 371–400.

Leclercq, Jean. "Experience and Interpretation of Time in the Early Middle Ages." *Studies in Medieval Culture* 5 (1975): 9–19.

———. "Le Thème de la jonglerie chez S. Bernard et ses contemporains." *Revue d'histoire de la spiritualité* 48 (1972): 385–99.

———. "St. Bernard's Attitude Toward War." In *Studies in Medieval Cistercian History,* no. 2, pp. 1–25. Edited by John Sommerfeldt. Cistercian Studies 24. Kalamazoo, Mich., 1976.

———. "Un formulaire écrit dans l'Ouest de la France au XIIe siècle." *Mélanges offerts à René Crozet.* Edited by Pierre Gallais and Yves-J. Riou. Vol. 2, pp. 765–75. Poitiers, 1966.

Leclerq-Kadaner, Jacqueline. "De la Terre-Mère à la Luxure." *Cahiers de civilisation médiévale* 18 (1975): 37–43.

Ledain, Bélisaire. *Histoire de la ville de Parthenay.* Paris, 1858.

Le Gentil, Pierre. *La Chanson de Roland.* Translated by Frances F. Beer. Cambridge, Mass., 1969.

*Le Istituzioni ecclesiastiche della "Societas Christiana" dei secoli XI–XII: Diocesi, pievi e parrocchie.* Miscellanea del centro di studi medioevali 8. Atti della sesta Settimana internazionale de studio, Mendola, 1974. Milan, 1977.

Lejeune, Rita, and Stiennon, Jacques. *La Légende de Roland dans l'art du moyen-âge.* 2 vols. Brussels, 1966.

————. "Le Héro Roland, 'Neveu de Charlemagne,' dans l'iconographie médiévale." In *Das Nachleben.* Edited by Wolfgang Braunfels and Percy Ernst Schramm. Pp. 215–28. *Karl der Grosse, Lebenswerk und Nachleben,* vol. 4. Düsseldorf, 1967.

Lemay, Richard. "A Propos de l'origine arabe de l'art des troubadours." *Annales, économies-sociétés-civilisations* 21 (1966): 990–1011.

Leriche-Andrieu, Françoise. *Itinéraires romans en Saintonge.* La-Pierre-qui-Vire, 1976.

Le Roux, Hubert. "Les Enigmatiques cavaliers romans, St. Jacques ou Constantin?" *L'Archéologie* 20 (1977): 75–78.

Lesne, Emile. *Histoire de la propriété ecclésiastique en France.* 6 vols. Lille and Paris, 1910–43.

*Les Trésors des églises de France.* Musée des arts decoratifs. 2d ed. Paris, 1965.

Lethaby, W. R. "Byzantine Silks in London Museums." *Burlington Magazine* 24 (1913–14): 138–46.

Levine, R. "Ingeld and Christ: A Medieval Problem." *Viator* 2 (1971): 105–28.

Lévi-Strauss, Claude. *Myth and Meaning.* New York, 1979.

Lewis, A. R. *The Development of Southern French and Catalan Society, 718–1050.* Austin, 1965.

*Liber Floridus Colloquium.* Edited by Albert Derolez. Ghent, 1973.

Little, Lester. "Pride Goes before Avarice: Social Change and the Vices in Latin Christendom." *American Historical Review* 76 (1971): 16–49.

Little, Lester, and Rosenwein, Barbara. "Social Meaning in the Monastic and Mendicant Spiritualities." *Past and Present* 63 (1974): 4–32.

Longhurst, M. H., and Morey, C. R. "The Covers of the Lorsch Gospels." *Speculum* 3 (1928): 64–74.

Lopez, Robert S., and Raymond, Irving W. *Medieval Trade in the Mediterranean World.* New York, 1955.

Lotz, Wolfgang. "Zum Problem des karolingischen Westwerks." *Kunstchronik* 5 (1952): 65–71.

Louis, René. "L'Epopée français est carolingienne." *Coloquios de Roncesvalles,* pp. 327–460. Zaragoza, 1956.

Lourie, Elena. "A Society Organized for War: Medieval Spain." *Past and Present* 35 (1966): 54–76.

Lubac, Henri de. *Exégèse médiévale: Les Quatre sens de l'Ecriture.* 2 vols. Paris, 1959.

Lyman, Thomas W. "Arts somptuaires et art monumental: Bilan des influences auliques pré-romanes sur la sculpture romane dans le sud-ouest de la France et en Espagne." *Les Cahiers de Saint-Michel de Cuxa* 9 (1978): 115–27.

————. "L'Intégration du portail dans la façade méridionale." *Les Cahiers de Saint-Michel de Cuxa* 8 (1977): 55–68.

————. "The Sculpture Programme of the Porte des Comtes Master at Saint-Sernin in Toulouse." *Journal of the Warburg and Courtauld Institutes* 34 (1971): 12–39.

McGinn, Bernard. "*Iter Sancti Sepulchri:* The Piety of the First Crusaders." *Essays on Medieval Civilization.* Walter Prescott Webb Memorial Lectures. Edited by Bede K. Lackner and Kenneth R. Philp. Pp. 33–71. Austin, 1978.

McKitterick, Rosamond. *The Frankish Church and the Carolingian Reforms, 789–895.* London, 1977.

Magnou-Nortier, Elisabeth. *La Société laïque et l'église dans la province ecclésiastique de Narbonne de la fin du VIIIᵉ à la fin du XIᵉ siècle.* Toulouse, 1974.

Maillard, Elisa. "La Façade de l'église romane de Saint-Jouin-de-Marnes en Poitou." *Gazette des beaux-arts,* 5th ser., 9, pt. 1 (1924): 137–50.

————. "Les Sculptures de la façade de l'église Saint-Pierre-de-Parthenay-le-Vieux." *Bulletin de la Société des antiquaires de l'Ouest,* 3d ser., 5 (1919): 237–48.

Mâle, Emile. *Art et artistes du moyen âge.* Paris, 1927.

————. *Religious Art in France in the XIIIth Century.* Translated by D. Nussey. London, 1913.

————. *Religious Art in France, the Twelfth Century: A Study of the Origins of Medieval Iconography.* Edited by Harry Bober and translated by Marthiel Mathews. Bollingen Series 90:1. Princeton, N.J., 1978.

Martindale, Jane. "Conventum inter Guillelmum Aquitanorum comes et Hugonem Chiliarchum." *English Historical Review* 84 (1969): 528–48.

————. "The French Aristocracy in the Early Middle Ages: A Reappraisal." *Past and Present* 75 (1977): 5–45.

Mattingly, Harold. *Coins of the Roman Empire in the British Museum.* London, 1940.

————. *Roman Coins from the Earliest Times to the Fall of the Western Empire.* London, 1928.

Maury, Jean; Gauthier, M.-M.; and Porcher, Jean. *Limousin roman.* 2d ed. La-Pierre-qui-Vire, 1974.

Mayo, Penelope C. "The Crusaders under the Palm: Allegorical Plants and Cosmic Kingship in the *Liber Floridus.*" *Dumbarton Oaks Papers* 27 (1973): 29–67.

*Mélanges de langue et de littérature médiévales offerts à Pierre Le Gentil.* Paris, 1973.

*Mélanges offerts à René Crozet.* Edited by Pierre Gallais and Yves-J. Rioux. 2 vols. Poitiers, 1966.

*Mélanges offerts à Rita Lejeune-Dehousse.* 2 vols. Liège, 1969.

Mendell, Elizabeth L. *Romanesque Sculpture in Saintonge.* New Haven, Conn., 1940.

Messerer, Wilhelm. *Romanische Plastik in Frankreich.* Cologne, 1964.

Metlitzki, Dorothee. *The Matter of Araby in Medieval England.* New Haven and London, 1977.

Meyendorff, John. "Byzantine Views of Islam." *Dumbarton Oaks Papers* 18 (1964): 113–32.

Michaud, Jean. "Dédicaces en Poitou: Faste des cérémonies (c. 800–1050)." *Bulletin de la Société des antiquaires de l'Ouest,* 4th ser., 14 (1977): 143–63.

Mickel, E. J., Jr. "Christian Duty and the Structure of the Roland." *Romance Notes* 9 (1967): 126–33.

————. "Parallels in Prudentius' *Psychomachia* and *La Chanson de Roland.*" *Studies in Philology* 67 (1970): 439–52.

Monroe, James T. "Hispano-Arabic Poetry during the Almoravid Period: Theory and Practice." *Viator* 4 (1973): 65–98.

————. "The Historical Arjūza of Ibn 'Abd Rabbihi, a Tenth-century Hispano-Arabic Epic Poem." *Journal of the American Oriental Society* 91 (1971): 67–95.

Montesquiou-Fézensac, Blaise de. "L'Arc de triomphe d'Einhardus." *Cahiers archéologiques* 4 (1949): 79–103.

————. "L'Arc Eginhard." *Cahiers archéologiques* 8 (1956): 147–74.

————. *Le Trésor de Saint-Denis.* 3 vols. Paris, 1973–77.

Montesquiou-Fézensac, Blaise de, and Gaborit-Chopin, Danielle. "Camées et intailles du Trésor de Saint-Denis." *Cahiers archéologiques* 24 (1975): 137–62.

Moralejo Alvarez, Serafín. "Pour l'interprétation iconographique du portail de l'agneau à Saint-Isadore de Léon: Les Signes du zodiaque." *Les Cahiers de Saint-Michel de Cuxa* 8 (1977): 137–73.

Morris, Colin. "*Equestris ordo:* Chivalry as a Vocation in the Twelfth Century." In *Religious Motivation: Biographical and Sociological Problems for the Church Historian.* Edited by Derek Baker. Pp. 87–96. Studies in Church History 15. Cambridge, 1978.

Mütherich, Florentine. "Die Buchmalerei am Hofe Karls des Grossen." In *Karolingische Kunst.* Edited by Wolfgang Braunfels and Hermann Schnitzler. Pp. 9–53. *Karl der Grosse: Lebenswerk und Nachleben,* vol. 3. Düsseldorf, 1965.

Munro, Dana C. "The Western Attitude toward Islam during the Crusades." *Speculum* 6 (1931): 329–43.

Murphy, Thomas P., ed. *The Holy War.* Columbus, Ohio, 1976.

Nelli, René. *L'Erotique des troubadours.* Bibliothèque méridionale, 2d ser., 38. Toulouse, 1963.

Nelson, D. "Animal Imagery in Marcabru's Poetry." *Studies in Medieval Culture* 11 (1977): 51–55.

Nelson, Janet. "Ritual and Reality in the Early Medieval Ordines." In *The Materials, Sources and Methods of Ecclesiastical History.* Edited by Derek Baker. Pp. 41–51. Studies in Church History 11. Cambridge, 1974.

*New Catholic Encyclopedia.* 16 vols. New York, 1967–74.

Nichols, Stephen G., Jr. "A Poetics of Historicism? Recent Trends in Medieval Literary Study." *Medievalia et Humanistica,* n.s., 8 (1977): 77–101.

————. "Canso-Conso: Structures of Parodic Humor in Three Songs of Guilhem IX." *L'Esprit Créateur* 14, no. 1 (1976): 16–29.

————. "The Interaction of Life and Literature in the *Peregrinationes ad Loca Sancta* and the Chansons de Geste." *Speculum* 44 (1969): 51–77.

————. "The Rhetoric of Recapitulation in the Chansons de Guillaume." *Studies in Honor of Tatiana Fotitch.* Edited by J. M. Sola-Solé, A. S. Crisafulli, and S. A. Schulz. Pp. 79–92. Washington, D.C. [1975].

————. "The Spirit of Truth: Epic Modes in Medieval Literature." *New Literary History* 1 (1970): 365–86.

————. "Toward an Aesthetic of the Provençal Lyric II: Maracabru's *Dire vos vuoill ses doptansa."* In *Italian Literature: Roots and Branches,* pp. 15–37. New Haven, Conn., 1976.

Niles, J. D. "The Ideal Depiction of Charlemagne in 'La Chanson de Roland.'" *Viator* 7 (1976): 123–39.

Noack, Ferdinand. "Triumph and Triumphbogen." *Vorträge der Bibliothek Warburg* [vol. 5], 1925–26, pp. 147–201. Edited by Fritz Saxl. 9 vols. Leipzig, 1923–32.

[Nogent, Guibert de.] *Self and Society in Medieval France.* Edited by John F. Benton. New York, 1970.

Nordström, Folke. *Virtues and Vices on the Fourteenth Century Corbels in the Choir of Uppsala Cathedral.* Stockholm, 1956.

Nye, Phila Calder. "Romanesque Signs of the Zodiac." *Art Bulletin* 5 (1922): 55–57.

Olson, Susan. "Immutable Love: Two Good Women in Marcabru." *Neophilologus* 60 (1976): 190–99.

O'Meara, Carra Ferguson. *The Iconography of the Façade of Saint-Gilles-du-Gard.* New York, 1977.

Oursel, Raymond. *Haut-Poitou roman.* La-Pierre-qui-Vire, 1975.

Owen, D. D. R. "Charlemagne's Dreams, Baligant and Turoldus." *Zeitschrift für romanische Philologie* 87 (1971): 197–208.

———. "The Secular Inspiration of the Song of Roland." *Speculum* 37 (1962): 390–400.

Pächt, Otto. *The Rise of Pictorial Narrative in Twelfth-Century England.* Oxford, 1962.

Painter, Sidney. "Castellans of the Plain of the Poitou in the Eleventh and Twelfth Centuries." In *Feudalism and Liberty.* Edited by Fred A. Cazel, Jr. Pp. 17–40. Baltimore, 1961.

Panofsky, Erwin. *Renaissance and Renascences in Western Art.* Icon Edition. Stockholm, 1960.

Pariset, François-Georges. "Les Eglises de Chadenac et de Pérignac." *Congrès archéologique* 114 (1956): 245–66.

Pasero, Nicolò. *Poesie Guglielmo IX: Edizione critica.* Modena, 1973.

Pearsall, Derek, and Salter, Elizabeth. *Landscapes and Seasons of the Medieval World.* Toronto and London, 1973.

Pei, Mario. *French Precursors of the Chanson de Roland.* New York, 1948.

Peters, E., ed. *The First Crusade: The Chronicle of Fulcher of Chartres and Other Source Materials.* Philadelphia, 1971.

Pfister, M. "La Langue de Guilhem IX, Comte de Poitiers." *Cahiers de civilisation médiévale* 19 (1976): 91–113.

Pfister, R. "Les Tissus orientaux de la Bible de Théodulf." *Coptic Studies in Honor of Walter Ewing Crum. Bulletin of the Byzantine Institute* 2 (1950): 501–30.

Pickering, F. P. *Literature and Art in the Middle Ages.* Coral Gables, 1970.

Pierce, R. "The 'Frankish' Penitentials." In *The Materials, Sources and Methods of Ecclesiastical History.* Edited by Derek Baker. Pp. 31–39. Studies in Church History 11. Cambridge, 1974.

Pinder-Wilson, R. H., and Brooke, C. N. L. "The Reliquary of St. Petroc and the Ivories of Norman Sicily." *Archaeologia* 104 (1973): 261–305.

Platelle, H. "Le Problème du scandale: Les Nouvelles modes masculines aux XI<sup>e</sup> et XII<sup>e</sup> siècles." *Revue belge de philologie et d'histoire* 53 (1975): 1071–96.

Poey d'Avant, Faustin. *Monnaies féodales de France.* 3 vols. Paris, 1858–62. Reprinted Graz, 1961.

Poignat, Maurice. *Parthenay et le quartier Saint-Jacques.* Niort, 1976.

Pon, Georges. "L'apparition des chanoines réguliers en Poitou: Saint-Nicolas de Poitiers." *Bulletin de la Société des antiquaires de l'Ouest* 4th ser., 13 (1975): 55–70.

Porter, A. Kingsley. *Romanesque Sculpture of the Pilgrimage Roads.* 10 vols. Boston, 1923. Reprinted (10 vols. in 3) New York, 1966.

Powell, James M., ed. *Medieval Studies: An Introduction.* Syracuse, N.Y., 1976.

Preus, J. S. "Theological Legitimation for Innovation in the Middle Ages." *Viator* 3 (1972): 1–26.

*Prudentius.* Edited and translated by H. J. Thomson. 2 vols. Loeb Classical Library. Cambridge, Mass., and London, 1962.

Quicherat, Jules. "De l'architecture romane." *Revue archéologique* 8 (1851): 145–58.

Ragusa, Isa. "*Terror demonum* and *terror inimicorum:* The Two Lions of the Throne of Solomon and the Open Door of Paradise." *Zeitschrift für Kunstgeschichte* 40 (1977): 93–114.

Rahman, Fazlur. *Islam.* 2d ed. Chicago, 1979.

*Ramon Vidal, Poetry and Prose.* Edited by W. J. W. Field. University of North Carolina Studies in Romance Languages and Literatures 110. Chapel Hill, N.C., 1971.

Richard, Alfred G. *Histoire des comtes de Poitou, 778–1204.* Paris, 1903.

Riché, Pierre. "Trésors et collections d'aristocrates laïques carolingiens." *Cahiers archéologiques* 22 (1972): 39–46.

Richter, Gisela M. A. *Catalogue of Engraved Gems: Greek, Etruscan, Roman.* Rome, 1956.

Richmond, I. A. "Adamklissi." *Papers of the British School at Rome* 35, n.s. 22 (1967): 29–39.

Riley-Smith, Jonathan. *What Were the Crusades?* Totowa, N.J., 1977.

Riou, Yves-Jean. "Le prieuré Notre-Dame d'Oulmes (Charente-Maritime)." *Bulletin de la Société des antiquaires de l'Ouest,* 4th ser., 13 (1975): 165–87.

Robertson, Anne S. *Roman Imperial Coins in the Hunter Coin Cabinet, University of Glasgow.* 4 vols. Oxford, 1962–78.

Robinson, I. S. "Gregory VII and the Soldiers of Christ." *History* 58 (1973): 169–92.

Rolland, Henri. *L'Arc de Glanum. Gallia* supplement 31. Paris, 1977.

———. *Le Mausolée de Glanum. Gallia,* supplement 21. Paris, 1969.

*Romans and Barbarians.* Boston, 1976.

Roques de Maumont, H. von. *Antike Reiterstandbilder.* Berlin, 1958.

Rosenblum, Robert. *Transformations in Late Eighteenth Century Art.* Princeton, N.J., 1967.

Rosenwein, Barbara H. "Feudal War and Monastic Peace: Cluniac Liturgy as Ritual Aggression." *Viator* 2 (1971): 129–57.

Ross, James Bruce. "A Study of Twelfth-Century Interest in the Antiquities of Rome." *Medieval and Historiographical Essays in Honor of James Westfall*

*Thompson*. Edited by James Lea Cate and Eugene N. Anderson. Pp. 302–21. Chicago, 1938.

Roy, Jean Henri and Deviosse, Jean. *La Bataille de Poitiers, octobre, 733*. Paris, 1966.

Ruiz Maldonado, Margarita. "La Contraposición 'Superbia-Humilitas': El sepulcro de Doña Sancha y otras obras." *Goya* 146 (1978): 75–81.

———. "El 'caballero victorioso' en la escultura románica española. Algunas consideraciones y nuevos ejemplos." *Boletín del Seminario de Estudios de Arte y Arqueologia*. Universidad de Valladolid. 45 (1979): 271–86.

Ruiz Montejo, Maria Ines. "La Temática obscena en la iconografía del románico rural." *Goya* 147 (1978): 136–46.

Runciman, Steven. "Byzantine Art and Western Medieval Taste." In *Byzantine Art: An European Art*. Athens, 1966.

Rupprecht, Bernhard. *Romanische Skulptur in Frankreich*. Munich, 1975.

Russell, Fredrick M. *The Just War in the Middle Ages*. Cambridge, 1975.

Salet, Francis. "Cluny III." *Bulletin monumental* 126 (1968): 235–92.

Salin, Edouard. *La Civilisation mérovingienne d'après les sépultures, les textes et le laboratoire*. 4 vols. Paris, 1949–59.

Salviat, François. "La Sculpture pré-romane en Provence." *Dossiers de l'archéologie* 35 (June 1979): 31–51.

Salvini, Roberto. *Medieval Sculpture*. History of Western Sculpture. New York, 1969.

———. "Pre-Romanesque Ottonian and Romanesque." *Journal of the British Archaeological Association*, 3d ser., 33 (1970): 1–20.

Sanderson, Warren. "The Sources and Significance of the Ottonian Church of St. Pantaleon at Cologne." *Journal of the Society of Architectural Historians* 29 (1970): 83–96.

Sanfaçon, Roland. *Défrichements, peuplement et institutions seigneuriales en Haut-Poitou du X^e au XIII^e siècle*. Quebec, 1967.

Sauer, Joseph. *Symbolik der Kirchengebäudes und seiner Ausstattung in der Auffassung des Mittelalters*. Freiburg, 1924. Reprinted Münster, 1964.

Sauerländer, Willibald. *Gothic Sculpture in France*. Translated by Janet Sondheimer. London, 1972.

———. "Sculpture on Early Gothic Churches: The State of Research and Open Questions." *Gesta*, 9, no. 2 (1970): 32–48.

———. *Skulptur des Mittelalters*. Ullstein Kunstgeschichte. Berlin, 1963.

———. "Über die Komposition des Weltgerichts-Tympanons in Autun." *Zeitschrift für Kunstgeschichte* 29 (1966): 261–94.

Saunders, J. J. "The Crusade as a Holy War." *Aspects of the Crusades*. University of Canterbury Publications 3. Christchurch, N.Z., 1962.

Sauvel, Tony. "Les Lions romans de Chadenac et ceux de St-Aubin d'Angers." *Bulletin de la Société des antiquaires de l'Ouest*, h.s., 1949, pp. 47–50.

Saxl, Fritz. "Lincoln Cathedral: The Eleventh-century Design for the West Front." *Archaeological Journal* 103 (1946): 105–17.

Schaeffer, Herwin. "The Origin of the Two-Tower Façade in Romanesque Architecture." *Art Bulletin* 27 (1945): 85–108.

Schapiro, Meyer. "The Angel with the Ram in Abraham's Sacrifice: A Parallel in Western and Islamic Art." *Ars Islamica* 19 (1943): 134–47.

————. *Romanesque Art*. New York, 1977.

————. "The South Transept Portal of St-Sernin at Toulouse." *Parnassus* 1 (1929): 22–23.

Scher, Stephen K. *The Renaissance of the Twelfth Century*. Providence, R.I., 1969.

Schnitzler, Hermann. "Das karolingische Kuppelmosaik der Aachener Pfalzkapelle." *Aachener Kunstblätter* 29 (1964): 17–44.

————. "Die Komposition der Lorscher Elfenbeintafeln." *Münchner Jahrbuch der bildenden Kunst*, 3d ser., 1 (1950): 26–42.

Schramm, Percy Ernst. *Herrschaftszeichen und Staatsymbolik: Beiträge zu ihrer Geschichte vom dritten bis zum sechzehnten Jahrhundert*. 3 vols. Schriften der Monumenta Germaniae historica 13. Stuttgart, 1954–56.

Schramm, Percy E., and Mütherich, Florentine. *Denkmale der deutschen Könige und Kaiser*. Munich, 1962.

Schuchard, B. "Architecture, littérature et art figuratif dans la France du XII^e siècle." *Les Cahiers de St-Michel de Cuxa* 4 (1973): 48–67.

Schürenberg, L. "Die romanischen Kirchenfassaden Aquitaniens." *Das Münster* 4 (1951): 257–68.

Seidel, Linda. "Constantine *and* Charlemagne." *Gesta* 15 (1976): 237–39.

————. "Holy Warriors: The Romanesque Rider and the Fight against Islam." In *The Holy War*. Edited by Thomas P. Murphy. Pp. 33–77. Columbus, Ohio, 1976.

————. "Romanesque Capitals from the vicinity of Narbonne." *Gesta* 11, no. 1 (1972): 34–45.

Setton, Kenneth M., ed. *A History of the Crusades*. Vol. 1: *The First Hundred Years*. Edited by Marshall W. Baldwin. Madison, Wis., 1969.

Shepherd, Dorothy G. "Banquet and Hunt in Medieval Islamic Iconography." In *Gatherings in Honor of Dorothy E. Miner*. Edited by Ursula E. McCracken, Lilian M. C. Randall, and Richard H. Randall, Jr. Baltimore, 1974.

Shepherd, Massey H. "Liturgical Expression of the Constantinian Triumph." *Dumbarton Oaks Papers* 21 (1967): 59–78.

Short, Ian. "Roland's Final Combat." *Cultura Neolatina* 30 (1970): 135–55.

Sivan, Emmanuel. *L'Islam et la croisade: Idéologie et propagande dans les réactions musulmanes aux croisades*. Paris, 1968.

Skubiszewski, Piotr. "The Iconography of a Romanesque Chalice from Trzemeszno." *Journal of the Warburg and Courtauld Institutes* 34 (1971): 40–64.

Smalley, Beryl. *Historians in the Middle Ages*. London, 1974.

Smith, E. Baldwin. *Architectural Symbolism of Imperial Rome and the Middle Ages*. Princeton, N.J., 1956.

Smith, Macklin. *Prudentius' "Psychomachia": A Reexamination*. Princeton, N.J., 1976.

Smith, Molly Teasdale. "The 'Ciborium' in Christian Architecture at Rome, 300–600 A.D." [dissertation summary]. *Marsyas* 14 (1968–69): 84.

Smyser, H. M. , ed. *The Pseudo-Turpin*. Mediaeval Academy of America Publication, no. 30. Cambridge, Mass., 1937.

Snijder, G. A. S. "Antique and Medieval Gems on Bookcovers at Utrecht." *Art Bulletin* 14 (1932): 14–18.

Sommerfeldt, John. "The Social Theory of Bernard of Clairvaux." In *Studies in*

*Medieval Cistercian History,* no. 1, pp. 35–48. Cistercian Studies 13. Kalamazoo, Mich., 1971.

Sourdel-Thomine, Janine, and Spuler, Bertold. *Die Kunst des Islam.* Vol. 4: *Propyläen Kunstgeschichte.* Berlin, 1973.

Southern, R. W. *Western Views of Islam in the Middle Ages.* Cambridge, Mass., 1962.

Stapert, A. *L'Ange roman dans la pensée et dans l'art.* Paris, 1975.

Stern, Henri. "Nouvelles recherches sur les images des Conciles dans l'Eglise de la Nativité à Bethelehem." *Cahiers archéologiques* 3 (1948): 82–105.

Stettiner, Richard. *Die illustrierten Prudentiushandschriften.* 2 vols. Berlin, 1895, 1905.

Stillman, N. A. "The Eleventh Century Merchant House of Ibn 'Awkal." *Journal of the Economic and Social History of the Orient* 16 (1973): 15–88.

Stock, Brian. "The Middle Ages as Subject and Object: Romantic Attitudes and Academic Medievalism." *New Literary History* 5 (1974): 527–47.

Storch, R. H. "The Trophy and the Cross: Pagan and Christian Symbolism in the Fourth and Fifth Centuries." *Byzantion* 40 (1970): 105–18.

Stroup, T. B. "Ritual and Ceremony in Drama." *Comparative Drama* 11 (1977): 139–46.

Stuard, Susan Mosher, ed. *Women in Medieval Society.* Philadelphia, 1976.

*Studies in Memory of David Talbot Rice.* Edited by Giles Robertson and George Henderson. Edinburgh, 1975.

Swarzenski, Hanns. *Monuments of Romanesque Art.* Chicago, 1954.

Swiechowski, Zygmunt. "La Formation de l'oeuvre architecturale au cours du haut moyen âge." *Cahiers de civilisation médiévale* 1 (1958): 371–78.

Szittya, Penn R. "The Angels and the Theme of *Fortitudo* in the *Chanson de Roland.*" *Neuphilologische Mitteilungen* 72 (1971): 193–223.

Taralon, Jean. "La Majesté d'or de Sainte-Foy du trésor de Conques." *Revue de l'art* 40–41 (1978): 9–22.

Tate, George S. "Chiasmus as Metaphor." *Neuphilologische Mitteilungen* 79 (1978): 114–25.

Thérel, M.-L. "*Caritas* et *Paupertas* dans l'iconographie médiévale inspirée de la Psychomachie." *Etudes sur l'histoire de la pauvreté: Moyen âge–XVI<sup>e</sup> siècle,* pp. 295–317. Paris, 1974.

Thiersch, H. *Pharos in Antike: Islam und Occident.* Leipzig and Berlin, 1909.

Thomas, Lucien-Paul. *Le "Sponsus": Mystère des Vierges sages et des Vierges folles.* Paris, 1951.

Throop, Palmer. *Criticism of the Crusade: A Study of Public Opinion and Crusade Propaganda.* Amsterdam, 1940.

Thrupp, Sylvia. *Society and History.* Edited by Raymond Grew and Nicholas H. Steneck. Ann Arbor, Mich., 1977.

Tonnellier, Chanoine. "L'Art roman en Saintonge." *Bulletin du Centre international d'études romanes,* 1964, pp. 18–37.

———. "L'Art roman en Saintonge." *Richesses de France: La Charente-Maritime* 75 (1968): 56–69.

Toubert, Hélène. "Aspects du renouveau paléochrétien à Rome au début du XII<sup>e</sup> siècle." *Cahiers archéologiques* 20 (1970): 99–154.

Toynbee, J. M. C. *Death and Burial in the Roman World.* London, 1971.

Tyson, Diana B. "Patronage of French Vernacular History Writers in the Twelfth and Thirteenth Centuries." *Romania* 100 (1979): 180–222.

Uitti, Karl D. *Story, Myth, and Celebration in Old French Narrative Poetry.* Princeton, N.J., 1973.

Ullman, B. L. "Classical Authors in Certain Mediaeval *Florilegia.*" *Classical Philology* 27 (1932): 1–42.

———. "Tibullus in the Mediaeval *Florilegia.*" *Classical Philology* 23 (1928): 128–74.

Ullmann, Walter. *The Carolingian Renaissance and the Idea of Kingship.* London, 1969.

Vance, Eugène. "Roland et la poétique de la mémoire." *Cahiers d'études médiévales* 1 (1974): 103–15.

Van de Kieft, C. "La Seigneurie de l'abbaye de Saint-Jean d'Angély au milieu du XIe siècle." In *Miscellanea mediaevalia in memoriam Jan Frederik Niermeyer,* pp. 167–75. Groningen, 1967.

Verdier, Philippe. "La Colonne de Colonia Aelia Capitolina et l'*imago clipeata* du Christ-Helios." *Cahiers archéologiques* 23 (1974): 17–40.

———. "Deux plaques d'ivoire de la résurrection avec la représentation d'un Westwork." *Zeitschrift für schweizerische Archäologie und Kunstgeschichte* 22 (1962): 3–9.

Verdon, Jean. "La Femme en Poitou aux Xe et XIe siècles." *Bulletin de la Société des antiquaires de l'Ouest,* 4th ser., 14 (1977): 91–102.

———. "La chronique de Saint-Maixent et l'histoire du Poitou au IXe et XIIe siècles." *Bulletin de la Société des antiquaires de l'Ouest,* 4th ser., 13 (1976): 437–72.

———. "Une Source de la reconquête chrétienne en Espagne: La Chronique de Saint-Maixent." *Mélanges offerts à René Crozet.* Edited by Pierre Gallais and Yves-J. Riou. 1:273–82. Poiters, 1966.

Vergnolle, E. "Les Arcs polylobés dans le centre Ouest de la France." *L'Information d'histoire de l'art* 5 (1969): 217–23.

Vieillard-Troiekouroff, May. *Les Monuments religieux de la Gaule d'après les oeuvres de Grégoire de Tours.* Paris, 1976.

Vielliard, Jeanne. *Le Guide du pèlerin de Saint-Jacques de Compostelle.* Mâcon, 1960.

Villard, F. "Guillaume IX d'Aquitaine et le concile de Reims 1119." *Cahiers de civilisation médiévale* 16 (1973): 295–302.

Vogel, Cyrille. "La Réforme liturgique sous Charlemagne." In *Das Geiste Leben.* Edited by Bernhard Bischoff. Pp. 217–32. *Karl der Grosse, Lebenswerk und Nachleben,* vol. 2. Düsseldorf, 1965.

Vryonis, Speros, Jr. "Byzantium and Islam, Seventh to Seventeenth Century." In *Byzantium: Its Internal History and Relation with the Muslim World.* London, 1971.

Waddell, Helen. *The Wandering Scholars.* 3d ed. Boston, 1927.

Wallace-Hadrill, J. M. *Early Medieval History.* New York, 1976.

Walpole, Ronald N. *The Old French Johannes Translation of the Pseudo-Turpin Chronicle.* Berkeley and Los Angeles, 1976.

Waltz, J. "Carolingian Attitudes Regarding Muslims." *Studies in Medieval Culture* 5 (1975): 33–40.

Warmé-Janville, Jeanne. "L'Eglise Notre-Dame de Villesalem, l'harmonie de son décor et ses liens avec l'art roman de la région." *Bulletin de la Société des antiquaires de l'Ouest*, 4th ser., 15 (1979): 279–96.

Warren, Larissa Bonfante. "Roman Triumphs and Etruscan Kings: The Changing Face of the Triumph." *Journal of Roman Studies* 60 (1970): 49–66.

Watson, Katherine. "French Romanesque and Islam: Influences from Al-Andalus on Architectural Decoration." *Art and Archaeology Research Papers* 2 (1972): 1–27.

Webster, James Carson. *The Labors of the Months in Antique and Medieval Art to the End of the Twelfth Century.* Princeton, N.J., 1938.

Weisbach, Werner. *Reforma Religiosa y Arte Medieval.* Translated by H. Schlunk and L. Vazquez de Parga. Madrid, 1949. (Published as *Religiöse Reform und mittelalterliche Kunst.* Einsiedeln, 1945.)

Weitzmann, Kurt. "Byzantine Miniature and Icon Painting in the Eleventh Century." In *Studies in Classical and Byzantine Manuscript Illumination.* Edited by Herbert L. Kessler. Pp. 271–313. Chicago, 1971.

———. "Icon Painting in the Crusader Kingdom." *Dumbarton Oaks Papers* 20 (1966): 49–84.

———. "*Locu Sancta* and the Representational Arts in Palestine." *Dumbarton Oaks Papers* 28 (1974): 31–55.

Wentzel, H. "Portraits 'à l'antique' on French Medieval Gems and Seals." *Journal of the Warburg and Courtauld Institutes* 16 (1953): 342–50.

White, Beatrice. "Saracens and Crusaders: From Fact to Allegory." In *Medieval Literature and Civilization: Studies in Memory of G. N. Garmonsway.* Edited by D. A. Pearsall and R. A. Waldron. Pp. 170–91. London, 1969.

White, Lynn. "Cultural Climates and Technological Advance in the Middle Ages." *Viator* 2 (1971): 171–201.

———. *Medieval Technology and Social Change.* Oxford, 1962.

Wilhelm, James. *The Cruelest Month.* New Haven, Conn., 1965.

Wolff, Philippe. "L'Aquitaine et ses marges." In *Personlichkeit und Geschichte.* Edited by Helmut Beumann. Pp. 269–306. *Karl der Grosse: Lebenswerk und Nachleben*, vol. 1. Düsseldorf, 1965.

Woodruff, Helen. "The Illustrated Manuscripts of Prudentius." *Art Studies* 7 (1929): 33–79.

Zarnecki, George. *Art of the Medieval World.* New York, 1975.

———. *Later English Romanesque Sculpture.* London, 1953.

———. *Romanesque Art.* New York, 1971.

———. *The Monastic Achievement.* New York, [1972].

Zeilinger, Roswitha. "Eginhard et la sculpture carolingienne." *Dossiers de l'Archéologie* 30 (1978): 104–12.

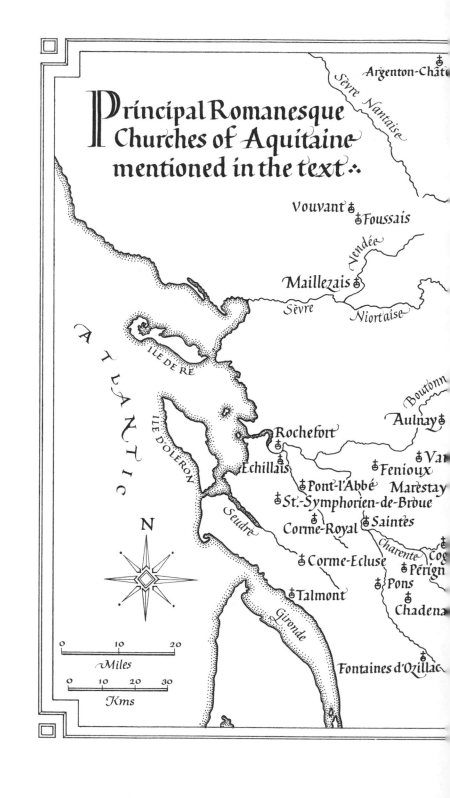

Principal Romanesque Churches of Aquitaine mentioned in the text ∴

Argenton-Chât

Sèvre Nantaise

Vouvant ⚓ ⚓Foussais

Vendée

Maillezais ⚓

Sèvre

Niortaise

ATLANTIC

ÎLE DE RÉ

Boutonn

Aulnay ⚓

ÎLE D'OLÉRON

Rochefort ⚓

⚓Va

Echillais ⚓ Fenioux ⚓

⚓Pont-l'Abbé  Marestay

⚓St.-Symphorien-de-Brdue

N

⚓Corme-Royal  ⚓Saintes

Seudre

Charente  Cog

⚓Corme-Ecluse  ⚓Pérign

⚓Pons

⚓Talmont  Chadena

Gironde

0        10        20
Miles

0    10    20    30
Kms

Fontaines d'Ozillac

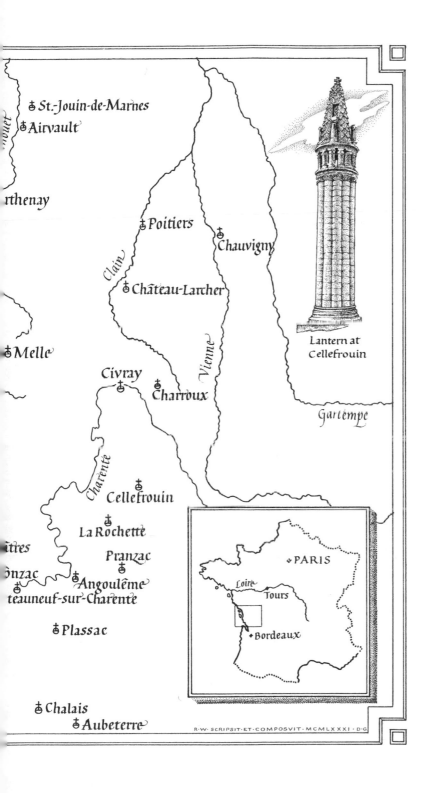

St.-Jouin-de-Marnes
Airvault

rthenay

Poitiers
Chauvigny

Clain

Château-Larcher

Vienne

Melle

Civray
Charroux

Gartempe

Lantern at
Cellefrouin

Charente

Cellefrouin

La Rochette

tres

Pranzac

nzac
Angoulême
teauneuf-sur-Charente

Plassac

Chalais
Aubeterre

PARIS

Loire
Tours

Bordeaux

R·W· SCRIPSIT·ET·COMPOSVIT· MCMLXXXI · D·G

Fig. 1. Notre-Dame de l'Assomption at Châtres

Fig. 2. Saint-Cybard at Plassac-Rouffiac

Fig. 3. Notre-Dame at Corme-Ecluse

Fig. 4. Saint-Jacques at Aubeterre

Fig. 5. Notre-Dame-la-Grande in Poitiers

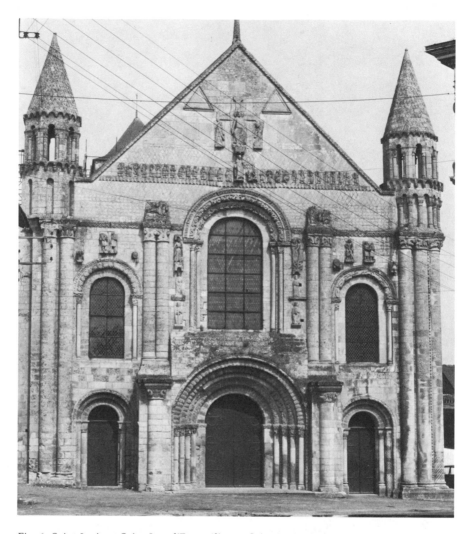

Fig. 6. Saint-Jouin et Saint-Jean-l'Evangéliste at Saint-Jouin-de-Marnes

Fig. 7. Abbaye-aux-Dames at Saintes

Fig. 8. Saint-Pierre at Parthenay-le-Vieux

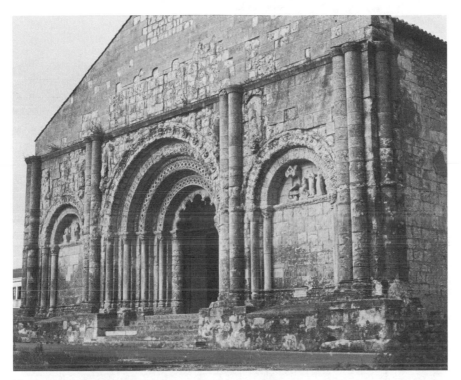

Fig. 9. Saint-Martial at Chalais

Fig. 10. Notre-Dame-de-la-Couldre at Parthenay. (Bildarchiv Foto Marburg)

165

Fig. 11. Notre-Dame at Fenioux

Fig. 12. Notre-Dame at Echillais

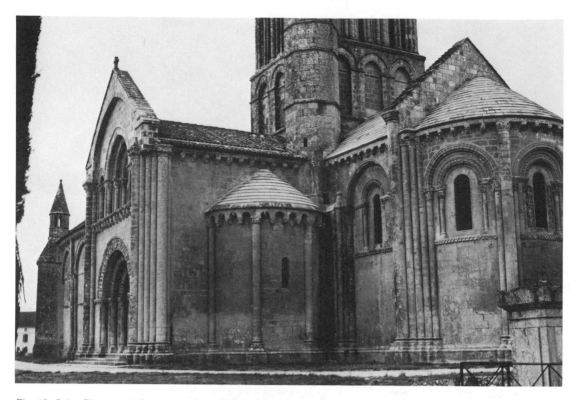

Fig. 13. Saint-Pierre at Aulnay, seen from the southeast

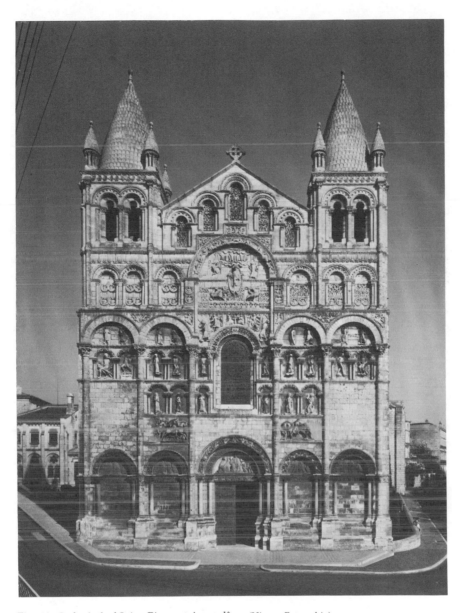

Fig. 14. Cathedral of Saint-Pierre at Angoulême (Hirmer Fotoarchiv)

Fig. 15. Gatehouse at Lorsch Abbey, Germany (Bildarchiv Foto Marburg)

Fig. 16. Arch of Constantine, Rome (Bildarchiv Foto Marburg)

Fig. 17. Arch of Einhard; drawing of a lost Carolingian reliquary base, Bibliothèque nationale, Paris, Fr. 10440 f.45 (Phot. Bibl. nat. Paris)

AD TROPAEVM AETER
NAE VICTORIAE SVSTI
NENDVM EINHARDVS
PECCATOR HVNC AR
CVM PONERE AC DEO
DEDICARE CVRAVIT

Fig. 18. Arch of Titus, Rome (Bildarchiv Foto Marburg)

174

Fig. 19. Christ and angels; ivory cover (back portion) from the Lorsch Gospel Book in the Vatican Library (Biblioteca Apostolica Vaticana)

175

Fig. 20. Emperor on horseback between trophies; reverse of a sestertius of Claudius commemorating Nero Drusus' victory over the Germans (Trustees of the British Museum)

Fig. 21. Escrain of Charlemagne; drawing of a lost Carolingian shrine in the Bibliothèque nationale, Paris, Recueil Le 38 c. (Phot. Bibl. nat. Paris)

176

Fig. 22. *The Mass of St. Giles* by the Master of St. Giles; 15th century painting showing the altar frontal of Charles the Bald (National Gallery, London)

177

Fig. 23. Funerary pyre; reverse of a sestertius of Commodus.
(Trustees of the British Museum)

Fig. 24. Mausoleum of the Julii, Saint-Rémy (Bildarchiv Foto Marburg)

178

Fig. 25. Crucifixion and Three Marys at the Tomb; ivory plaque from a bookcover (Walters Art Gallery, Baltimore)

Fig. 26. Lantern of Bégon, tower reliquary in the Treasury at Sainte-Foy in Conques (Joubert/© C.N.M.H.S./ S.P.A.D.E.M.)

Fig. 27. Cemetery lantern at Fenioux

Fig. 28. Archivolts over the central door at Saint-Martin at Chadenac

Fig. 29. Archivolts over the southern door at Saint-Mandé-sur-Brédoire

181

Figs. 30 and 31. Archivolts over the central door at Notre-Dame-de-la-Couldre, Parthenay; detail of fig. 10

Fig. 32. Marys at the Tomb; façade capital at Chadenac (Photo Lila Lang)

Fig. 33. Weighing of the souls; façade at Corme-Royal

184

Fig. 34. Wise and Foolish Virgins; archivolt above the central door on the façade at Corme-Royal; detail of fig. 37

Fig. 35. Archivolts over the central door at Fenioux; detail of fig. 11

185

Fig. 36. Mask capital from the entry into the bell tower of Saint-Martin at Périgné

Fig. 37. Saint-Nazaire at Corme-Royal (Bildarchiv Foto Marburg)

Fig. 38. Archivolts over the central door of Saint-Pierre at Pont-l'Abbé-d'Arnoult

Fig. 39. Detail of the central door at Notre-Dame-de-la-Couldre, Parthenay; compare figs. 10, 30–31

Fig. 40. Archivolts over the central door at Saint-Gilles at Argenton-Château

Fig. 41. Keystones of the archivolts over the central west door at Saint-Pierre, Aulnay;
detail of figs. 48, 51 (Photo Lila Lang)

Fig. 42. Christ ascending surrounded by angels; detail of the upper portion of the façade at Angoulême (Photo Lila Lang)

Fig. 43. Music-making angels; detail of an archivolt at Saint-Nicholas in Civray

Fig. 44. The Last Supper; detail of an archivolt on the façade at the Abbaye-aux-Dames, Saintes

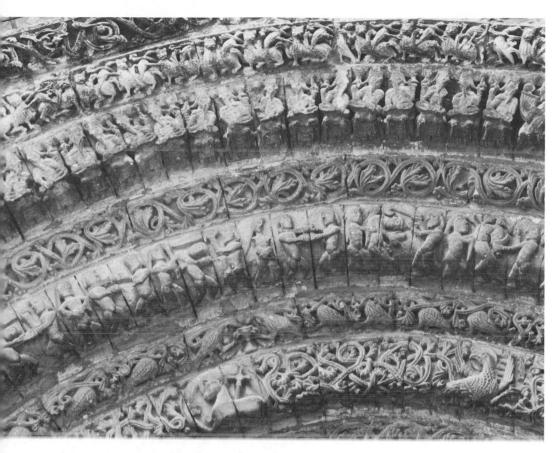

g. 45. Detail of the archivolts around the central door at the Abbaye-aux-Dames, Saintes

195

Fig. 46. Façade of the Hospice at Pons

Fig. 47. Apsidal capital at Saint-Pierre at Dampierre-sur-Boutonne

Fig. 48. Saint-Pierre at Aulnay (Photo Lila Lang)

Fig. 49. Victorious figures; ivory plaque in the Museo nazionale, Florence (Photo: Alinari)

Fig. 50. *(a)* Arch supporting chariot and two equestrian figures; reverse of denarius of Septimus Severus. *(b)* Paired victories holding a shield; reverse of a solidus of Constans. *(c)* Victory writing on a shield; reverse of a coin of Gratianus. *(d)* Emperor victorious over a barbarian; reverse of a medallion of Constantinus II. *(e)* Emperor galloping; reverse of a sestertius of Trajan (Courtesy Museum of Fine Arts, Boston)

Fig. 49

Fig. 50a–e

Fig. 51. Central door on the west façade at Saint-Pierre, Aulnay (Photo Lila Lang)

Fig. 52. Reverse of the lead seal of William, count of Forcalquier, 1150–1208 (Trustees of the British Museum)

Fig. 53. Equestrian figure on the façade of Saint-Pierre at Parthenay-le-Vieux

Fig. 54. Saint George on a tympanum from Saint George's Church, Brinsop, Hereford-shire (National Monuments Record, London)

Fig. 55. Riders accompanied by women; capital on the façade of the Abbaye-aux-Dames, Saintes

Fig. 56. Woman in a litter; detail of a scene on a Persian bowl depicting a siege (Courtesy of the Smithsonian Institution, Freer Gallery of Art, Washington, D.C.)

Fig. 57. Luxuria riding and dancing; British Library, Add. MS 24199, fol. 18r (Reproduced by permission of the British Library)

Fig. 58. Luxuria attacked by serpents; detail of a capital from the façade of St-Pierre, Parthenay-le-Vieux

Fig. 59. Loving couple on a corbel from Saint-Sulpice at Marignac

206

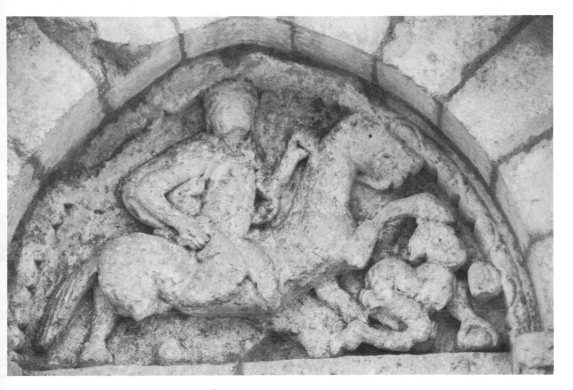

Fig. 60. Equestrian figure on the façade at Ĺa Rochette

Fig. 61. Hispano-Arabic ivory box (Victoria and Albert Museum, London. Crown copyright)

Fig. 62. Detail of the façade of the town house at Saint-Antonin

Fig. 63. Equestrian hunter from a house in the Caucasus (The Metropolitan Museum of Art, Rogers Fund, 1938)

# Index